RUINS OF A SOCIETY AND THE HONORABLE

A Prison Story and Autobiography

By

Al Bermúdez Pereira

ISBN: 978-0578043432

Printed in the United States of America
ID: 1-275929551

www.RuinsOfaSociety.com

Special Thanks

Lydia Bermúdez, my wife, whose assistance in the creation of the front cover brought to surface her ability to see nature's beauty and capture it instantaneously. Special thanks to those depicted on this cover; NYC police department, Brooklyn south division, Patrolman Joe Pagan, The NYS correction's emergency response team of Albany, NY., NYC firefighter and former NYC Patrolman Gregory Santangelo and his father; FDNY fire squad executive officer, and Columbia Association President, of Gerritsen Avenue Brooklyn, NY, Buddy Santangelo.

Furthermore, displayed on the cover are The Ruins of Krzyztopor Castle in Ujazd, southern Poland. Built in 17th century, it was destroyed by Swedish Army ten years after it was elevated.

Dedication

To all the active and fallen correction officers, law enforcement officers, firefighters and US soldiers worldwide who for the sole purpose of keeping us all safe and free in our homeland, gave their lives without prejudice. We as a society in this great nation of freedom tend to forget the many lives lost, families shattered and dreams cut short by their courageous and ultimate sacrifices, they deserve better government care.

This book is also dedicated to another group of special people who we also tend to forget, the crime and terrorists victims of our nation. They too are families with shattered dreams cut short by the lowlife criminals of our society.

To our doctors, nurses and paramedics throughout America who subject themselves to the daily experiences of tragedy, the airborne diseases that sometimes claim their own lives and the rude patients who make their ability to care for others almost impossible. They are the frontline of our society and at times forgotten.

For all the memorable moments, I also dedicate this book to the following Foxwood Drive families of Newburgh, New York and their children; William and Lily McKinley, Joe and Nadine Gizzarelli, Mark and Jo-Ann Pugh, Richard and Marilyn Verrette, Tom and Carrie Quinn, Jeff Jackson, Roger and Brenda Ramjug, Michael and Vanessa Allen, John and Lorie Coombs, Bill and Stacy Drew, Janie Joyce, Michael and Karin McCartney, Effie Miller Keith and Mary-Jo Rauscher, Thomas and Angela Smith.

65th Infantry WWII, Korean, Vietnam and Iraq

A special dedication to our relatives, and all others of Vieques, Puerto Rico and the United States who served, continue to serve and were wounded or killed in action.

Pvt. FC.	L. Bermúdez	No. Korea	WIA
Pvt.	D. Bermúdez Ortiz	WWII	KIA
Pvt. FC.	E. Bermúdez	Company B	WIA
Pvt.	D. Bermúdez, Jr.	Army	Brother
Corporal	R. Bermúdez	So Korea	WIA
Corporal	A. Bermúdez	Company A	KIA
Corporal	C. Bermúdez	Company B	1953
Corporal	Jose Pereira	Army	Uncle
Unknown	Victor Pereira	Army	Uncle
Unknown	Liberato Bermúdez	Army	Uncle
Unknown	Pedro Bermúdez	Army	Uncle
Unknown	Thomas Guadalupe	Viet. WIA	Cousin
Sgt. FC	Jeff Santana	Army Act.	In-law
Mst. Sgt	Albert R. Bermúdez	Bronze Star	Meritorious
Pvt.	Jeremy Alvarez	Army Act:	Nephew

Fallen Brother Officers of Sing-Sing and Downstate Facilities, 1985–2010 Rest in Peace

I. Boyd	Murdered	Active Officer
L. Valdistino	Murdered	Active Officer
G. Rawl	Murdered	Active Officer
J. Kane	Murdered	Active Officer
B. Rodriguez	Drowned	Active Officer
J. Santoro	Drowned	Active Officer
T. Connaire	Suicide	Active Officer
J. Colon	Suicide	Active Officer
M. Mullen	Suicide	On Duty Officer
J. Rosado	Accident	On Duty Trooper
E. Johnson	Accident	Active Officer
R. Ruiz	Accident	Active Officer
E. Torres	Natural	On Duty Officer
A. Lyons	Natural	Active Officer
E. Montalvo	Natural	Active Sergeant
E. Burns	Natural	Active Warrants
W. Vega	Natural	Active Officer
H. Cheaham	Natural	Active Officer
A. Reed	Natural	Active Officer
R. Haynes	Natural	Active Officer
A. Sementini	Natural	Active Captain
F. Frank	Natural	Active Officer
H. Day	Natural	Active Officer
S. Ebron	Natural	Active Officer
D. Keenan	Natural	Active Officer

M. Harper	Natural	Active Officer
K. Bentley	Natural	Active Officer
C. Carabeo	Natural	Active Officer
C. Drake	Natural	Active Officer
D. Macintosh	Natural	Active Officer
C. Kerr	Natural	Active Officer
J. Tabasco	Natural	Active Officer
S. Martinez	Natural	Active Officer
J. Holman	Natural	Ret. Lieutenant
C. Johnson	Natural	Ret. Sergeant
M. Brown	Natural	Ret. Sergeant
D. Austin	Natural	Ret. Sergeant
B. Madden	Natural	Ret. Sergeant
C. Taylor	Natural	Ret. Sergeant
J. English	Natural	Ret. Officer
R. Brown	Natural	Ret. Officer
S. Montgomery	Natural	Ret. Officer
W. Reich	Natural	Ret. Officer
R. Santiago	Natural	Ret. Officer
M. Green	Natural	Ret. Officer
D. Gant	Natural	Ret. Officer
D. Navarro	Natural	Ret. Officer
W. Murphy	Natural	Ret. Officer
R. Williamson	Natural	Ret. Officer
J. McGue	Natural	Ret. Officer
J. Gooden	Natural	Ret. Officer
A. Sportiello	Natural	Ret. Officer

Introduction

Ruins of a Society and the Honorable, is an autobiography and short story based on real-life circumstances as I lived it and remember it to the best of my recollection. Many names have been changed to protect sources from reprisals and legalities. Real names contained in this book were either approved by the individuals; were parts of a publication made available to the public and encrypted in citations, or were spoken of in honorability. Others are based on personal opinions. This book contains incidents, which took place in one day and a half while at Sing-Sing prison where I worked, and outside the prison's environment.

It then sidetracks to speak of other stories, voice opinions and reflects on my life as a young Latino growing up in Brooklyn and abroad. This book honors many who crossed paths with me during my lifetime, who inspired me and whose recognition is well deserved. Honorableness can be described in many definitions and involve many different circumstances, which led me to honor who I felt deserves to be honored, and indeed, an honor for me to do so. Many in this book are and were correction officers. They are unfortunately looked down upon by many in other fields of law enforcement, despised by criminals and unappreciated by most. They deserve better, "Not in my opinion, but as a matter of fact."

Although seventy-five percent of the book is based on prison experiences, other parts of this book relate to the many life encounters, we've all experienced in our own lives. In reference to autobiographies and real prison life stories, this will be Al Bermudez's final book. Throughout the book, the actual story stops with an asterisk, (*) to voice an opinion or explain a different set of circumstances; it then continues on to the story with the words, (STORY CONT).

Chapter One

~~~

It's Saturday, five a.m., as I exit my home in preparation for work at Sing-Sing maximum-security prison. Before entering my vehicle, a blue Delta 88, 1988; I took notice of a parked blue Cadillac with its engine running directly in front with four Latino occupants inside. This was unusual, since we're the only Latinos in a predominately Italian neighborhood of Gravesend, Brooklyn. I proceeded to enter my vehicle parked directly behind them. I turned on my ignition, my headlights and opened my passenger-side window. I pulled out my off-duty weapon, the most widely used law enforcement weapon at the time; the Glock model-17. I placed it on the seat to my right, keeping my finger along side of the trigger guard, just in case. I then cautiously moved up to their driver-side window. I notice the driver reach down beneath his seat. He looked out of his window and in a boisterous manner yelled out.

"What's up Papa, you want something?"

I can see a very large scar on the left side of his face running from the top of his head down to his neck. I answered back.

"How are you guys doing?"

"What's up, you want something," asked the driver again.

I can feel the tension in the air, almost as though we were two western cowboys preparing for a showdown at OK-Corral.

1

"Are you guys waiting on my nephews?" I asked cautiously as I surveyed the others in the car. I knew my nephews were much too young to be out at five a.m., let alone with a group of thugs that quite obviously was up to no good.

"Nah, we're waiting on a girl name Shelly," yelled out one of the passengers.

Living over ten years in the neighborhood and knowing ninety percent of my neighbors, I knew there was no resident named Shelly.

"Oh, yeah, Shelly, I know her she lives right there."

Pointing to a building where no women have occupied in the last two years.

"Yeah, right there," said the driver.

"Ok, I have her home number. I'll give her a call from the public telephone at the corner and let her know you guys are waiting. I'll be right back."

I drove up to 86th Street and turned right, then turned left into a gas station and parked in the rear of the station on Boynton Place. This was an advantage point for me, since they couldn't see where I was parked. I had a clear view of five intersections; Avenue X, McDonald Avenue, 86th Street, Shell Road and Boynton Place. I sat there and within three minutes, I saw the blue Cadillac approach the intersections. They turned up 86th Street towards the Marlboro housing projects, and were gone in the early-morning dusk. I holstered my weapon, exited my vehicle and walked to a public telephone at the gas station. I dialed 911 for good measure and gave a full description of the blue vehicle and its suspicious occupants. I then called my family and instructed them to be on their toes.

'*One could never be too precautious,*' I thought to myself.

I waited twenty minutes. It was now five-thirty and I was running a little behind. I left the gas station and drove up McDonald Avenue. As I approached every intersection with a red light I cautiously proceeded through making sure no other vehicles were in sight. I didn't like the idea of waiting at a red light in a commercial area with an elevated train at five in the morning. I guess my conscience wouldn't allow me to place myself at a disadvantage should a criminal decide to either car jack me or shoot me in the head while the overhead train passed and muffle the sound of gunfire.

2

I finally made a right turn onto Cortelyou Road where I would then proceed to Ocean Parkway and turn left heading toward the Prospect Expressway. As I was approaching the intersection of Ocean Parkway, I can see ahead of me many flashing emergency lights. I then began seeing lights on my rearview mirror quickly approaching. As they got closer I can hear the sounds of police sirens increasing all around me. As the police cars suddenly approached my immediate area, I reached underneath my seat for a hand scanner. My brother Cruz, (The Moe) Morales was a New York City police officer at the time and was assigned to the area. I wanted to monitor the police frequency, in case he was involved in an incident and needed help, when suddenly I heard the screams, the yelling and instructions.

"Stop, put you're fucking hands where I can see them!"

Another voice yelled out.

"He was reaching underneath his seat for something, freeze motherfucker or I'll blow your fucking head off!"

Then a third voice continued.

"Go ahead; make my fucking day ass hole!"

It was me, they were yelling at. I immediately dropped my scanner, turned on my interior lights, opened my window and placed both of my hands on the steering wheel while letting out a great big smile, like Eddie Murphy in the movie, 'Trading Places.'

As the flashlights were beaming in my face from every direction, I immediately identified myself.

"I'm a state correction officer on my way to work officers. My shield and identification are in my right rear pocket along with my off-duty weapon."

A police officer stepped forward.

"Oh, Jesus, you don't know how close you came to getting shot. Keep your hands where we can see them. Do you know why we stopped you?"

"No officer I don't."

"You took about ten red lights back there, not to mention your vehicle match the description of a 911 call made earlier by an off-duty MOS, (Member of service). What's your name, officer?"

"Al Bermudez," I said, while shaking as though I was being electrocuted in an electric chair. Having numerous gun barrels pointed at my face and head wasn't something I could get use to.

"My brother, Cruz (The Moe) Morales is a police officer in your command" (Precinct).

"Ok, Al, slowly step out of your vehicle and show us your credentials."

Another officer stepped forward.

"You were reaching for something under your seat when we pulled up, what you were reaching for?"

"I carry a handheld scanner underneath my seat. I listen to it every once in awhile on my way to work, since my brother works this area. When I saw all the red flashing lights and heard the sirens, I thought of my brother possibly needing my help."

"Ok, that makes sense, but why did you take all the red lights back there?"

"I'm running a little late for work, and to be honest I don't like the idea of waiting at a red light in a poorly lit commercial area with an elevated train. However, I made absolutely sure there was no traffic in sight officers."

I surrendered my identification. It was confirmed, and I was instructed to leave, but not without one more word of advice from a sergeant who came on the scene.

"Mr. Bermudez, maybe next time you should try another way of getting to work, like the Belt Parkway. That is, if you don't like traveling through poorly lit commercial areas with an elevated choo-choo train and little bad men lurking about."

I felt my anger rising to its surface, and my first thought was to tell him to go screw himself, but considering I blew several lights back there, an insult was not a bad price to pay.

"Yeah, your right sarge, we'll do and my apologies."

"No problem, apology accepted. By the way, where do you work?"

"I work at Sing-Sing State Prison, where there are approximately two-thousand two-hundred-fifty little bad men lurking about."

The sergeant didn't like my answer and verbally shot back in his Irish accent.

"Oh, so now you're a wise guy?"

"No, sarge, it wasn't meant to be sarcastic, just a little humor."

"Oh, yeah, well I'm not laughing. So go-ahead to work and have yourself a good day before I change my mind and tag you with numerous red-light summonses."

No argument from me.

I finally drove off onto Ocean Parkway and toward Manhattan, where I would pick up a car pulling co-worker named Willie Marrero, before heading to Ossining, NY, where Sing-Sing prison is located. Born and raised in Puerto Rico, Willie was a tall, slim, well educated Latino, who for reasons unknown hated criminals with a passion. Willie was a by-the-book prison officer with no exceptions and no excuses. There was no negotiating and no finagling him. If you were found violating prison rules, you were going to receive the maximum allowable charge. Some convicts hated him. Others feared him, but most respected his professionalism. Willie always took pride of his Puerto Rican heritage and was knowledgeable on its history than most at the prison. His conversations, as I can remember, focused on the injustices endure by the people and the struggle of our forefathers in the prevention of colonialism. If you personally knew Willie, you would know he had a heart of gold. In actuality, his kindness superseded the tough-guy image he projected in a prison environment. *

Willie and I spoke many times concerning many things, from crime, to the economy, corruption, and the foreign invasions and injustices that plagued the islands of Puerto Rico. In one of those conversations of injustices, we spoke of my uncle Jose Pereira Torres from Monte Santo, Vieques Puerto Rico. He was forced out of Vieques during the US invasion of the 1940s. He migrated to St Croix, Virgin Island and ran for the Senate November 07, 1978. In May 1979, he was accused of conspiring to participate with a radical group in sabotaging US military vehicles, charges that were later proven false and eventually dismissed. The only violation committed by Jose Pereira was when he and twenty-one others were arrested for civil disobedience in a restricted US Navy bombing area, which was also the same year when the Crusade for the Rescue of Vieques was founded. However, the injustice against Jose Pereira and others didn't end there. Against his will and proclamation of innocence, my uncle was labeled a communist by US officials, but Jose Pereira saw himself as a freedom fighter and not an independentistas, (pro-independence). In his words, "independentistas concern themselves with too many issues beyond the problems of Vieques." Unlike the others, he acknowledged the existence of the court and made it clear this was not the problem.

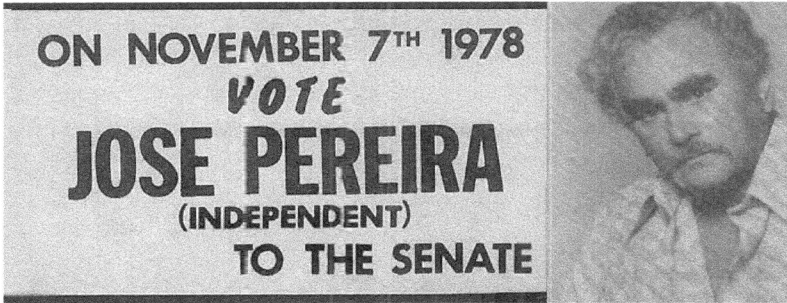

Jose Pereira Torres, 1978

"The bombardment, the injustices of our people, and the forcible migration of Viequsnses are my concerns. I'm here to prevent future generations from the humiliation we were all subjected to." Making it clear to his family; he accused the government of torture and experiment of others while incarcerated. Angel Rodriguez Cristobal, who was also arrested with Jose, was sent to a federal prison in Florida, two weeks later he was found dead in his cell. According to prison officials he committed suicide by hanging, but reports stated he had a large gash across his forehead ard a pool of blood beneath his feet where he hung in his cell. Jose Pereira returned to St Croix and later died of cancer. This sort of killing, torture and experiment was unfortunately common practice toward Puerto Ricans who were incarcerated during this period. Pedro Albizu Campos, a Lieutenant in the US Army and Graduate of Harvard University also alleged he was subjected to radiation experiments in prison. Although government officials stated he was not mentally stable while making those statements, an examination by President of the Cuban Cancer Association, Dr. Orlando Damuy, who traveled to Puerto Rico to examine Albizu Campos, found evidence of high levels of radiation in his skin and flesh. In 1932, Pedro Albizu Campos charged Cornelius Rhoades, an American doctor and pathologist of killing Puerto Rican patients during medical experiments conducted in San Juan's Presbyterian Hospital for the Rockefeller Institute by injecting them with live cancer cells. Although Rhoades and government officials emphatically denied the allegations, the American Association for Cancer Research in 2003, remove Dr. Rhoades's name from their annual award intended for meritorious achievement in cancer research, after conducting an independent investigation.

6

These were just some of the many injustices that natives of Puerto Rico like my uncle Jose Pereira and Pedro Albizu Campos objected to and tried to prevent. Although these inhumane practices no longer exist in Puerto Rico, the reminisce left behind by the constant years of US military exercises in bombing Vieques, still show signs of extremely high levels of radiation, lead contamination and cancer among many children throughout most of the island of Vieques, Puerto Rico.

STORY CONT:

I was now entering onto Manhattan Bridge and I am instantly captured, as I've always have been, by the spectacular luminosity of New York City skyscrapers. It's a never ending derived of sensory processes stimulating your mental contentment. But just as that moment was reaching its peak of excitation, a dark silhouette was vaguely approaching my car.

"What the heck is this," I unexpectedly ask myself?

An Asian woman was approaching my car on the middle of Manhattan Bridge. I could see she was wearing pajamas. I looked in my rear view mirror, saw no traffic behind me and came to a complete stop. I opened the passenger side window and she began speaking to me in Chinese. I had no way of understanding what she was trying say. She glanced at my uniform then scantily uttered her words.

"Police, you police."

"No lady I'm not the police. Get in the car before you get hurt out here."

She appeared discombobulated and handed me a small piece of paper with an address written on it.

"I go; I go," she said.

Unfortunately for her, I was not about to drive halfway across town in search of an address. It was quite obvious to me she was dropped off by a snakehead, (Chinese slang for human smugglers). I tried unsuccessfully to explain I was not going to take her to her destination. As I approached the end of the bridge I stopped on Chrystie Street, the road leading off the bridge.

"You have to go now," I said.

"No, I go, I go," she insisted while again attempting to hand over the piece of paper.

I turned off my car and removed the keys from its ignition. I stepped out, approached the passenger side door, and opened it.

"No, you go; I can't take you any further."

She finally understood what I was trying to say and exited the vehicle. Although I wished I could have helped her further, I also knew this was a Federal offense in progress I wanted no part of. *

Countless of people are smuggled into the US on a daily basis and many others never make it in. Many illegal immigrants drown when ships are capsized; others die in ship containers when the suns heat is too much for them to bear. Hundreds of others we never hear about have perished and will continue to perish for the sake of freedom. The human sacrifices made on a daily basis by these immigrants; whether it's from China, Mexico, Cuba or Africa, for the sake of giving their families a better way of life and the freedom we all take for granted, supersedes the fears and potential threat of death. While the US is slowly but surely losing all its farmers, farm lands, natural resources and the harvesting of millions of our fruits and vegetables, many of us (Americans) concern ourselves with illegal immigrants who are picking those fruits and vegetables in our own homeland.

Not to mention we are now importing wheat into this country from other countries and seeing a shortage of food, something not seen since the Second World War. I have driven throughout many New York counties, and one which comes to mind is Westchester County, a prestigious and preppy little territory just thirty minutes north of New York City. Many living there are lawyers, doctors, judges, politicians, stock market brokers, actors and other high end level careers. The taxes are high, its residential landscaping are immaculate and homes are; to say the least, very expensive. Many homes have beautiful natural field stones beautifying its curb appeal and architectural designs not seen anywhere else. Although I must admit Lake Mary in Florida comes close. The landscaping alone is time consuming and requires years of hands-on experiences, *ever wonder where the labor come from?*

During a winter's day, I was once asked on my day off by a co-worker to help in constructing a garage made of natural field stones and clay roof tiles for a gentleman in Westchester. This garage was constructed for three vehicles; it had a beautiful curved stairwell leading to an upstairs office with three-quarter inch hardwood flooring throughout and a spectacular stone fireplace towering approximately twenty-five feet high. The garage doors were constructed to resemble a Victoria antique look, and every exterior detail was made to match the existing Victorian home. The lawn was imported from Ireland, and while everyone else's lawn appeared fatigued, pounded and pulverized by the winter's cold. This lawn was plush green as though it was springtime in New York, *ever wonder where the labor comes from?*

This guy was a Wall Street self-made millionaire, so I later learned. He was accused of having an affair with a known Playboy Bunny. He allegedly gave her insider trading tips, and she was discovered while in the process of implementing her scheme by Federal authorities. She eventually gave up her source. He was removed from Wall Street, placed on house arrest with an ankle bracelet, removed as chairman from a nearby country club and made to pay back restitution. His garage was finally finished, and it resembled a beautiful Victorian home build in the early 1900s. Many other homes in Westchester County and surrounding counties are just as spectacular; *ever wonder where the labor comes from? I'll answer that.*

Having the pleasure of knowing and witnessing firsthand the many years of construction productivity, and working side by side with these people, I can honestly say the Mexican people, South American Latinos and Italians. Those are the ones responsible for this labor and in helping to beautify, not only this New York County, but many other counties throughout the United States. While attending a Central Florida University, and having a class discussion on illegal immigration, a student who was originally from Los Angeles now residing in Florida, stood up from his chair and courageously stated,

"We need to build a Noah's Ark, gather up all these Mexicans, who are taking our jobs and sending their money back home, and ship them back to their damn country!"

9

Quite naturally, being of Latino descent, the statement disappointed me.

"Take all the Mexicans, put them on a Noah's Ark, and ship them back to their damn country? And how do you propose we remove twelve million plus Mexican people who are working and spending their money at your local Wal-Mart stores or supermarkets without having a catastrophic effect on our US, economy?"

The majority of immigrants come here with good intentions. They come to work and seek the same freedom in which all of our ancestors sought before us. Some monetarily provide what little they can to their love ones back home, not to stabilize Mexico's economy. We leave that to the American families and business corporations which spend on average approximately ten-thousand dollars to vacation in Cancun. We in America are so focused on the most ridiculous issues that we lose sense and sight of what's important. We fail to see what's really going on around us and what's happening to our own American people. Politicians in Congress are being given CEO positions throughout our nation's health care industries and others being promoted to medical directors by many hospitals simply because they have the gut and lack of remorse to turn away qualifying patients who are terminally ill or possess a preexisting condition. We live in the most powerful country in the world, yet London, Panama City, France, Canada and Cuba, are just some of the countries where medical health care is absolutely free.

The photograph of the young lady holding her son is that of Eileen Pagan Bermudez, and six-year-old son Alex Abreu, Jr. Eileen use to live a Central Florida, but in 2004, she moved back to New York after losing her fiancé Alex Abreu, Sr., who went to sleep one night on his thirty-third birthday and never woke again. Eileen experienced countless of medical care refusals in Florida. She suffered from diabetes since childhood, which required constant attention. One day while enjoying the sun at a Miami Beach with her family, Eileen suffered a diabetic seizure and was immediately taken to a local Miami Beach hospital by her father-in-law Gonzalo Abreu. Miami hospital personnel refused to treat Eileen, who unfortunately had no medical health insurance.

Eileen Pagan and Alex Abreu, Jr

Other local hospitals also refused to take her in as well, and Gonzalo Abreu was forced to drive to Hialeah, Florida. During this journey, Gonzalo's nerves were tested to the up most extreme, and Eileen almost died on this day. Mr. Gonzalo Abreu was no stranger to devastation and extreme circumstances in his own life. He was once a farmer and land owner in Cuba, and lost all he had to the new communist assumption of power by Fidel Castro and his regime. Although sadden and devastated by his lost in Cuba, Gonzalo moved on. He eventually pioneered his way into the United States, and made a successful and productive life for himself and for his family.

He's one of the most decent and honorable men I know. It was this same courage, dedication and love for others; in addition to his driving skills, that would subsequently save Eileen's life on that long and devastating trip. On January 12, 2005, Eileen went through a major transplant operation and received a kidney and pancreas at New York Presbyterian Hospital, and we're all extremely grateful for that. However, on February 12, 2005, just before St. Valentine's Day, she was readmitted to New York Presbyterian Hospital with physical complications. After one week of hospitalization, she was told by doctors, she was well enough to go home. Although she was being released, she suspected there was something physically wrong with her, leaving a recorded phone message to her father Pedro Pagan, stating those facts. She arrived home one hour and half later in Brooklyn. She was met and welcomed by her family and her son Alex, who waited on top of the stairs to greet his mommy with a St. Valentine's Day heart shaped candy box. She smiled and began walking up the steps, but stopped and stated to her mother Joanna Pagan Bermudez, "Mom we're going to have to move from here. These stairs are to too much for me." Immediately, after that statement Eileen collapsed, released a loud exhale and died at the bottom of those steps in front of her family and six-year-old son. Eileen was thirty years old, and she was my first niece. An autopsy later revealed Eileen's heart was double the size of a normal heart. Now we had a six-year-old boy without parents and a grandmother that will be subjected to hospitalization bureaucracy. A bureaucracy in whom all underprivileged Americans, who will seek healthcare, will inevitability be subjected to. I once viewed a televised commercial in central Florida, paid for by a local politician running for office who was criticizing his or her opponent. The announcement stated,

"By sympathizing with illegal immigrants, the opponent was breaking our most fundamental laws."

Is that right, let's be realistic about this for a moment, not taking under consideration the former New York's Governor prostitution scandal, New Jersey's Governor homosexual scandal, Illinois's Governor corruption scandal, South Carolina's Governor infidelity scandal and the hundreds of other politicians and county commissioners sex and corruption scandals throughout our nation.

If the United States President signed a bill into law making the violation of fundamental laws a class, (A) felony with no possibility of parole, our court rooms on all government levels, private corporations and construction industries would be affected in one form or another. Many of our judges, attorneys, stock market brokers, doctors and this particular politician would be under my supervision at Sing-Sing prison eating out of a styrolfoam tray. Far from the caviar usually served as hors d'oeuvre in their fancy little local restaurants. Don't tell me they're not conscious of their surroundings or what's going on in their own back yard, with respect to landscaping and construction performed by immigrants. We as Americans in this country almost always attempt to benefit by the misfortune of others, and/or profit from the extreme cheap slave labor that comes with being an immigrant. It's the American way.

It was no different in the early 1900s, at Ellis Island during the arrival of the Polish, Swedish, Russian Jews, French, German, Irish, Italian, Czechoslovakian and Hungarian immigrants. Unlike today's immigrants, America allowed them entry then profited from their slave labor as well. Other than being allowed entry into the US, the only difference with the immigrants during the 1900s, and today's immigrants, there was no public picketing or protesting their arrival, no protesting the possibility of losing their jobs to lower labor wages as we see today. Not to mention there were much fewer factories, corporations and jobs available during the early 1900s. Many Americans like to complain, but love to profit from those immigrants. When that doesn't work, other methods of profiting are implemented. Using our freedom of information tactics we search our local town clerks, municipal buildings, banks and newspapers in hopes of finding someone whose home may be in foreclosure as a result of losing a love one, lost of employment, inability to make mortgage payments, taxes, low wages or victims of a poor economy. I've personally witness many South American Latinos, Italians and Mexican immigrant workers involved in upscale construction projects who successfully completed work assignments with time to spare and who were not paid. Not paid by contractors or employers simply because they were people who did not possess a green card.

Mr. Wallison and Mason Crew, 2008

However, these scam practices by contractors and corporations are not only limited to immigrants. Here in central Florida I had the honor and privilege of meeting and hiring an Afro American masonry crew, who's been in the business since the mid 1960s. According to its owner Mr. Wallison, they were hired and contracted by the most famous theme park in central Florida during the 1960s. The contractual agreement was to create architecturally designed concrete structures in different locations throughout the park at a specified time. After months of hard work, dedication and successful work accomplishments, executive members of this theme park refuse to pay the mason crew over one hundred thousand plus dollars in labor cost and materials. Making excuses involving time frame and poor concrete material used on architectural designs, which still stand today, forty plus years later. Although their spirits were harmed, and souls impaired by the ignorance of these so-call entrepreneurs, Mr. Wallison and his crew, with one hundred thirty years of combined experience, moved on. Through it all, they manage to keep the business, maintained their honorableness, integrity and courtesy toward their customers. A lesson we all can learn from.

14

However, let's not forget or confuse discrimination with ignorance, like the Noah's Ark story mentioned previously. An ignorant individual no matter what skin color, is an ignorant individual, and I personally like many others, don't like ignorant individuals. We need not to concern ourselves with those immigrants who enter the US for the sole purpose of survival, but celebrate them, their success and contribution to this country and its people, like American Engineer and NASA Astronaut, José Moreno Hernández and Former US Attorney General, Alberto Reynaldo Gonzales.

STORY CONT:

After dropping the Asian woman off in her pajamas, I finally reached Willies home on Allen Street in Manhattan, and honked my horn informing him of my arrival. As I sat there staring at the ground. I can see hundreds of street rats running endlessly in every direction. Some actually huddle in groups as though they were sharing a meal, while others gathered like neighbors having a neighborhood chat. A whistle startled me momentarily and startled the rats. It was Willie from his window above.

"I'll be right down Bermudez, give me a minute?"

"Al, Al, call me Al, when we're off-duty," I said.

"Ok big Al, give me a minute."

I knew the request wouldn't last, since we're so governmentally institutionalized and use to addressing one another by our last names. Willie finally came down.

"Hello, Mr. Bermudez, and good morning sir."

"Good morning, Mr. Marrero," I replied knowingly.

We began the journey up East Houston Street toward the FDR, (Franklin D. Roosevelt) expressway. We stopped at a red light on Columbia Street intersection and were met with a New York City patrol car, which pulled up alongside of us. As they slowly proceeded through the intersection I looked over to the patrol car and could see two male police officers with what appeared to be a female prisoner in the rear seat.

15

Al and Willie Marrero, 1988

"Oh, shit!"

"What's wrong Bermudez?"

"See the Asian woman in back of the patrol car?"

"Yeah, I do, what about her?"

"I dropped her off on Chrystie Street a few minutes ago. She was in the middle of the road on the Manhattan Bridge wearing pajamas."

"We see many Asian people walking around this neighborhood in the early-morning hours. I think they're smuggled here and dropped off on the bridges."

It appeared as though the patrol car was heading toward the FDR.

"Are there any police stations nearby?"

The closet station is in the opposite direction. Did she tell you where she wanted to go?"

"She tried giving me a piece of paper with an address written on it. I think she wanted me to take her to that location, but it was way across town."

"They're probably going to drop her off."

Having traveled across the FDR and Major Deegan expressways, we were now entering the Sprain Brook Parkway, one of many convenient routes; we took to the prison to help us break up the same-old driving routine.

"I see you're carrying a large bag, what's for lunch?"

"Bermudez let me tell you what I have here. Un poquito de todo, (A little bit of everything). Pollo frito, totones con ajo y arroz con habichuelas, (Fried chicken, fried plantation bananas in garlic with rice and beans).

I looked at Willie with a disgusting look.

"Coño, Willie, tu come como un Rey y de pues te queja, (Damn, Willie, you eat like a king and like to complain).

"Dicen que la manera al corazón de un hombre es por el estómago. Algunas mujeres verdaderamente creen eso," (They say a way to a man's heart is through his stomach. Some women actually believe that).

"I don't know Willie; some women can't cook if their children lives depended on it."

"Yeah, that may be true, but as long as my wife, and I can cook that's all that matters."

And the conversation slowly ended as Willie began dosing off. We were now entering route 117, a dark and winding road with an abundance of wildlife; especially deer, that is usually standing off the side of the road or gingerly walking across. Route 117 has very narrow lanes, rolling hills, and lots of vacant land with trees that can topple at any given time. It's a hazardous road on raining days and treacherous in snowy conditions. It's one of those roads which demands respect and complete attention to unforeseen circumstances. Willie was now deep in his sleep, and I had the Kenny G music playing on my cassette tape. Nothing unusual and the road seemed quiet and well lit; that is until a human silhouette appeared directly in front of the car. '*Not again,*' I said to myself, remembering the Chinese woman on the bridge. This time, it was a man directly in front of me, a short distance away. I immediately applied the brakes, pulled onto the shoulder and brought my vehicle to a completely stop.

"Oh, shit… what was that?" I said in confusability.

"What was what, what happen?"

"I saw someone on the road, but he's no longer there."

"There's no one there Bermudez."

"Yes, I know. I can see there's no one there, but I'm sure I saw someone. He was an elder guy, wearing a short dungaree jacket and blue jeans. He turned his head to look over at the car."

Still trying to understand what just occurred, I stood there wondering and looking around for a pedestrian who obviously wasn't there.

"Hey, B, (Short for Bermudez) you're scaring me."

Willie couldn't comprehend, and neither could I.

"Sorry, Willie, let's get out of here."

I drove away locking continuously in my rearview mirror, but nothing appeared. For the life of me, I couldn't understand what just happened.

Willie gave me a strange look.

"No me digas que tu eres una de esas personas que ven cosas que no está allí," (Don't tell me you're one of those persons who see things that aren't there).

"No, I'm not, but I know what I saw. There was a man on the roadway walking with his back to us. He turned to look as though the car's headlight got his attention."

I didn't expect him to understand, sure as heck I didn't. Willie looked at me with a strange stare again, and in a somber voice said, "Hey, brother, let's hurry up and get to the prison. I rather see living breathing bodies. You're starting to scare me and do me a favor, don't pick me up tomorrow."

I laughed and instantly knew Willie was not the hardcore officer he portrayed himself to be. We were finally entering Ossining, where the prison is located and stopped for a coffee at Gino's Deli off route 133. We walked in and greeted Gino.

"Hey, Gino, what's going on?"

Gino began speaking in Italian.

"Ehi, Al, buon giorno, ciò che fa lei dice?" (Hey, Al, good morning, what do you say)?

"Good morning, Gino," said Willie, as he headed toward the newspapers, something he does every morning religiously and right to the sport section.

"Che farà lei gli individui hanno questa mattina?" (What will you guys have this morning)?

"Hey, Gino, thanks for the education in Italian language, but we don't speak Italian. We're learning though," I said.

"Hey, fellas, a little Italian speaking on a daily basis and by the end of the year you'll have sentences others will understand," said Gino. *

Gino was an Italian gentleman from Yorktown Heights, in Westchester County, who recently opened his deli. When Gino served you breakfast you were sure to leave his establishment content and with a protuberant belly. Entering Gino's deli on any given day and smelling those Italian cheeses hanging from its racks, in addition to the lingering aroma of morning coffee, always brought me back to the old Italian neighborhood of Bensonhurst, Brooklyn. I was once employed by an old Italian shoemaker named Ciro, who also owned a shoe store off Avenue U, in Brooklyn, next to the Avenue U train station. He was a frequent visitor of an Italian cafe and deli. The café had many little flags of green, white and red colors flying in the wind with several outdoor tables and chairs available only to those who frequented the establishment. Outside the business looked old and outdated. Some pedestrians would walk by and never take a second look, but inside was a completely different story. The floor was that of Italian marble from Carrara, Italy, I later learned. Wood inlays, iron and marble detailing added an authentic stylish touch. Stone wrapped on walls create the kind of rustic quality one would expect from an old Italian building. Other sections of the walls had pine paneling, similar to the wainscoting we see today. The ceilings were high and architecturally designed. The counter panels and base were solid mahogany with granite top, unusual for those times. Several columns decorated the café, and a stunning rotunda, intended to give the business a historical sense of place with an old world feel. The espresso machine was an old Italian antique dating back to the 1930s. It was made of cooper and brass with a finished polish shine. The owner was a tall, Italian old man named Vito, from Siracusa Sicily, who spoke severe broken English. He sported a white curled up handlebar mustache, always wore a white apron and rarely was seen without his Toscano Originale cigar, handmade in Lucca, Italy. Other old timers sat inside the establishment on rounded tables and in clouds of cigar smoke; while having their espresso and Italian pastries, cannolis were the favorite.

Vito called me over to the counter.

"Hey, you wanna espresso?"

"Sure," I replied.

He walked over to the coffee machine placing his cigar on an ashtray.

"You see-ah this-ah ashtray, this-ah antique ashtray was-ah made in Murano, Italy."

"Nice ashtray," I replied not realizing the value of his description. Walking into his establishment was like heading back in time. The words vintage and antique covered every inch of the cafe.

"What part of Italy yo-u family from," asked Vito in his broken English.

"I'm not from Italy sir. I'm from Brooklyn, and my parents are from Vieques."

I remembered Vito's puzzled look trying to understand what I said.

"Vieques, what-ah part of Italy is-ah, Vieques?"

"No, Mr. Vito, Vieques is not in Italy. It's an island just off Puerto Rico."

"Puerto Rico!" he shouted, as though he was completely taken off guard.

"Ehi, Ciro, lei porta uno Spagnolo bambino qui!" (Hey, Ciro, you bring a Spanish boy here!)

"Non preoccuparsi Vito è un bambino buono," (Don't worry about it Vito, he's a good kid).

Vito's eyes began to squint. He picked up his cigar from the ashtray and put it in his mouth. His lips tilted and he brightly let out a smile.

"You look-ah, like-ah Italiano and its-ah good enough for me."

He handed me a double espresso and in one shot, I took it down. Vito didn't know I was a coffee fanatic and came from a family who loved coffee with an immense passion; of course, Café Bustelo being the favorite.

"Minga, beve il caffè come un Italiano," said Vito. (Damn, he drinks coffee like an Italian).

I had an idea of what was being said, since there are many similarities in dialogues between the Italian and Spanish languages.

I too became a regular at Vito's café and deli. I eventually got to know all the old-timers that frequent the place. I later moved from the neighborhood, never to return, but always remembered and took with me, the stories told by these Compatrioti Italiani, (Italian countrymen). Living and working in Gravesend and Bensonhurst, Brooklyn as long as I have, makes it almost impossible not to cross paths with an Italian family. I was sincerely privileged in my life to have been able to live in an Italian neighborhood. I was born and raised in a ghetto, lived fairly close to a Jewish neighborhood, and spent many school vacations as a child in Vieques, Porto Rico. This diversified way of living helped me, not only to understand the many different cultures and traditions, but respect the way of live life and conditions of everyone else's.

STORY CONT:

After having breakfast and filling our tummies at Gino's Deli, with home-fries, eggs, bacon, toast bread, orange juice and coffee, Willie and I were tempted to call in sick and head back home. We were now a couple of living breathing zombies, with basketball shaped stomachs and absolutely no energy for a conversation. We left and drove up to route 9, then State Street and onto Hunter Street, arriving at the prison parking lot. We momentarily sat in the car and looked at one another.

"Well, Mr. Marrero, we're here. Are you ready to go in?"

"Not really, the breakfast made me lazy and sleepy. I tell you what, I feel like going back home. I hate this damn place."

"Yeah, I know exactly what you mean. Who doesn't hate coming to a place like this, so what do you want to do?"

"Coño, yo no se, (Damn, I don't know). Come on let's go to work."

"Ok, if you say so."

I smiled while exiting the vehicle. We approached the facility arsenal, where Willie and I surrendered our weapons." *

Sing-Sing's arsenal stores many firearms and other important equipment, rifles, gas guns, gas masks, shotguns, service revolvers, chemical agents, (tear gas), chemical projectiles, handcuffs, leg irons, ammunition, departmental radios, thousands of keys and much more. It is an area of extreme importance and requires the officer's complete and full attention to detail. It is not the place for mistakes, and if you are one who wishes to make it your permanent place of work, you must familiarize yourself with its rules and regulations, with its policies and procedures, pertinent directives and job descriptions. The issuing of equipment and firearms is not the only comprisable activity that takes place. Arsenal officers also have to monitor radio communications, listen to alarms, which may be activated, and respond accordingly, effectively and immediately. In addition to documenting all equipment surrendered, transportation records and daily activities conducted are also logged. Officers who work this hectic and chaotic environment in most cases burn out and subconsciously develop attitudes toward others, but understandably so. Other officers don't understand how crucial it is or don't understand the responsibilities that come with working a facility arsenal. Many officers, including myself, took matters personal when confronted with an attitude or became impatiently agitated when delays were caused at the arsenal window, not realizing or taking under consideration the magnitude of responsibilities an arsenal officer has to undertake. If all that responsibility wasn't enough, in 1989, an arsenal officer who had successfully completed the weapons manufactures armored school, along with training officers, were also responsible for the cleaning and repairing of those weapons as well. My hat goes off to those officers who worked and continue to work Sing-Sing's arsenal and other facility arsenals throughout the country. And who manage to keep their sanity intact at the end of the workday.

STORY CONT:

We're now entering the prison's front gate after submitting our weapons. We reached into our pockets, produce our shields, with identification cards and opened any carrying bags for contraband search by the gate officer before making full entry.

22

We then looked up at the green chalkboard directly in front of us for photos of decease officers which may have been posted by the previous shift. Other than the front gate officer, the photograph of a deceased officer is the second face you'll probably see upon entry. We then walk into the time card room; pull out our time cards from its slots and slipped it into the time clock for a date and time computation. Our next step is to enter the lineup room and submit our time cards to the attending assistant watch commander, (a sergeant) for a signature and attendance check. Willie placed his hands behind himself before entering the lineup room, positioned himself like an ice skater and skated on the slippery floor making his way up to the sergeant's desk. This was something he did every morning. Everyone in the lineup room smiled and others laughed. After getting his time card signed, Willie skated around several officers and supervisors before exiting the lineup room.

The many years of pretending to ice skate have caused Willie to perfect this act. When you saw him skate into the lineup room, it actually looked as though he was gracefully skating on a sheet of ice. Another of Willie's comical act was his ability to speak in sentences, or call out people's names while at the same time sounding like a sheep or a goat. We both went downstairs to the locker room where we had lockers next to one another. We were met by other officers who were already there in the same isle and engaged in hot conversations. Soon, the conversations turned into laughter as Willie ludicrously began his playful insults by calling out officer's names in his famous sheep impersonation. Officer Rolando Gonzales (aka Gonzo) was the first victim of the day.

"Gon-za-liiii-toooo - Gon-za-liiii-toooo."

Gonzo was a tall Latino man, over two-hundred pounds, mild mannered, yet able to lose his cool at the drop of a hat. He didn't like Willie's joke and shot back in Spanish.

"Oye, Marrero, que te pasa, tu quieres una pela," (Hey Marrero, what's wrong, you want an ass kicking).

Willie began laughing and Gonzo looked at him with an intense stare. He began shaking his chest muscles in an intimating manner, and again, he verbally shot back at Willie.

"You want some of this Fifi? You want some of this? Do me a favor, you want to impress me? Go to the blocks and fight your own fight, don't let my man Bermudez do all the fighting for you."

The name Fifi was given to Willie by block officers because he came to work one day while sporting jerry curls and white socks with his dark uniform pants. The fashion statement only lasted eight hours, thanks to peer pressure. Willie's jerry curls and white socks were never worn again. Willie's attempt to anger others always worked. He knew exactly how to get underneath someone's skin. Right at that same moment another officer walked in, Emil Mejia and Willie began his verbal sheep attack.

"Me-jiiii-aaaa - Me-jiiii-aaaa, good morning Me-jiiii-aaaa."

Officer Mejia, originally from Long Island, was an extremely funny character and able to make people laugh with just one look, but like many others, Willie was not one Emil took lightly to.

"You piece of shit, get a life!"

And he walked over to his side of the locker room with nothing further to say. Willie thrived on this reaction and for some unknown reason, officers didn't like it when Willie called out their names or tried to converse with them while at the same time imitating a sheep. I personally didn't have a problem with it. As a matter of fact, I enjoyed every minute of it, and at times I couldn't stop laughing about it. For years Willie continued his verbal assault and torment on others. We were now done putting on our uniforms and made the trip back upstairs to the lineup room for roll call and briefing. Willie entered the lineup room again in his famous ice skating performance. As we both walked inside the lineup room, I saw a ten-dollar bill on the floor. No one in the immediate area seems to be aware it was there, nor did anyone stepped forward to claim it. So I bend over to pick it up and the ten dollar bill instantly pulled away from me, "Oh, shit" I said. Puzzled by how fast it slipped out of my hands. *

Behind a wall was practical joker Frank Diaz, who had the ten-dollar bill affixed to a string with a retractable spring loaded mechanism. Everyone in the lineup room was in on the gag, and laughter surfaced from every corner of the room. One officer yelled out, "Aw, you poor bastard, guess you'll have to wait for a union raise." While another added a few words of his own, "or wait for a uniform allowance."

Born and raised in Porto Plata, Dominican Republic, (La Hispaniola) Franky Diaz worked in B-block with the rest of us. Franky was a jokester and always had a trick up his sleeve.

Soft-spoken and mild mannered, Franky always managed to suppress his anger and maintain complete control of himself and of his surroundings. A lesson we all could have benefited from, although some supervisors and convicts saw this as a weakness. I once witnessed a confrontation involving officer Frank Diaz with a convict. The convict was yelling at the top of his lungs while using threatening gestures. Franky stood his ground allowing the convict to continue his verbal assault until he was blue in the face. The convict apparently knew his tantrum and wolf tickets, (Slang for threats) were not resulting in retaliation. He finally stopped the yelling and like a professional boxer who recognizes defeat, the convict took a look around his immediate area, found a seat and sat himself down in a sweat. Franky, on the other hand, approached the convict and with his velvety voice said,

"Hey, you want some water?"

The convict's facial expression toward Franky was a classic. The convict had an expression of complete regret and remorse, almost as though he just verbally insulted the Catholic Pope. Officer Diaz had a way with self-control, willpower and level headedness. However, it didn't always work in his favor. Like many others, he later sustained serious physical injuries in another unrelated incident. A convict apparently kicked a steel door shut while Frank's arm was positioned between the steel door and an eight inch thick concrete wall. He sustained numerous fractures on his arm requiring surgical reconstruction, using stainless steel screws and brackets for repair and stability. His ability to use his arm under normal circumstances would never be the same. After seeking disability retirement and subsequently receiving a denial, Frank Diaz against all wishes, returned to work and continues to work today as a result of poor legal representation of counsel. Incidents like this are all too common throughout the United States in our correctional institutions. Correction officers throughout the US, and almost on a daily basis are stabbed, slashed, punched, kicked, slapped, stomped, bitten, struck with dangerous instruments, held hostage and subjected to urine and feces throwing. They're verbally harassed, spit upon, threaten and families are also threatened. They're tormented, sexually abused, extorted, manipulated, screamed upon, set up, tricked, fooled and murdered.

During my career, I worked with approximately forty plus correction officers who unfortunately died of heart attacks, strokes or cancer; while active on the job. Others died immediately after retirement or committed suicide. While many in legislative and administrative positions, law offices, courts and labor relations board are convinced correction officers are paid enough to tolerate these threatening behaviors and assaults, nothing could be further from the truth. In December of 2000, the National Institute of Justice, for the US Department of Justice, released a publication series, "Addressing Correctional Officer Stress, Programs and Strategies." This publication was designed to inform administrators of correctional institutions throughout the US, to develop programs in preventing and treating officer stress. Through in-house training, counseling, peer support and other services. Although these services are not that of a psychiatrist, psychotherapist or any other mental health practitioner, the services are provided by fellow officers of all ranks and readily available to an officer at their facility. It's accessible daily and in some cases immediately following an incident.

In Sing-Sing, many of those officers, who were assigned to help you, also spread rumors and gossip concerning your personal dilemma. As it presently stands, many of our nation's state and local correction officers, troopers, police officers, peace officers, deputy sheriffs, probation officers, parole officers, detention deputies, firefighters and paramedics are not aware the US Department of Justice has in place a Public Safety Officers Disability Benefits Program.

Enacted in 1976, with injuries later added November 29, 1990, the program covers all who suffered a death or permanent and total disability as the direct result of an injury sustained while in the line of duty. Anyone with a legitimate claim of disability which led to retirement and family members on behalf of an officer's death must file within three years. If you had no knowledge, such a program existed you may file a written request for an extension or call 888-744-6513. According to the US Department of Justice, Bureau of Justice Assistance Program, the following chart indicates the amount all states and local public safety officers are entitled to. For each death and disability claim the award amount is solely determined by the actual date of officer's death or disability, not retirement date.

DATE OF DEATH	BENEFIT AMOUNT
9/26/76 to 5/31/88	$ 50,000
6/01/88 to 9/30/88	$100,000
10/01/88 to 9/30/89	$103,890
10/01/89 to 9/30/90	$109,460
DEATH OR INJURY	BENEFIT AMOUNT
10/01/90 to 9/30/91	$114,235
10/01/91 to 9/30/92	$119,894
10/01/92 to 9/30/93	$123,520
10/01/93 to 9/30/94	$127,499
10/01/94 to 9/30/95	$130,416
10/01/95 to 9/30/96	$134,571
10/01/96 to 9/30/97	$138,461
10/01/97 to 9/30/98	$141,556
10/01/98 to 9/30/99	$143,943
10/01/99 to 9/30/00	$146,949
10/01/00 to 12/31/00	$151,635
01/01/01 to 9/30/01	$250,000
10/01/01 to 9/30/02	$259,038
10/01/02 to 9/30/03	$262,100
10/01/03 to 9/30/04	$267,494
10/01/04 to 9/30/05	$275,658
10/01/05 to 9/30/06	$283,385
10/01/06 to 9/30/07	$295,194
10/01/07 to 9/30/08	$303,064
10/01/08 to 9/30/09	$315,746
10/01/09 to 9/30/10	$311,810
10/01/10 to 9/30/11	$318,111
10/01/11 to 9/30/12	$323,035

This onetime payment benefit will not affect or offset your monthly benefits with SSA, your disability pension or workers compensation benefits, nor is it taxed by the Internal Revenue Service, (IRS). Most employees are not aware such support program or disability benefits exist for correction officers.

Not to say these programs don't exist, it quite obvious they do, but in Sing-Sing, the implementation in making the information available to everyone does not happen. Correction officers play a vital role in the assistance of mental health observations and interventions, in addition to successful collaboration, communication and cooperation between officers and mental health personnel. Correction officers are trained and know these are the important elements needed in contributing and managing mental disorders in convicts, all part of the custody, care and control philosophy. These exercises and techniques are conducted daily with success and without any expression of discontent by most. However, when the shoe is on the other foot, ever wonder who will be there for the law enforcement officers who find themselves hopeless, helpless and desperate for answers? Unlike those who work in private sectors or civilian capacity, a law enforcement officer who seeks psychotherapy, psychiatry or other mental remedy is automatically labeled by its administration as unfit for duty, and in most cases at risk of losing their jobs. Adding to an already hardship circumstance and thus forcing many not to seek help in the first place. Not to mention weapons are also taken away or firearm permits rejected upon an officer's retirement. Something the NYS Labor Relations Board thrives on. Many in our society are under the misconception that a law enforcement uniform is somehow an erasability of life's disreputable hardships. Alternatively, that the existence of emotional distress, physiological distress, financial difficulties or your common family matters doesn't exist within a law enforcement officer's household. The fact of the matter is— many law enforcement officers who work the prison system or patrol our streets and highways are actually experiencing detrimental perplexities in their personal lives, from having children with cancer, irreversible brain disease, heart disease, severe autism and mental depressive illnesses. Law enforcement officers, whether within the confines of a prison or on public streets, have a sworn duty to protect others from harm or harm to themselves. What many of us don't know and at times will find out when it's too late—is that our own family members are sometimes forgotten and they, like everyone else, suffer from these unfortunate crises. We need to remember as law enforcement officers, we are not immune from such crisis. As a parent or spouse, we're equally sworn to protect our own love ones.

Unfortunately, many of Sing-Sing officers and law enforcement officers throughout our nation seek a remedy through substance abuse and the overindulgence of alcohol. This behavior can be attributed to many different factors; wanting to fit in with a particular group of officers or supervisors. Trying to forget the prison environment and all its negative elements associated with it, attempting to camouflage the stress or pain inside your soul, an energy boost at the end of your workday or the prison and home environment is characteristically similar. I've been there, and I too found myself in the overindulgence of alcohol during my career. However, the substance abuse doesn't end at the level of officers. Many supervisors are in the same unpleasant predicament which only decreases any chances of hopeful correspondence for an officer who may be in need of help. Although there were many supervisors experiencing substance abuse or personal problems in Sing-Sing, many others were willing to put themselves in your shoes, thus eliminating any complex interaction between the individuals. Then you had the other kind of supervisors with substance abuse problems who use their supervisory authority through verbal alleviation. Alternatively, whose sole purpose was to relieve themselves from their inner guilt's and anger by making your day incredibly difficult; adding to an already chaotic environment.

If NYS and other states throughout our nation were to implement a mandatory drug test effective immediately upon all officers and supervisors, more than fifty percent of all examined would fail. Either through positive urine, blood or some form of elevated SGPT, (an enzyme found within the liver cells which indicates the liver cells are damaged as a result of large quantity of alcohol consumption). Although ignored by the general public, forgotten by many and looked down upon by most, correction officers just like our police officers, firefighters, nurses, doctors and soldiers, are an extreme important part of our lives. We are an intelligent society living in modern times with electric razor fencing, infrared cameras and motion sensors in the prevention of escape and protection of our public. Implementations of helpful and advance knowledgeable programs that can successfully and prematurely extinguish any signs of substance abuse, financial hardship and family matters for correction officers are just as important in the prevention of escape and protection of our general public.

A sound body and mind, healthy, proud, educated and a financially stable correction officer, is a professional with endless years of loyalty and dedication, not only to his or her department, but to society as a whole.

STORY CONT:

Officer Frank Diaz emerged from behind the wall with his retractable device and reached out a handshake in a friendly forgiving gesture.

"Perdóneme mi hermano eso fue una broma," (Forgive me brother it was a joke).

I maturely reached out my hand in forgiveness and to my surprise was once again met with another practical joke, the classic hand buzzer. It's a ring that slips over a finger with a buzzer seated on the palm of the hand. It gives the victim a small electrical shock. I was again taken off guard.

"Tu eres una plasta de mierda," (You're a mass piece of shit). Practical jokes and humorous conversations were Frankie's MO, (Method of operation). It actually helped to break up the morning tension and temporarily allowed us to forget where we were for those several minutes before the completion of the lineup and the long walk up to the prison blocks. I walked away from Franky and sat down with Willie on our favorite wooden bench where we had a view of the entire lineup room and all the employees who entered. We began conversing, but ending the intellectual conversation was the morning yell of a supervisor.

"Listen up officers, on the lineup, on the lineup," (Roll call attendance).

Like dope fiends in search of a drug fix, officers ran up to one another asking for collar brass, (insignias) and other uniform equipment. Lineup was now in progress, and attendance was being conducted. Sergeants were making their way through the lines surveying the officer's uniforms. Sergeant Marcus Rivera made his way to officer, Eddie Villanueva. He stopped and looked up and down at the officer. Villa lets out a smile knowing full well his appearance couldn't be questioned by his superiors, so he verbally lets the sergeant have it.

"Sigue por alli sargento, que aqui no hay nada," (Keep going sergeant, there's nothing here).

Sergeant Rivera smiled at his remarked, walked over to Willie Marrero, and stopped to survey his uniform. Willie looked at the sergeant and began doing what he liked best, verbal tormenting.

"Hey, Sergeant Rivera, can I ask you question?"

"Sure, Marrero, what's up?"

"I was wondering sergeant, you like girls?"

"What?"

The sergeant was totally confused and caught off guard by the question.

"You like girl's sergeant?"

"You are a sick little fucking puppy. What kind of question is that? Of course, I like girls."

This was a question Willie asked everyone every now and then. It always confused the person and there was no rhyme or reason to Willie's unpredictable questions.

"I just wanted to know if you like girl's sergeant, because if you don't, I have a handsome macho I can introduce you to who's standing right next to me."

Willie looked over at me, and I quickly responded in defense. "Jesucristo, no le aga caso sargento que ese tipo está enfermo de la cabeza, (Jesus Christ, don't listen to him sergeant, that dude is sick in the head).

Willie continued.

"I tell you what sergeant, if you're not into little guys like Bermudez, how about that great big pretty Puerto Rican standing right over there," pointing toward Gonzo.

Gonzo immediately replied with a threat.

"Oye, Marrero, tu esta buscando que yo te rompa en dos," (Hey, Marrero, you're looking for me to break you in two).

Sergeant, Marc Rivera smiled at Willie and Gonzo, while quietly instructing them to keep it down.

"You guys are crazy. Keep it down the lineup is still in progress." Sergeant Rivera walked away.

Attendance is called for those who did not submit their time cards or have not yet made it to work. Although Willie already submitted his time card for a signature and made his presences known to the attending sergeant, his name was called anyway. Some sergeants liked how Willie answered to his name during attendance. His name was called.

"Officer Marrero," called the sergeant.

Willie replies in his famous sheep impersonation.

31

"Heeerre Seerrrgggeant."

The entire lineup room began laughing, stopping sergeant Rivera dead in his tracks. He looked over at Willie, but had nothing to say since his name was purposely and officially called by the assistant watch commander.

"Alright now, that's enough with the morning's entertainment. Let's get back to the attendance," announced a lieutenant. However, the damage was done and some officers couldn't stop laughing. Some tried hard to hold it in, but with the silence came another outburst of laughter. The laughter was similar to that of a celebrity who's trying to get their lines spoken, but fails to complete the sentence when the smallest of things makes them laugh. Some supervisors, mostly lieutenants, were getting annoyed and began reading out loud the latest in departmental policies and procedures. Other supervisors, who did not want to be seen holding back the laughter, covered their mouth and walked out of the lineup room. The jokes ended, and lineup attendance completed. Willie somehow managed to slip away from the formation and quietly exited the lineup room to the arsenal window at the rear corridor. Sergeant Rivera was given the honors of dismissing the lineup room and sending the officers to work.

"Officers, attention, go to work!"

Officers rushed to the arsenal window for last minute pickup of equipment and keys. As we approached the window, we could hear Willie calling out to the civilian phone operator in his verbal sheep imitation.

"Oooperaaator, good morning, Oooperaaator!"

Willie picked up the equipment, and we began the long walk up to the prison block. We reached the gates at five building and finally B-block housing unit. Several officers from the previous night shift were standing at the gates hugging the bars and waiting to leave. As soon as the eco of voices are heard in the corridor, officers hug the exit doors like thoroughbred horses at a starting gate, and who can blame them, eight hours in a prison is enough for anyone to hug any gate leading to civilization.

"On the gate, the 7-3 officers are here! How are you guys doing? It's always nice to see you guys."

Willie scowled.

"How was the night shift?"

"All the convicts are sleeping."

"Sure they are, or dead and stinking."

The nightshift officers ignored him, and we walked in. Officers assigned to galleries pick up their radios and swap their batteries. Keys are then collected. A list of confined convicts is received, and information is exchanged by relieved and relief officers. Officers without permanent assignments stand by for further instructions while others reported to their locations. Willie and I are assigned to keeplock recreation, (recreation for confined convicts). Our next step is to obtain a list of those disciplinary convicts, put them on our list and visit each cell for recreation confirmation, (We basically ask if they will attend recreation or not). Willie will cover the front side of the housing unit galleries, Q-R-S-T-U, and I was to cover the back side, V-W-X-Y-Z. Our daily method of operation was to start on top galleries first and work ourselves down, always meeting at the center of the gallery for note comparison before moving on to the next tier. The least amount of convicts we had for recreation, the better our day would be. Most convicts asked about the weather, and the answer was always the same, cold and wet. Even if the sun was expected to rise, and temperature was expected to be mild or warm. The answer was always the same, cold and wet. We were correction officers, not weathermen. Fewer convicts in recreation equaled fewer problems. On this day only seven volunteered for recreation, making for an easy afternoon. We went down to the office and compared notes making certain convicts who volunteered for recreation were not confined for fighting one another.

"How many convicts do you have for recreation Bermudez?"

"I have four convicts who want Rec, (Recreation).

"I only have three, why do you have four, didn't you tell them its cold and wet outside?"

"Does it matter three or four? We're usually escorting fifteen in the morning and ten in the afternoon."

"Yeah, you're right. There are no fighters on our list, so we can take them all out in the morning and goof off in the afternoon."

"Sure, no problem, unless of course, an escort is needed in the afternoon, then we'll have to take turns in escorting them."

"Bermudez, you'll escort the first convict who needs to go somewhere; I'll take the second?"

"Coño, hermano, (Damn brother) why is it, you have to make the rules?"

33

"I have one-month seniority over you. You came in August, and I came in July."

Sensing he proved his point, Willie laughed, launched out of the office and walked off to the coat room where coffee was brewing. We began drinking coffee and a yell from above distracted our morning conversation.

"CO, put me down for rec, I want to go!"

Willie stepped out of the coatroom and yelled back.

"What cell are you in?"

"I'm in S-100, and no one asked me if I wanted to go out!"

Willie momentarily reviewed his list and answered back.

"I went to your cell, and you said you didn't want recreation, so you can't go!"

"Yo, co, don't fuck with me man, I want my rec!"

"Like I said, you said no!"

"Yo, co, check this out, when I get out of this cell, I'm going to fuck you up. That's my word!"

"Yeah, whatever you say schmack-da-vic!"

Schmack-da-vic was a word created and used by Willie to camouflage the true meaning of its definition, "Schmuck."

The convict continued yelling and began rattling his cell door for attention.

"Yo, sergeant, I want my fucking rec, or I'm going to burn this fucking cell!"

I told Willie I would go up and see what I can do to calm down the potential firebug. Willie snapped.

"You're getting soft on me Bermudez, the heck with that prick. He said he didn't want recreation, and I wrote his refusal down. If we start giving recreation to every schmack-da-vic like him who wants to change their minds every time they feel like it or discover they're buddy is going to recreation, we'll never get our work done!"

"I'm going upstairs and calm him down that's all. I'm just trying to make it easier for the gallery officer, so he won't have to put up with the convict's bullshit the rest of his shift."

The convict yelled again.

"CO, I want my fucking rec!"

"I'm going up there so stop the damn yelling!"

I went up to S-gallery and approached the screaming convict only to find myself speechless.

"I know you. You're from Coney Island."

"Yeah, officer, I know you too. You live in Carey Gardens, what's up dog?"

"Dog...the name is Bermudez. What are you doing in state prison tough-guy?"

"It's a long story; something happened that shouldn't have happened."

"Yeah, something like what?"

"I got life in prison; you know what I'm saying?"

"Life, what the hell did you do kill a cop?"

"Yeah, something like that."

"Either you did or you didn't?"

"It was an accident; we didn't mean to kill him."

"Oh, shit, you killed a cop. What the hell were you thinking, what happened?"

The convict stated that one early morning, he and his crime partners all from Brooklyn, entered a McDonald's restaurant they thought was empty, but to their surprise, there were workers still inside. They forced everyone at gunpoint into a room and while attempting to open a safe. One of the workers managed to slip away. Moments later, officers arrived and he was immediately apprehended, but his crime buddies ran up to the roof with one cop in hot pursuit. The officer fell into a shaft and unfortunately died as a result of his fall. *

According to a local paper, Anthony T. Dwyer, twenty-three years old, and several other police officers interrupted a robbery at a McDonald's restaurant. All four robbers described as career criminals were charged with his death. First Deputy Police Commissioner Richard J. Condon said at a news conference that one of the four, E. Matos, twenty-one years old, said he fought with the officer on the roof moments before the officer fell into the twenty-five-foot shaft. After nearly a half-hour of efforts to lift Officer Dwyer from the shaft, Emergency Service officers broke through a ventilation duct near the bottom and carried him through the basement of a neighboring restaurant to an ambulance. Their efforts were in vain. Officer Dwyer was pronounced dead at Bellevue Hospital. The first man arrested, T. Harris, thirty, of W. 23d Street in the Coney Island, was taken into custody inside the McDonald's. The three other men were arrested in Coney Island that afternoon.

35

They were identified as J. Bullock, forty, of W. 23d Street, Matos and Samuel Torres, thirty-five, both of W. 23d Street. All were charged with murder, burglary, attempted robbery, assault and possession of a deadly weapon. A police spokesman, Sgt. Raymond O'Donnell, said that about three-fifteen a.m. Harris, Bullock and Matos used a twelve-pound sledgehammer to smash a glass door of the McDonald's, at Seventh Ave near 40th Street. They surprised a worker laying tiles and five janitors. The robbers herded the janitors at gunpoint into a back room, where they tried to open a safe, but the man laying tiles slipped out and ran out to Times Square, where he found Officer Dwyer, Sgt. Thomas Flannagan and Officer Kevin Labrecht. When the officers crawled through the shattered door, Harris ran into a basement locker room, where he was arrested by Sergeant Flannagan, Officer Labrecht, and Sergeant O'Donnell. Matos and Bullock meanwhile, scrambled up a steel ladder onto the roof, with Officer Dwyer in pursuit. Matos and the officer struggled, and the officer fell over a two-foot railing into the shaft. However, it was unclear whether Bullock was present during the scuffle. Torres had been sitting in a getaway car in front of the McDonald's and drove off at some point. Raymond Rivera, one of the first paramedics at the scene, said Officer Dwyer was conscious and mumbling at the bottom of the shaft, "he was twisted like a pretzel against the wall," he said. Inspector Mayronne said the first two police officers to reach Officer Dwyer said he told them he had been pushed down the ventilation shaft, (*NY Times 1989*).

I knew exactly who this convict was talking about. I knew of the incident and knew of the officer's death. My brother Cruz 'The Moe' Morales was officially stationed at the fallen officer's home in a patrol car, where his wife was expecting a child. A child officer Dwyer would never get to see and enjoy. Cruz told me of the constant cries and yells that penetrated the walls of Dwyer's home and how it somehow entered his patrol car overpowering all other sounds around him and of the endless family visits with devastated faces and looks of uncertainty in what the future held for those he left behind. Cruz later left the NYC police department and became a Florida resident. He founded a cyber cafe, Lan-Gamerz and a private investigation business.

Cruz 'the Moe' Morales Pereira

Giving up those businesses, he then founded two companies: DBA Right Image Investigations, specializing in investigating compensation-related injuries and death cases—and the Insurance Workshop, (TIW) in Longwood, FL. Cruz also when on to join the rank and files of the Florida Highway Patrol. He is now the leading investigator in the hiring application process for six counties throughout Central Florida. Counties include Brevard, Volusia, Lake, Seminole, Orange and Osceola. Although his ability to reach entrepreneurship is at his disposal, the importance of life's normality supersedes the potential balance of power.

STORY CONT:

Now here I was faced with the decision of either giving a cop killer his one hour of recreation, as mandated by NYS, or deny him the recreation, since he refused it in the first place. A decision needed to be made with the knowledge that he knew exactly where I lived. He knew who my family members were and knew what kind of car I drove. He also knew what floor my mother lived on and knew her apartment number. All it takes from them (convicts) is one call from prison to their people on the outside and before you know it, crime-scene tape is scattered all around your residents and detectives labeling the crime scene as a drug-related homicide until proven otherwise.

'Heck with it, he refused his recreation, so I'll stretch out my refusal in the form of a conversation.' I subconsciously said to myself.

"Jesus Christ, so you and your buddies were responsible for the death of a police officer, and now you're here at Sing-Sing asking me for an hour of recreation that you previously refused to attend?"

"Come on, officer Bermudez, I'm paying my debt to the man, and you know me from the streets. I'm no cop killer."

"I hear you, I tell you what. Let me talk it over with my partner first."

"Who's your partner?"

"My partner is officer Marrero."

"Officer Marrero! Yo, that fucking co doesn't like me. If I was to kill a cop, I swear he would be the kind of cop I would kill. I can't stand him, and he can't stand me."

"Wait a minute, wait a minute! I'm not going to stand here and listen to this bullshit. I don't give a damn where you and I come from, or how long we've known one another. You understand? I've worked with this officer long before you decided to kill a cop and come to prison. We've been through a lot as brother officers."

The convict interrupted with an apology.

"I'm sorry officer. I didn't mean it that way."

"You're sorry, I tell you what. I'm going to forget what you just said about my partner, and you're going to forget about recreation, understand?"

"Damn, officer Bermudez, it's like that?"

"I'm afraid so, it's like that. You mentioned a threat on an officer's life in my presents and given your conviction history, as you just previously stated to me, I have to take this threat seriously and inform my superiors."

"Aight, aight, (Slang for understood). I didn't threaten him. I just said I would kill someone like that if I had to…never mind. I'll take my rec tomorrow, damn man! Are you going to write me up?" (Issue a misbehavior report).

"As long as you keep it down and forget what was said, no. However, just as soon as I get the word that you flew off the handle, I'm putting it in a report."

"No problem Bermudez, I'll just go back to sleep, but what if I have a problem with that same officer tomorrow?"

"You won't have a problem with him tomorrow or anyone else, for that matter, just as long as you're sure of your answer for recreation."

"Aight then, but before you leave officer, check this out. For the record, I'm no angel, and I've done a lot of bad stuff in my life, but I didn't kill that cop in New York, you know what I'm saying? No one did. It was an accident."

"I really don't know what to say, I'm not the judge or the jury. What's done is done and the bottom-line is, it was your action and the actions of your crimeys, (Slang for partners in crime) which led to his demise, regardless if you were in the immediate area or not."

And like a sign from heaven, an announcement was made over the PA, (Public address) system.

"Officer Bermudez and officer Marrero report to the OIC office or call the assistance watch-commander!"

I immediately informed the convict I had official work to conduct and the conversation ended. Willie and I met at the office, and I made the call to the sergeant.

"This is officer Bermudez returning your call sergeant."

"Yes, you and Marrero drove up together correct?"

"Yes we did sergeant, why?"

"You guys put in a PL, (Personal leave request) thirty days ago. I know you guys are already here, but would you guys like to take the day off and go home?"

"You don't have to ask me twice, hell yeah!"

"How about Marrero, does he want to go?"

"Don't worry about him sergeant; he's out of here too."

"Good, let the OIC officer know that two officers are on the way up and will be taking your place?"

"No problem sergeant thanks," and I hung up.

"Oye, (Listen) Willie, we're out of here. El sargento nos dio el resto del día libre, (The sergeant gave us the rest of the day off).

"Are you kidding me?"

"Nope, the personal leave slips submitted thirty days ago were approved."

"Damn, I forgot all about those slips, well let's get the hell out of this place?"

"We'll have to wait for our relief. They're on the way up."

The relieving officers arrived moments later. We exchanged all related information, informed them of the keeplock recreation list, of the screamer on S-gallery, surrendered our equipment, our duties and left with no hesitation. We arrived at the front gate. We showed our shields, identifications cards and approved slips with a great big smile. We stopped at Ray's deli off Springs Street for a coffee and continued on our way. We finally reached the Third Avenue Bridge an hour later, then onto the FDR Expressway only to be halted by traffic. However, it was ok because we were going home, and it was Saturday morning. The sun was out, and the day was clear. Our wives were home and nothing else mattered. Even so, something was bothering me. I still had to work the next day, Sunday.

"Oye, Willie, tu sabe algo, me olvidé de dar un PL para mañana, Domingo, (Hey, Willie, you know something. I forgot to submit a PL for tomorrow, Sunday).

"Yo puse el mio y fue aprobado esta mañana," (I put mines in and it was approved this morning).

"Que gato de yarda tu eres y cuando tu me lo y vas a decir?" (What an alley cat you are and when were you going to tell me)?

"I thought you submitted one last month."

"No I didn't. I forgot and now I have to work tomorrow."

"Mira hermano, mañana es Domingo, Salsa con Polito Vega, La Mega 97.9. Encuentrate un lugar donde tu puede relajarse y escuchar la música, el día se va rápido," (Look brother, tomorrow is Sunday, Salsa with Polito Vega, La Mega 97.9. Find yourself a place where you can relax and listen to the music, the day will go fast). *

40

La Fania, Courtesy of Izzy Sanabria, 2009

Somehow, I allowed Willie to convince me tomorrow wouldn't be so bad. I did enjoy listening to legendary radio talk show host Polito Vega. The classical salsa music on 97.9, La Mega, was something I looked forward to every Sunday. Although many songs are played by many different artistes, most of the music was by Fania. During the early 1960s, a military veteran of the Korean war and former New York City police officer Jerry Masucci, an Italian American that had a profound taste for the flavor of Latin Music, got together with legendary composer Johnny Pacheco, and created an entertainment organization that will forever be engraved in our history books, in our hearts and in the memories of millions, La Fania. The Fania consisted of many legendary talented musicians like; Larry Harlow, (who was the first to enter Fania) Ray Barretto, Bobby Valentin, Willie Colon, Hector LaVoe, Roberto Roena, Jorge Santana, Celia Cruz, Barry Rogers, Ismael Quintana, Ismael Miranda.

Others were Bobby Cruz, Cheo Feliciano, Pete "El Conde" Rodriguez, Justo Betancour, Santos Colon, Yomo Toro, Ruben Blades, Mongo Santamaria, Richie Ray, Joe Bataan, Papo Lucca, Adalberto Santiago, Eddie Palmieri, Tito Puente, Andy Montañez, Louie Ramirez, Jimmy Sabater, Orestes Vilato, Manu Dibango, Luis Perico Ortiz, Bobby Rodriguez, Renaldo Jorge, Hector Bomberito Zarzuela, Manu Dibango, Larry Spencer, and of course, the founders of Fania, Jerry Masucci and Johnny Pacheco.

The history of Fania All Stars is the man behind the scenes. Jerry Masucci. After attending college at night; he took a leave of absence from NYPD, and attended Mexico City College where he played halfback with their football team while earning a degree in business administration, majoring in foreign trade, and graduating first in his class with cum laude honors. He then returned to the police department as a plain clothes policeman and attended New York Law School during the day. He graduated from New York Law School in 1960, and thereafter received a Doctor of Law Degree. Jerry then resigned from the police department and worked in Havana, Cuba, as assistant to the Director of Public Relations in the Department of Tourism. Masucci partnered with Pariser and started the Pariser and Masucci law firm. In 1962, Johnny Pacheco used Masucci for his divorce, and Masucci saw a business potential in the Latin music scene. Jerry Masucci would eventually become the sole owner of Fania Records and the numerous other labels and umbrella labels in South America that he acquired and created. Jerry recognized the talents of his stars. He signed and owned them. His money and business acumen launched unknowns to stardom. He put together his entire artist's and invited others outside of his label to sing with Fania artists. Masucci was a clever man from lawyer to record producer, to promoter and feature film Maker. Masucci had Pacheco to direct stage productions and Larry Harlow directing the artist in the studio. In 1968, with the record label garnering more acclaim and a troupe of emerging artists, Masucci and Pacheco decided to create an ensemble of the most well-known and innovative Fania artists, a continuously-revolving line-up of entertainers known as the *Fania All-Stars*. Especially during the 70s, the star-studded group became renowned worldwide for their spectacular musical performances, (*Izzy Sanabria, 2009*).

Salsoul music was also making the music scene and sweeping many New Yorkers off their feet. With singers like Joe Bataan - Mujer Mia, Latin Struck, Muchacho Ordinario; Malo – Suavecito; Jimmy Sabater – To Be With You; Paul Ortiz – Tender Love and Sweet Caresses; Bobby Rodriguez - Latin from Manhattan; Ralfi Pagan – El Hijo De Mama; and many more. Latinos were discovering a new form of Salsa that contained all its musical and percussional rhythm. But Fania kept its music coming and it was a nonstop shower of música hitting the radio stations, concert halls and local clubs throughout the country with songs like Ismael Miranda's - Asi Se Compone Un Son; Andy Harlow – La Loteria; Ismael Quintana – Mi Debilidad; Ray Barretto – Vive y Vacila; Bobby Valentin – Guaraguao; Willie Colon – Abuelita; and so many more. Before the disco explosion of the 1970s, Fania's explosion was ten years ahead of its time and like a revved up locomotive at full throttle with no brakes, it swept through the 1970s, music revolution, 1980s, hip-hop and 1990s, rap. Although Fania may presently seem to be slowly fading away, Fania still continues its compatibility with Reggaeton on Sunday's radio shows. Fania's magical contemporary style of Salsa music touched many generations of all ages and even now in 2010; we listen faithfully as though it was yesterday. Times have changed and so have the morals and values of people. Many musicians today don't possess the caliber and cooperationist, held by the Fania musicians. To form a new Fania will take a miracle. Continuous dedicatory, genuine commitment in partnership, workmanship and total cooperation in every aspect of entertainment and management are the DNA molecules which created and kept together this legendary organization for so many glorious years.

STORY CONT:

Willie and I were now exiting Houston Street, from the FDR Drive. We couldn't tell if it was morning or mid afternoon. The streets were crowded with people walking endlessly, playing dominos and listening to music. All the vegetables from local bodegas, (grocery stores) were out on display. Plátanos verdes, (green bananas) batatas, (sweet potatoes) guineos pequeños, (small bananas) and the Piraguero in his sombrero de paja, (Spanish Icy Man in his straw hat) was out in full force.

We stopped at Katz's Delicatessen for a couple of pastrami sandwiches. Katz's is the Coney Island version of Nathans on the lower eastside of Manhattan and notorious for their sandwiches. We finally reached Willies place of residents off Allen Street where I dropped him off. After our good-byes, I continued toward the Brooklyn Battery Tunnel, then Gowanus Expressway and finally the Belt Parkway. As I approached the Verrazano's Narrows Bridge, I can see the many kites flying in the wind. Many of those kites were spectacular in color and design; some were worth hundreds of dollars. The rainbow color's lid up the sky and children faces could be seen paste on their car windows as they drove by. However, the numerous complaints of small aircraft pilots and automobile accidents took its toll on the kite flyers. The premier kite-flying venues of the 1990s, came to end when Mayor, Rudy Giuliani gave the order to stop the kite flying, although kites can still be seen today making its way across the Verrazano Brooklyn skies. I finally reached home where I was met by family and friends who were visiting. I looked up and saw my wife smiling back at me from a window, '*A sight for sore eyes on any given day,*' I thought to myself. I went upstairs and like usual, received a passionate kiss. I would now enjoy what little time was left in the day. As I looked out of my window and gazed at my family below, I then thought to myself.

'No matter how little time was left in a day and no matter how good your day went in a prison environment; it couldn't compare to even one minute of being around family.'
Next Day:

Nothing interesting occurred at work the previous day, Sunday. It's now Monday, and again, I awake at four a.m. in preparation for work. The travel from Brooklyn to Ossining New York, where the prison is located is approximately two hours sometimes less. Ossining is one-half hour north on route 9 from the historic Sleepy Hollow, Village of the Headless Horseman, and one half hour south of Bear Mountain and Indian Point Nuclear Center. Every morning before leaving, I look out of my window for night burglars or car thieves that hanged around from the previous night. I've caught a few in their act of criminal mischief. I remember catching one particular guy red handed exiting my vehicle with stolen Kenny G audiotapes. Let's just say, if he ever decides to enter another vehicle he'll probably run away just as soon as he sees Kenny G audiotapes lying around.

The bottom line is, you can mess with my car, but don't mess with the only thing that unwinds me at the end of a prison day, my Kenny G music. The neighborhood is known for night thieves, since we live in a mostly commercial area. There's also an elevated train over the street. In most cases, what crooks like to do is wait for the train to pass then try to camouflage the sound of breaking glass with the passing noise of the train. What the crooks don't know is; any noise outside of what's normally heard by passing trains will automatically catch the attention of any neighborhood resident who has lived long enough in the area to distinguish the difference between the two sounds. I begin the drive north as I've done many times before; Belt Parkway to Gowanus Expressway, to Brooklyn Bridge, to FDR Drive to Interstate 87 north then route nine Tarrytown exit. While driving on Interstate 87, I see on the side of the road a familiar character I've seen once before. Just yesterday, Sunday, I pulled over to help a stranded motorist, a gentleman wearing a tan trench coat, over a dark suit with a white shirt and red tie. He had an Audi sedan parked off to the side of the road just before Yankee Stadium with its hood wide open. I approached the gentleman and offered my help. He stated his car was not turning on, and he wanted to leave the area and find another way home, but only had a checkbook and no money. He asked if I could lend him ten dollars, and he would write me out a check for fifteen dollars as a token of his appreciation. I reached inside my pocket and came out with a twenty-dollar bill, but it was the only thing I had, so I told him I would be right back. I began my journey in search of an open store at five a.m. in hopes of breaking my twenty-dollar bill for two tens. After several minutes of searching, I couldn't find an open business and returned to the stranded motorist. I explained I couldn't change the twenty-dollar bill, and he asked for the whole twenty.

"Can I have the whole twenty dollars?"

"I'm sorry buddy, if I could I would, but I can't. It's all I have," I said.

Then off I went with a guilt feeling strapped to my conscience. Here, we are the following day Monday, the same guy and same Audi sedan, on the same road just two miles further north on Interstate 87, closer to Yankee Stadium. A NYC cab driver appears to be handing over some money. I immediately pulled over and approached the cab driver.

"Hey, that guy was here yesterday asking for money. He told me his car wouldn't start, that he only had a checkbook and no way to get home!"

As the cab driver turned around to look at him, the crook had already silently closed his hood, was inside his Audi, and just like that, he sped away.

"How much money you gave him?"

"Twenty damn dollars!"

"Better catch him," I said.

The cabby ran into his yellow cab and sped off after him. I always wondered if he ever caught up to him and got his money back. I finally pulled up to the prison parking lot, and I sat in my vehicle for several minutes while drinking a coffee from Ray's Deli. I subconsciously asked myself.

'What the hell am I doing here? Do I really want to go inside that damn rat hole or should I call in sick from my cell phone and make the two-hour trip back home?'

Whatever my decision would be I knew the whole process would repeat itself again the following day. My decision was made; I'll go to work and call in sick tomorrow instead. Like so many others, I'm sure; I begin to psychologically pump myself up for the prison environment. As I sat there with my coffee, I began to project an image of a tough no holds barred prison officer. *

Many correction officers who worked within the prison system learn how to create and project an image of a tough officer, outside their normal way of life. This behavior by most helped us get through the day. Although the quality or state of being kind is another method you can adapt to, you will quickly learn how fast the word, 'kindness' will be misconstrued and how harmful it could be to your tour of duty, not to mention your career. To try and project an image of another correction officer in hopes of getting the cooperation, he or she may be successful with, will only result in an unfavorable outcome for you. Different officer's project different images, what may work for them, may not always work for the next individual. Most officers who show respect to convicts may get very little respect in return. Then there are those officers who show no respect and in some cases, get the respect in return. A convict, like any other human being, is more likely to assault or attempt to intimate an officer who stands five feet tall than one whose stand six feet tall.

They are most likely to assault or try to assault an officer whose one-hundred pounds in weight, in contrast to one who's two-hundred plus pounds. It's human nature. Although most convicts will not verbally tell an officer, they actually appreciate an officer who does his or her job and are firm in their position. It makes them feel safe and give them a sense of security. In other cases, a correction officer, whose nationality is Puerto Rican, quite obviously will have something in common with a convict who's also Puerto Rican, and in most cases will receive the respect and cooperation than that of an Afro American or Caucasian officer; the same theory applies to all other nationalities. Nationality, physical appearance, things in common and professionalism, all play a vital role in being a correction officer and in successfully exercising interpersonal communication. In projecting an image, some correction officers reward convicts by sharing his or her home-cooked meal, yet being firm in their position. It works every time; I've done it with unbelievable results. A convict who's been incarcerated several years and has not had a home cooked meal, is a convict at your command, and in some cases, they'll even keep the petty crooks and extortionist away from your gallery or housing unit. However, beware of those convicts who will file a cause of action against you and the state for developing a tummy ache as a result of your home-cooked meal. In our free society money talks, in prison food is just as powerful. A slice of pizza to you and I is just that, a slice of pizza, but to man who has not had pizza in years. It's like having a lobster, and no convict wants to lose that kind of meal connection. Projecting an image in prison for an officer can take on many different forms. For example, you have officers who physically discover themselves in a prison environment. They begin workout regiments, building their bodies in competition with other officers or convicts. I personally don't see a problem with this since building up physical strength helps the officer's condition. It also prepares them for possible future confrontations and gives them a strong psychological advantage over others. Then there are those who pretend to work out or work out for five minutes and think they have enough muscles on the surface to walk around the prison like a NYC pigeon, with their chest protruding outward and heads bopping back and forth. This is mostly an ego trip, subconsciously warning others to stay away. Then you have correction officers who project images of being cool, down to earth or even sexy.

For example, like shaking hands with convicts in a show of support or solidarity, having long personal conversations and exchanging family photographs, magazines, music tapes or gifts. Like one particular officer from A-block who brought audio cassette tapes for convicts. He was never caught by prison officials, as did his partner at another facility. He later resigned and joined the rank and files of NYC police. This behavior is quite possibly to prevent harassment, to fit in, avoid confrontations and/or hide their inner fears. This behavior gains no respect from convicts or fellow officers and can only lead to corruption and serious injuries. It breeds hatred among real hardcore criminals and in most cases, this behavior is seen as a sign of weakness or insecurity and many convicts thrive on weaknesses, insecurity and low of self-esteem.

Good example of projecting an image in a group was the one-to-nine shift officers of Sing-Sing during the early 1990s. Although not all, many who entered Sing-Sing as rookie officers thought they had all the intricate answers to daily prison operations and personal communication skills with convicts, simply because the environment they grew up in, was that of the environment where many of the convicts grew up in, NYC. Their cocky attitudes, lack of respect and common sense was something we always looked forward to daily. In some individuals, we knew exactly who lacked the courage and knew who would make the extra effort to help a fellow officer. As the officer in charge I had the privilege of assigning these one-to-nine officers to job locations throughout the housing block, which didn't always go well. During the summer months, some refused to work the gym because it was too hot or couldn't take the smell of men perspiration. To others, the convict to the officer ratio, which was approximately four officers to two-hundred convicts, made them apprehensive.

Others refused to work the yard during the summer because of the sun's heat or too cold during the winter months. Then you had others who just didn't want to work or be assigned to any specific location. They instead wanted to walk around the facility with their little posse where they felt safe and secure. Not surprisingly enough, as a result of their inability to function among men, most of these one-to-nine shift perpetrating officers lost their jobs, due to criminal activities, stupidity and time abuse.

Some transferred to different prisons where the convict population and temptations was much less and where the risk of getting a foot up the ass, either by a convict or an officer, was almost nonexistence. Those one-to-nine officers who continue to work today at Sing-Sing are the few good officers who manage to keep their heads up, avoid temptation, corruption, and never allowed their stupidity to dictate a common sense decision. In projecting an image, some officers discover religion in prison and while on duty begin sporting dreadlocks and kufi's, simply because convicts wore them or wore it to avoid harassment. Other officers preach the bible for eight hours in hopes of saving lives. Convicts in any correctional setting thrive on lack of morale, unification and weak personalities.

In 1997, I can recall meeting a Caucasian male correction officer at Downstate facility who was an extremely large man. If I'm not mistaken, his height was approximately six-foot-five and appeared to weigh over two-hundred-fifty pounds, nothing fat about this guy. I entered his unit; complex 2, on an official capacity and his first words to me was in the form of a question.

"What are you, a fucking Mexican officer?"

For that split second, I stood there wondering and thought to myself.

'He's a big guy, and I'm only five-foot-six, so I knew I couldn't be a physical threat to his well being. This could quite possibly be a joke, or maybe he's a ruthless officer and/or borderline racist. Or he could be just a six-foot-five coward trying to project an image in front of his convicts.'

So I played along and called his bluff, I answered him in the form of a question as well.

"What does a fucking Mexican officer looks like tough-guy?"

He gave me the facility count slips, stepped out of his unit bubble and told me to get the fuck out of his complex. He also threatened to do me bodily harm at the end of our shift at the facility parking lot. I was ok with that, since I knew my trusted companion, the 9mm, Glock, would be concealed on my waist side to protect me from all harm. Nothing ever happened on this day, but his empty verbal threats continued, not only with me, it continued with others as well. Until one glorious day he decided to threaten an Afro American officer who happened to be his own size.

The word was out throughout the facility, and everyone knew the parking lot was where the action would be at three o'clock sharp. And just like clockwork, they met toe to toe. Some words were exchanged, and the Black officer let him have it. One closed fist to the jaw. I knew this would be one hell of a thunder fight, two large men at six plus feet and over five-hundred, pounds combined. The Thrilla in Manila was the first thing I thought of, but it never happened. Like in the Damon Wayans movie, "I'm Gonna Git You Sucka," whose gangster character was cornered in a dark alleyway while a female with her period slapped him around, the six-foot-five officer, who we'll call Manic…panicked. He let out a girlie scream, grabbed his cell phone and called state police, so much for projecting an image of a ruthless and barbaric Scandinavian Pirate.

Females who project an image discover their looks and instantly begin sporting different hair styles and ridiculous hair colors while in uniform. Extremely tight uniforms pants, unbuttoned shirts exposing cleavage, lots of perfume, pounds of lipstick, makeup, and anything else you can think of which may put a smile on a convict's face and give the green light of confidence for a recreational convict to officer approach. Which reminds me; I once had the pleasure of knowing a female officer at Downstate, who walked around the prison with convicts who perpetrated being Muslim bodyguards. She too considered herself Muslim, but was far from it. Coward was more of her description. She entered my unit while her two perpetrating Muslim bodyguards stood watch on my front entrance, like two Buckingham Palace Guards in London. She acknowledged herself to me and went up to a cell for a one on one recreation visit with a convict who was convicted of robbing and raping elderly women in NYC. Of course after seeing the extra security planted on my unit's front door, I had to do taxpayers a favor, and I got rid of the two perpetrating palace guard pricks. She somehow thought in her deranged mind that by walking around with convict bodyguards it would somehow give her a sense of security and get her respect of others, "Disgrace was more like it." Projecting an image to make your day productive and safe is one thing, lacking common sense and being down right ignorant is completely another. These are the kind of employees who think they'll be spared from a hostage situation, spared from physical attacks, or in some cases the possibility of rape.

The fact of the matter is; it's completely the opposite, and no one is safe within the confines of a correctional institution on any security level. Unfortunately, this kind of behavior is not only limited to security staff. Many others in civilian capacity are also doing the exact same thing, from counselors to nurses, teachers and maintenance workers. Not all the correction officers or civilians do this, most are professional civil servants, but unfortunately for them, those mentioned above are the ones who give an entire department, on any government level throughout the US, a bad name. It also labels many others, who are otherwise professionals in every sense of the word. However, not all women in corrections display this corrupt and cowardly behavior. Some were actually hardcore and better at their jobs than most men I worked with.

A case in point was when I entered the administration office at Sing-Sing during the 1980s. I approached a young lady on an official capacity who was a civilian employee. Her smile told me she was probably good-hearted and kind. She asked me several questions concerning the responsibilities of being a correction officer. She stated she took the exam, passed it, and was scheduled for the Academy in a few months. I asked her what facility she planned to work and she answered, Sing-Sing. As she continued talking, I looked at her and wondered how in the world, she was going to control a convict who's was out of control at her height and weight. She appeared to weigh ninety-nine pounds soak and wet and barely five feet tall. Breaking up a fight between two men who are six feet and two-hundred pounds of solid muscles take a lot of energy and strength, not to mention one whose focus on hurting you. She finally went through her Academy and became a correction officer at Sing-Sing. Her personality was genuine and her ability to pick up on prison procedures was a cut above many. She went through several months with no incidents and pulled through her probation period with flying colors. While working in B-block messhall one day a convict decided to approach her. With his two hands, he grabbed both of her breasts and squeezed them. She immediately fought the convict off, secured her area and took the convict's identification card. She knew an incident in the messhall can easily escalate out of control, so she patiently waited for him to exit the messhall to make her move. With a fearless heart and no fear projected upon her face, she confronted the convict.

51

She let him have it verbally and personally escorted him down to the office where she eventually took him down, and we helped her brand her initials in his mind, (MV). This was the first unusual incident I encountered with this officer, but it would not be my last.

In 1999, we were both working at Downstate correctional facility and stationed at complex 2. While escorting a group of thirty-six, convicts back to their housing unit, one convict decided to break away from his formation and attempt to assault me for reasons still unknown. As we struggled in the corridor, I was beginning to lose the edge over the much bigger convict when in that instance, someone came launching from behind me like a football player in desperate need of a reputational tackle. Before we knew it the force brought us both down to the concrete pavement. I immediately looked down and saw the female officer tightly holding on to the convict's legs with a vise grip. I couldn't believe what I was seeing and couldn't believe it was she who actually made us fall and hit the floor. I felt some sense of relief, but nothing could explain what I felt after that incident and the immense respect I felt for that officer. Her name was Maria Velardo, The little Italian Mare from Ossining, NY. Her projection of an image didn't exist in her heart. Her ability to maintain a daily character and not sidetrack from her personality worked fine for her and made her a cut above the rest. I miss her dearly, and although I never had the honor and privilege of ever thanking her personally for her loyalty and help; this dedication is in her honor and in the honor of all women like Maria, who never get the chance at recognition.

STORY CONT:

As I'm looking in my rear-view mirror and psychologically pumping myself up for the prison environment, a loud knock to the window startled me and caused me to spill the coffee on myself.

"Hey, hammerhead…you think you're Robert DeNiro or something? Let's get to work, cupcake!"

"You damn Irish prison guard!" I yelled out startlingly. It was a buddy coworker named Jimmy Carmody, the pride of Ireland with hair so red he looked like a walking human lipstick. *

Raised in the Bronx, Jimmy was the kind of guy you liked being around with and one you can depend on. Regardless of the circumstances, he'd be there for you in a heartbeat. The only catch with Jimmy was, if he watched your back, you can rest-assured you'd owe him a beer by the week's end.

Jimmy and the guys often met up the road from the prison at a bar called Izzy's for drinks and to share some prison stories. Whenever Jimmy was present, you were guaranteed a laugh. Jimmy's last name, Carmody, (Similar to comedy) was the perfect name for his humorous character. I can recall one of many stories told by Jimmy. Was it true, who knows? He was sent to a maximum-security prison in upstate New York to pick up an ill convict. Upon arrival, Jimmy entered the prison unit and requested to identify the convict before the trip. A sergeant informed him the convict was dressing up. Jimmy began chatting with other officers while he waited. The convict was finally brought over to Jimmy for the transport. The only problem was, the convict was strapped onto a wheelchair like you would strap someone to an electric chair for an execution. There was a large bed sheet wrapped around his waist with a large bow tied in front, and little bows tied to each wrist. Jimmy took a second look and began talking to the convict.

"Hey, are you all right? Wake up."

But there was no reply.

"This guy is not talking. I think there's something wrong with him sergeant."

"Nah, he's probably just sleeping."

"I'll tell you what; let me call my supervisor before I transport this guy?"

The call was made to Sing-Sing's watch-commander.

"Hey, Lou, (short for Lieutenant) this is officer Carmody. I'm calling from Upstate prison. The convict I'm supposed to transport doesn't look good Lou. I mean they got this guy tied to a wheelchair, and he's not responding to anything I say. I think this convict is either dying or already dead."

"Get the hell out of there. Don't transport that guy and get your ass back here," said the lieutenant.

Jimmy went back and informed the officers, he couldn't take this convict, since he appeared too ill for transportation.

"There's nothing wrong with this guy, look here."

The sergeant tried waking the convict up by talking to him and tapping on his boots, but the convict didn't move.

"This doesn't look good sergeant, I got to go."

"No officer, take him with you, he's just sleeping."

"No, that's okay sergeant. You guys stay with him."

Jimmy took off like a bat out of hell and went back to the facility. Upon his arrival, Jimmy stated to his superiors, "The guy was tied up like a Christmas present with pretty holiday bows."

It was later discovered the convict was in his last stages of AIDS, and too frail, even for a conversation. Another of my many personal experiences with Jimmy was during a transportation trip with Jimmy to Downstate correctional facility. We had two convicts to transport. The first convict was a small Hispanic male, approximately five feet tall and one-hundred pounds soaking wet. The other convict was an African-American male about six feet, four inches tall and two-hundred seventy-five pounds of solid muscles. He had long dreadlocks tied up in a ponytail with a rubber band. The small stature Hispanic convict had a face that screamed innocence of guilt, while the other convict had a face of a notorious and ruthless killer. We began the trip up to Downstate facility. Every now and then, I looked back at the convicts for security observation. The bigger convict appeared to look even more ruthless than before, and his face was becoming downright scary at times. I even thought of unsnapping my holster, just in case I had to shoot myself with it. Quite frankly, I didn't think the bullets were going to penetrate this guy. Halfway through the trip Jimmy looked over at me with a peculiar look on his face.

"Hey, Al, what the heck is that smell?"

"Don't know, but I smell it too."

"Open the damn windows Al."

The Hispanic convict called out to us.

"Yo, officers, that's me man. I shitted on myself, I couldn't hold it in. I knew I had stomach pains, but didn't know I had diarrhea."

"What...dammit, we have another thirty-five minutes to get there," said Jimmy.

All of a sudden it hit me, what if the bigger ruthless looking convict gets pissed off and wants to kill the other guy in the back seat?

54

Jimmy on left and partner Joe, September 2004

I turned around, looked to the rear at the ruthless convict and saw he was sitting there as though the whole world just caved in on him. His complexion didn't look good and his lips looked dry and pale. His eyebrows were tilted to the side, almost parallel with his ears and a facial expression similar to that of a little dog begging for a bone. The notorious, ruthless, and scary killer look was now covered with a look of mercy and pain.

"Damn, are you okay?"

The convict looked at me with a pitiful look.

"This shit got to be worse than the damn electric chair. Shoot me in the fucking head officer, and put me out of my misery."

We began laughing, and Jimmy continued.

"Hey, look at it this way, this could quite possibly be the next form of crime deterrent for convicts, and unlike the electric chair, the smell won't kill you."

Jimmy Carmody served many years as a member of the correction emergency response team and member of the fugitive warrant squad, which covers the five boroughs of New York City and all of New York State.

He later became a NYS court officer, and was present during the 9-11, terrorist attacks. Many of us were not aware several court officers were sent to the World Trade Center during those attacks, never to return. Like thousands of other civil servant workers and volunteers, Jimmy was placed in the heart of ground zero. He courageously dedicated most of his family time in the recovery efforts and as a result, in 2010, Jimmy discovered he now has cancer. Comical, but tough and honorable is my philosophy in describing Mr. Jimmy Carmody. He continues serving as a court officer and unlike correction officers, he's stacking up on commendation bars for his extraordinary and courageous service. Alternatively, as he once explained it to me while pointing to his commendation bars.

"This one is for falling down the stairs, this one is for falling up the stairs, and this is one is for buying everyone lunch."

This one is for you buddy…

God, hear our prayer, and let our cry come to you.
Do not hide from us in the day of our distress, but turn to us and speedily answer our prayer.
Eternal God, source of healing, out of our distress we call upon you.
Help Jimmy to sense your presence at this difficult time.
Grant him and us patience when the hours are heavy.
In hurt or disappointment give him the courage.
Keep him and us trustful in your love.
Give us strength for today, and hope for tomorrow.
To your loving hands we all commit our spirit when asleep and when awake.
You are with us; we shall not fear.
Most merciful Father, it is you and only you who can place you're healing hands upon Jimmy Carmody and every one of us.

Amen

Chapter Two

~~~

STORY CONT:

After cursing Jimmy and wiping myself from the spilled coffee, I exited my vehicle and made my way across the parking lot toward the facility arsenal when I was approached by Officer Villanueva. We began to chat for a short while. Villa had a voice like singer Barry White, but unlike Barry White, Villa couldn't sing if his life depended on it. With military creases, spotless shinny law enforcement shoes, polished insignias with a clean-cut look and by the book attitude, Eddie Villanueva like many others was a prime example of what professionalism in appearance was meant to be. *

Also born and raised in south Bronx, Villa served in the United States Armed Forces, USS South Carolina, before becoming a NYS correction officer. His past military experience showed in his discipline. Villa was also a member of the correction emergency response team and member of the fugitive warrant's squad. He eventually left Sing-Sing and is now a lieutenant at a Virginia, Regional Jail. The majority of Latino officers in Sing-Sing, like Eddie Villanueva, were from the Bronx. The Bronx unlike other city boroughs has the largest group of Latinos.

Lieutenant Eddie Villanueva in white, 2011

According to Bronx President, Adolfo Carrión, Latinos have increased steadily as a percentage of the US population and become the largest minority group in the country. The 39 million Latinos in the US now account for 13 percent of the U.S. population, a 74 percent increase since 1990, a gain of about 13 million people. Latinos have immense buying power in the nation as consumers, and currently control about $653 billion in spending power. Hispanics' economic clout has risen from $222 billion in 1990, to $504 billion in 2000, to $653 billion in 2003, and is projected to be $1,014.2 billion by 2008. The 2008 value will exceed the 1990 value by 357 percent a percentage gain that is substantially greater than the 148 percent increase in the buying power of all consumers combined. In terms of political influence, the number of Latino voters has jumped as well. 6.9 million Latinos voted in the 2004 November election - 6.1 percent of the nation's total electorate, an increase of 17 percent from the 2000 presidential elections. Latinos are now also the largest minority group in New York City, with a 27 percent share or 2.16 million people. There are 657,000 registered Latino voters today in NYC. Latinos voters accounted for 18 percent in the 2001 mayoral general election.

Nationally, there are 6,000 Latinos who are elected or appointed officials, most of them on local school boards. By the year 2025, Latinos will account for 18 percent of the U.S. population. And by 2050, the Latino population will almost triple; one out of every four Americans will be of Latino origin, (*Gabriela Remigio, 2005*).

This fact can also be seen in the dramatic increase of Latinos in US law enforcement agencies on all government levels throughout our major cities like; New York City, Newark, Los Angeles, Miami, Orlando, Houston and now newly appointed Justice of the Supreme Court of the United States, Sonia Maria Sotomayor. However, unfortunately for many of these Latino law enforcement officers a supervisory position will never be an option during the course of their career. Although many of these Latinos have the capabilities, courage or familiarity gained by experience, they are, nevertheless, passed on for supervisory positions, quite obviously an underrepresented matter in need of reparability. Naturally, we don't expect every Latino officer will become a supervisor in law enforcement during his or her career, or the next appointed US Attorney General, as did Alberto Gonzales. However, we also can't ignore, in some cases; the obvious practices of the bonds of family and common ancestry theory where, "blood is thicker than water," to play an unjustifiable role in departmental policies and procedures relating to equal opportunity. In a recent show of force, solidarity and partnership in Washington, DC, three influenceable organizations joined together, the National Council of La Raza, the Hispanic American Police Command Officers Association and the National Latino Peace Officers Association. Three powerful organizations unified in an attempt to stamp out the law enforcement administrative injustices, and problematic discrimination many Latino officers are experiencing throughout their career, and in some cases, the application investigative process. Not every Latino individual in law enforcement is subjected to discrimination. Here in Central Florida many Latinos are in supervisory positions. Some are even selected spokespersons for their department. A good example is the Orange County Sheriffs Office of Central Florida, who has several Latino spokespersons, Captain, Angelo Nieves, Lieutenant, Carlos Padilla, and Florida Highway Patrol Applicants Leading Investigator Cruz Morales Pereira, just to name a few.

59

There's a fine line between discrimination and stereotyping, we have to be educated enough to know the difference between the two. I once had the privilege of conversing with three recent police recruits who were subjected to different law enforcement investigative process and three different scenarios.

In 2007, a New York State Department of Correctional Services investigator questioned a Latino recruit.

"Have you ever smoked pot?"

The answer was no.

"Have you ever stolen anything?"

The answer was no.

"Have you ever been arrested or received any tickets?" Again, the answer was no.

The investigator apparently became irritable and his whole demeanor shifted from applicant investigator, conducting a recruit investigation, to a prosecution cross examination.

He continued.

"Let me be clear with you, I think your bull shitting me. I will find out if you're telling me the truth or not, you can count on it. Don't tell me you never got in trouble as a young man, because I will find out, so my advice to you is to come clean."

The recruit explained.

"My parents wouldn't put up with any misbehavior, and my uncles were law enforcement officers who didn't tolerate behavior closely resembling criminality. They were always around, use to give us advice and participated in sport activities, or took us on recreational trips."

A young Latino man, born and raised in New York City, without any problematic history was extraordinarily unusual to accept for the investigator. It upset me to learn that such stereotyping still exists today. I clearly understand the law enforcement funnel system in weeding out the bad apples, and I understand many candidates lie in their applications. It's a difficult investigative process, and the more lies presented to an investigator the more investigative techniques are implemented during their investigation. However, utilizing skin color as evidence of criminal involvement is not proper procedure in conducting an official recruitment investigation.

60

Al Pagan, photo by Bermudez

The recruit in question was my nephew Al Pagan, who went on to attend the New York State Corrections Academy, but resigned two weeks before his graduation for a position with the New York City transit authority as a train conductor. Now a Florida resident, he and his fiancée Nikki, a former New York City fire department paramedic and niece to retire professional baseball player Devon White, both attended Miami's Police Academy, graduated, and are now active members of Miami's finest. On the morning of September 11, 2001, terrorist high jacked an airline and crashed it into the World Trade Center buildings. Al Pagan, like many others, barely escaped with his life when plane debris came crashing into a restaurant where he worked. Has society forgotten, good young men and women still exist?

In 2007, another Latino recruits, born and raised in New York City, was put through the same investigative process with the New York City police department, but unlike his brother, Al Pagan, mentioned above, this recruit received a ticket during the course of his lifetime; for playing basketball in a public park after nine p.m.

61

Joe Pagan, photo by Bermudez

Fortunately for him, he was not subjected to the stereotype ringer and didn't experience the prosecution cross examination scenario. His New York City police investigator was quite clear and to the point, 'If you have anything to tell us, that you may have forgotten or not have mentioned in your application or previous interviews, do it now; because if you don't and we find out otherwise, you will, then be dismissed as an applicant and be denied any future possibilities of ever reapplying with our department.' According to the recruit; his investigative process was appreciative, proper and professional in every sense of the word. Aware of the manipulative and amateurish investigative techniques his brother, Al Pagan, previously encountered, he was happy to learn his investigator was professional in her questioning and happen to be of Latina descent.

I once asked Joe about the outcome of that ticket he received in the ballpark.

"The officers who came on the scene instructed me to shoot the basketball through the hoop, from the foul line, and they will forget about writing me a ticket. So I did, and it went through the hoop, it was all net from the foul line; but they gave me the ticket anyway."

Goodness, did I laugh after hearing that one. The recruit in question was also my nephew Joe Pagan, who went on to attend the New York City Police Academy, graduated, and is an active member of New York City's finest.

In 2007, another young Latino recruit, born and raised in Bronx, NY, was subjected to a similar investigative process, but his case was of a much more serious and horrific one. Working the late shift, his home arrival time was always like clockwork, twelve-thirty-five a.m. The elevator doors opened to his floor, he exited the elevator and made his way to his apartment. Reaching his apartment door with keys in hand, he entered his apartment. An immediate sense of apprehension came upon him and before to can make sense of it all, he felt three continuous blows to the head. He was struck with a hammer by unknown assailants. As he regained consciousness, he can see there were three black males in his apartment. One of them pulled out a kitchen knife and began stabbing him, but the blade bent and broke off. Another suspect immediately armed himself with another kitchen knife and continued where the other attackers left off. The recruiter was helpless in defending himself, and lay on the floor pretending to be dead, as the assailants continued thrusting the knife into his back, neck and chest. The assault was over and the three lowlife pricks began to panic. They quickly walked out of the apartment, stood standing at the front door, and spoke quietly while planning their next move. The recruit took advantage of this moment and locked his door from inside; preventing reentry for the lowlife pricks. When the area was clear, and he was sure it was safe to walk out, he quickly began knocking on neighboring doors yelling for help, but no one would open. Losing massive amount of blood, he walked over to the elevator, pressed the button and the doors opened, revealing his fiancée and her daughter who were both standing there with puzzled looks on their faces.

They apparently were downstairs in a laundry room, doing the laundry at twelve-thirty a.m. He was immediately taken to the hospital where he was hospitalized for a week, treated for three hammer wounds to the head and fifty stab wounds to the neck, chest and back; one stab wound puncturing his lung. His prognosis was not good and physical condition was frail, when his fiancée walked over to his bedside.

"Hey babe, where are the insurance papers?"

Having foreknowledge she was a suspect, she went back to the apartment, clean up the crime scene of all trace evidence and cleaned out his bank account. She has since disappeared with her daughter and hasn't been seen. The NYC detectives assigned to the case have no leads, and the case was placed on the back burner probably the day it arrived on their desk, in my opinion. Although NYC has many similar cases occurring every day, we all know how inexpensive Latino life is in NYC and how misrepresented they are. Unlike in black communities, which have a voice in American Baptist minister and civil rights-social justice activist Al Sharpton and Jewish communities which have a voice in American businessman philanthropist and NYC Mayor Michael Bloomberg, Latinos are not so privileged. A good example of that misrepresentation is the Palm Sunday massacre killer, Christopher Thomas. He killed two Latina women and eight children execution style in 1984; he's now eligible for parole? But regardless of all the clout and political activism representation, he survived his attack. His name is Eddie Ortiz, nephew to my sister Joann. Eddie also went on to attend the Los Angeles Police Academy in California. His investigative process brought to surface many questions. Was there drugs involved, was he a drug dealer, did he owe a debt, was he a gang member? None of those questions applied. He was a victim of his fiancée's financial greed. She conspired with others to have Eddie murdered and collect on his life insurance. Now the little slattern woman is on the lam with very few places to go and hide. While the public news media and television production companies glorify young criminals during their act of violence and allow them their fifteen minutes of fame, like the four lowlife pricks mentioned above, countless of other decent and productive young people are not given the time of day.

Brandon Gonzalez (Left) photo by Annie Leibovitz

In New York City, a brand-new skyscraper was under construction with seven-hundred thousand rentable square feet, thirty-two thousand square feet of rentable floor size, twenty-four thousand square feet of ground floor space, seven-hundred square feet of frontage, an overall building size of 1.6 million square feet and fifty-two stories high. It's the new; New York Times building finally completed in November 2007, and nestled in the heart of Midtown Manhattan. It's close to the ever popular 42nd Street, Madison Square Garden and within walking distance to the beautiful New York's central park. There were thousands responsible in the planning, engineering and development of this iconic structure designed by Italian architect, Renzo Piano. Although everyone involve deserves a story of their own, this story only focuses on one individual, my niece Elaine Bermudez Gonzalez's husband, Brandon Gonzalez. Making his way to work from Sheepshead Bay, Brooklyn, on a daily basis, he was one of many ironworkers responsible for assembling the massive steel beams that would eventually conform into an architectural skyscraper. Brandon was an ironworker apprentice, (Structural steel erector) certified in accordance with regulations under the apprenticeship and trades qualifications of New York State.

Like Brandon, I've worked construction for many years in the heart of Soho, New York City, converting old factories into lofts and store galleries. Starting as a laborer, I eventually worked myself up to a laborer foreman, carpenters helper and finally a full-fledged carpenter. With jobs that included sheet-rocking, sandblasting, hardwood floor installation and masonry. The promises of entering a carpenters union were endless, but the possibilities were hopeless. I slowly began realizing; a young Latino in NYC during the 1980s, with full carpentry capabilities, had no place in a carpenters union. Even as I almost lost my life seven stories above one early morning in Soho, when our scaffolding suddenly collapsed and left me hanging on a life rope, a carpenters union was still out of the question. Like every other courageous ironworker before Brandon, his responsibilities involved heavy lifting, welding, bolting and being able to perform a balancing act under extreme weather conditions, while also conducting other multi functional tasking high above everyone else. There aren't too many Latinos like Brandon, whose Cuban and privileged, not only to be a part of a powerful ornamental ironworkers union like Local 580, but to be a part of such extraordinary building accomplishments, in addition to being incorporated into the Empire State Building history books of architectural construction. He's one of very few young Latinos, that I know whose promise of a trade unionism became a reality. In 2006, New York Magazine featured Brandon and his coworkers that were interviewed by magazine editor, Arianne Cohen, and photographed by legendary photographer Annie Leibovitz. It takes lots of courage to work on the high beams, but courage doesn't stop on tall skyscrapers for ironworkers like Brandon, or in a boxing ring with another professional fighter. It doesn't develop behind the barrel of a gun while emptying the pockets of another. Courage is a quality of mind, a spirit, which enables the individual to challenge dangers head on. It's the absence of fear, an immense bravery incompatible with many others. Courage without honor can't exist, although courage is sometimes taught by others, true courage is immeasurable and stands alone. Women and men who voluntarily entered a job knowing the risk of losing their lives on a daily basis or who enter a job for the sole purpose of defending their country, make the ultimate sacrifice and should be held at the highest possible standards in our society.

Jeremy Alvarez Morales, photo by Bermudez

While the interpretation of courage is defined in many different ways, my next story is of three courageously important people of my life, and one who stand alone as a guardian angel.

The first is my nephew Jeremy Alvarez Morales; he's no exception to the rule. At the young and rightful age of nineteen, Jeremy entered the US Army, with no looking back and no regrets. He understood the magnitude of this responsibility and like thousands before him, it was his courage and honorableness, which dictated and drove his survival through the battles of Iraq.

In February 2009, while on a mission, a roadside bomb exploded killing several US military soldiers and injuring Jeremy, who sustained a concussion in the attack. Not fazed by the dangers of war, Jeremy continues serving in Iraq and has recently decided upon the completion of his military mission, to enter the Division of Alaska state troopers. However, this inheritance of courage should come as no surprise for those who know my nephew Jeremy.

The second is my sister and Jeremy's mother Milagros, (Millie) Morales, who was no stranger to devastation. She too experienced her share of death and ruins along with millions of others.

On the morning of September 11, 2001, while working in the World Trade Center for Morgan Stanley, a high jacked plane hit one of the skyscrapers. As chaos was all around her and while still in her office, screams filled the building hallways and streets below. Millie became confused and unsure of what to do next. While listening to repeated announcements over a PA system, not to evacuate and requesting that everyone return to their assigned offices, Millie decided that evacuating the building would be her best choice. She immediately began her exited down the stairs with many others and finally reached an escalator leading to the lobby. As she got closer to the main exits, she began to instantly realize the catastrophic magnitude of what was occurring. She ran as fast as she could toward the doors when she was ordered by a Policewoman to stop. She did, and at that precise moment, a human body, along with building and airplane debris, crashed onto the pavement directly in front of her. The second plane hit the building where Millie was working. It was the actions of this courageous officer which saved my sister's life. That woman officer, I later discovered, was killed in her quest of saving lives. I also later discovered she was a NYC police officer named, Moira Smith. Coincidently, she also have a brother who a correction officer in Virginia and works hand-in-hand with Lieutenant Eddie Villanueva. Millie finally made her way out of the building and ran toward the Brooklyn Bridge. Her fear only escalated when she felt the bridge begin to sway back and forth as a result of thousands of people running across. She was almost sure the bridge would collapse. I can't begin to imagine what she, and hundreds of others went through during that detrimental day. The pain I felt on this day, suspecting I may have lost my sister in those buildings was unbearable. However, even that feeling could not possibly compare with the thousands of others who lost a loved one, like our guardian angel, Moira Smith. My sister Millie never fully recovered from her devastating experience, but her survival capabilities and the courage to keep on going, no matter what; is fueled by the knowledge that others gave their lives so that she and many others like her can live on and live a good life in their honor, (*Rest in Peace-Moira Smith*).

68

STORY CONT:

After chatting with Villa and the fellas, I submitted my weapon at the arsenal. I approached the front gates and entered the facility lobby where we were met by several supervisors. It was quite obvious to me, it was employee frisk day. That meant we all had to empty our pockets and submit to a pat frisk by a supervisor for possible contraband introduction; like drugs, alcohol or weapons. I personally didn't have a problem with it and as far as I was concerned, they could perform it daily. I'm not opposed to anything, which helps to maintain the sanity and security of our prison system. That wasn't always the case with others, especially those who made a scene while walking in, then attempted to walk back out. Some of us already on the wall being frisked, looked at one another as others walked back out, and like little snitches, we yelled, "Yeah, that piece of shit walking out is dirty, get him sergeant!" Finally done with being frisked, we went to the time clock, punched in our time cards and took them to the assistant watch commander for a signature. *

If you didn't have a job bid the sergeant will assign you to a post. He would then sign your time card and literately tell you to go fuck yourself with a huge morning attitude. Unless of course, you had a nice pair of tits, nice lips and a southern glazed ham for booty; then he was at your command. Most officers kept shut, for fear of retaliation from this supervisor. Like being pulled from their bid jobs and sent to the poorest locations within the facility or being bounced around to different jobs throughout the entire shift for excising their freedom of speech. Some officers retaliated by putting their timecards back in different slots without having it signed. Then they head down to the locker room without making their presents known. That meant the sergeant would later have to search the entire rack and find the time cards of those who either didn't make it in to work or just didn't get their cards signed. This obnoxious behavior was a common practice with this particular sergeant who worked the six to two, day shift. He projected a real tough-guy image that didn't take any shit from those below his rank and was willing to step toe to toe with you if you didn't like it. Although I did personally see him get slapped in the parking lot from wall post thirteen by a transportation officer.

The last I heard he retired and during his retirement ceremony, he cried like a little rookie prostitute who was apprehended by police on her first prostitution arrest.

STORY CONT:

I went down the locker room and walked to my side of the lockers when I heard a familiar voice yelling out his usual morning greetings, "Hey, B, what's up dude? Look at this, look at this, B? You ain't got this, B!" *

The locker room was an old indoor firing range build in the early 1900s, with lots of humidity, leaky water pipes, and roaches that look like little walking footballs. In New York, they called them water bugs, in Florida, tropically enough, they call them palmetto bugs. I call them German roaches on steroids. The bathroom always stunk like urine and the showers were off-limits to any human being with common sense.

POINT OF INTEREST:

"Workers from several independent construction companies' plumbers, electricians and carpenters, refused to work this area and other areas throughout the facility. After submitting samples for analysis to an accredited testing laboratory, they discovered the insulation around the outdated water pipes and other areas, contained asbestos. In addition to this, the hundreds of paint applications throughout the facility were also discovered to contain extremely high levels of lead. This crucial information was not made available to the officers. As recent as 2000, some areas of Sing-Sing had asbestos removed by certified professionals." One officer, Eddie Jorge, who monitored the removal of asbestos and wore a mask, was ordered by his immediate supervisor to take off his mask, 'since this may cause an outcry among the convicts who saw him wearing it. Intelligently enough, Eddie refused and told his supervisor to take over his post without a mask if he indeed felt it was safe to do so. The sergeant refused and walked away with nothing further to say."

The familiar voice calling me 'B' was that of a Gonzo, short for Gonzales. A great big pretty Puerto Rican, who somehow discovered how to move his chest muscles up and down and use it as an intimidating gesture and morning greetings. I've always told Gonzo he was abnormal, simply because Puerto Rican men don't come that big and pretty. They're usually around my height and size five feet six inches tall with an average build. Someone fed this man Miracle Grow during his adolescence. Nevertheless, it didn't matter, because anything thrown at Gonzo was everything missed. Nothing fazed this dude unless you were Willie Marrero. I always wondered what it would be like to drop a brick on his head from a twenty-story-high building, not to see what kind of injuries he would sustain, but to see how high it would bounce from his head before it came crashing down on someone else's head killing them instantly. I went on with my business and somehow managed to allow Gonzo to distract me. I couldn't remember the combination to the lock.

"*Shit*," I confusingly said and yelled back at Gonzo.

"Oye, (Listen) I can't remember the combination to my damn lock. I hope you're happy?"

Gonzo replied with the shaking of his chest again.

"This shit will do that to you, B. This shit will do that!"

The similarity between Gonzo and celebrity Dwayne Douglas Johnson, (The Rock) was unbelievably similar. I walked away to the employee mailboxes and checked my mail for any prior approved personal leave slips. I began reading posted memorandums off the bulletin board on the latest policies and procedures when moments later a distinctive smell of men's cologne instantly invaded my immediate area. I turned around and saw it was Gonzo, smiling and leaving the locker room to the upstairs officer's lineup room. "See you upstairs B," he said while walking up. "B," was short for my last name, Bermudez. We were so institutionalized we never took the time to call each other by our first names. Neither did we call each other by our first name during family gatherings or union picnics, something I never understood. I went back to the locker and successfully managed to open my lock. Somehow Gonzo's absence brought me back to normalcy. I began removing my clothing with a hateful look upon my face as I surveyed the uniforms. *

Light blue shirts with apron pockets and no flaps for closing it. When officers ran on an emergency or struggled with a convict, everything contained in those pockets fell out. This was a big distraction and dangerous at times because we had to stop and pick up the fallen items when others were in need of our help. Every second during an emergency made the difference. Whoever came up with this idea was probably sentenced twenty-five years to life. The uniforms were so perfectly tailored that buttonholes didn't line up with its buttons. Some shirt collars were wide enough to fit two human heads and others were not centered with the shoulders. The collar brass insignia had a sharp-pointed stem which protruded through the locking mechanism and was capable of piercing into your collarbone like a finishing nail into a soft piece of wood. We actually had to bite off pencil erasers and insert them onto the sharp stem to prevent injuries. The arm patch and its colors were not bad, although I never understood where the word 'services' came from or its reason for being on the patch. Some say it was because of division of parole and other state agencies that worked hand-in-hand with correctional services. I later discovered it was exactly what we did on a daily basis, service the convicts. We served them toiletries, blankets for cold nights, soapies for their showers, tooth brushes, paper pads, cosmetics, and let us not forget their food in those little non-biodegradable Styrofoam trays. Convicts in other correctional facilities were responsible for the making and tailoring of officer's uniforms. And you can best believe these uniform discrepancies were not something done unintentionally. During the early 1980s, a convict tailored an erect penis on one of the female figures of liberty and justice of the great seal of NYS coat of arms patches. He apparently got away with it for quite some time before anyone noticed. Another convict stitched women's pleats on men uniform pants, while others labeled the sizes from medium to small and large to medium. I learned quickly and always double checked my uniforms for any irregularities, but it was quite obvious many others didn't, and lord knows they should have. Some officers looked like security guards in some run-down abandon bread factory. Like many others, I carried a dark blue and black thread for those pants that almost always and for some unknown reason, tore right down the middle at the slightest bend.

I kept many extra uniform pants, shirts and clean sweaters in my locker for that reason. While on the subject of lockers, let's briefly talk about lockers. Everyone's locker had a story to tell. Some guys had their family photographs posted on their locker doors; their beautiful children playing in the background, pretty little Christmas photos and kissing photos with their significant other. Other officers had photos of nude women, nude celebrities, sport heroes, race cars, mirrors, air fresheners, mug shots, wanted posters and many other surprising arts. One particular low-life prick surprised everyone with his collection of child pornography. This guy submitted a role of undeveloped film to a local Walmart store for development. An employee there discovered the photos and rightfully so, notified local authorities. The former correction officer, 'Lunschester the child molester' had twenty-plus years of service. He was later arrested, charged child pornography and convicted. While attending Harriman Training Academy, I once heard from a wise instructor named Richard S. Reed.

"There's a fine line between being a correction officer and being a convict, so don't make that easy, yet devastating transition, or you will be sorry."

He wasn't kidding. There were many wise instructors at Sing-Sing, who qualified officers in firearms, chemical agents and many other tactical training exercises. These were instructors who were professionals in their work and patient with their officers. After witnessing many other law enforcement instructors at work in other states, I don't think Sing-Sing instructors know just how valuable their skills really are. Their knowledge, levelheadedness, careful observations and strict firearm safety guidelines set them aside from many other departments. They are an asset to any law enforcement agency throughout the US.

Many of those instructors during my career are now retired, moved on to supervisory positions and transferred to other departments, but surely will not be forgotten. Those instructors responsible for making this all possible and responsible for the training, retraining and state certifications at the prison were, Theodore, (Teddy) Edlow Jr., Anthony, (Tony) Sportiello, Neil Ingenito, Gerald J. Ellerbe, Noel F. Morris, Richard S. Reed, James T. Hamlet, Julian Hampden and Dr. Curtis M. Johnson. These were the instructors of my time, individuals who didn't sidetrack from their character or way of life.

They were a special group of honorable men, the prison's front-line and first emergency responders you would probably see when all you have left is a prayer. In reference to training, state requirements for recertification are done on a yearly basis, twice a year if you were a member of the emergency response team and takes place on prison grounds during the course of one week. Many officers dread the one week of training with their instructors, never realizing or taking for granted the tranquility of its environment or the importance and long-term positive effects that come with possessing the knowledgeableness of its fortification. Firearm's training was at the top of my list, without a doubt, although I must admit those .38 Smith and Wesson service revolvers were well outdated. I can recall a news media interview by a deputy of administration at the prison during the 1990s. He stated to the media, "The new walls being built at Sing-Sing with the new razor wire, electric fencing and cameras, are symbols of change with the times." If this indeed was the case; whatever happen to replacing the revolvers and holsters that date back to the early 1900s? It was quite obvious, even to a blind man that those revolvers were outdated; although I must admit, I did love its accuracy and weight. During a training class, an instructor named Ted Edlow once stated about the revolver,

"Hey, I have six bullets in my revolver's cylinder, if I can't get you with one or two of those six, or all of those six, what makes you think I can get you with a fifteen round magazine. I just as well give up, run my skinny black ass down the street and look for help."

Knowledge of what is true or right coupled with just judgment as to action; is a statement that defines wisdom, which was indeed the case with instructor Theodore (Teddy) Edlow, Jr. Not realizing it until recently, Teddy was from the old stomping grounds of Brooklyn's, Bedford Stuyvesant, Tompkins housing projects to be exact. He served in the US military before entering the prison system in 1968; only back then the prisons were not called correctional facilities. His first stop was at Matteawan State hospital for the criminally insane, now known as Fishkill Correctional Facility. Teddy always had a great sense of humor and made your training day a knowledgeable and pleasurable one. His capabilities and knowledge as an instructor surpassed many others.

**L-R Top, Neil Ingenito, James Hamlet, Julian Hampden,
Andrew Sementini and Gerald Ellerbe**

Teddy once mentioned Matteawan had two kinds of criminals, the criminally insane and the insane criminal. I didn't comprehend that statement and didn't see any difference in the two, until his clarification.

"Hey, Al, always remember, the criminally insane are crazy before they enter the prison system and the insane criminals become crazy while in the prison system."

A spoken eulogy, probably not; words of wisdom and life experience that outweighs any eulogy is more like it. Without it, (wisdom and life experiences) our lives are absent from knowledge and passage to common sense impede. I've learned enough to last me a lifetime during my career with Teddy Edlow, and I've also learned never to forget the meaning and the honoring of great men like him.

Another instructor with a nonchalant mannerism who comes to mind and who moved up through ranks to captain was also knowledgeable and a professional instructor, his name was Neil Ingenito. Always on top of his game the Italian Stallion Ingenito was a mild-mannered man, until he made his presents known in class and on the firing range.

PAPD Police Sergeant, Julian Hampden

He was a by the book instructor and a naturally intelligent gentleman. His comprehension of state law was made clear to everyone who listened and heard Neil speak in class. In all the years I've worked in Sing-Sing, there was only one officer who never lost his cool while working the hectic and chaotic environment of Sing-Sing's arsenal, Neil Ingenito. His radio transmissions were always kept professional, limited and direct in communications. Many times I've duplicated those same transmissions in an attempt to sound like him. Neil Ingenito was also a man of honor and a man who showed great concern for others. I know; I've seen him go beyond his normal scope of duties in his numerous engagements of righteous conduct. Another young and dedicated instructor who I had the great pleasure of knowing was Julian Hampden.

He later left Sing-Sing for a position with the New York Port Authority police department. Adherence to moral and ethical principles is an understatement when describing this man. His ability to survive the most drastic of circumstances gives new meaning to the word inclination. After leaving Sing-Sing and while serving with the Port Authority police, Julian was one day enjoying a peaceful day at a park in Queens when he heard two shots being fired from a distance. Not knowing where the shots came from, or who may have fired the shots, Julian was surprised to discover he was the intended target. Someone fired into Julian's back, and the bullet ripped through his body exiting out of his chest. He miraculously survived the attack, but his brush with death didn't end there. On September 11, 2001, Julian, faith was again tested when two American jet liners were high jacked and intentionally crash into the World Trade Center buildings. He again survived and like many other courageous emergency personnel and volunteers, he ignored his own personal responsibilities and dedicated all of his time and energy in the rescue and recovery efforts of that faithful day. Although many of these instructors like Julian Hampden were not too far ahead in age, they still were a prime example of what I would have been or wanted to become, if I had ever made a New York State correctional and police instructor. Many officers take for granted or don't appreciate the "know how," passed on by these professionals, and I'm no exception. They are a rare breed of officers and whether you like it or not they are a cut above the rest.

STORY CONT:

I finally dressed up, left the locker room and went upstairs to the lineup room where everyone congregates and waits for attendance, assignments and briefing. As I walked in I could see to my left, most of the Latino officers to the front of the room, to the rear of the room on the left were the African-American officers and in two separated groups were the Caucasian officers from upstate and New York City region. All the brown noses, ass kissers and female sex slaves were piled up around the sergeant desk for the easy job assignments. You see; many officers didn't like working the back, (prison blocks) others didn't mind and others who refused to brown nose their supervisors didn't have much of a choice.

I sat down on the bench where a small space was left for me and began talking to my fellow comrades, 90 percent of whom had black hair pushed back and plenty of *grasa de pelo,* (hair grease). Those who were less fortunate were either half bald, had shaved heads or wore their caps. We discuss things like prison gossip, the latest Latin music available on the market or whatever came to mind on that particular day. Every now and then, each of us walked over to the African American side and chat with our fellow officers, and they would do the same. Then over to the New York City Caucasian side as well. Once the lineup was terminated, and it was time to work, we all became one big family quite naturally. The announcement was made by a supervisor, "On the lineup!" Everyone looked for their favorite spot in line. Some would stand to the rear so not to be seen and others close to the exit door in hopes of avoiding a line at the arsenal window for final equipment pickup. Names were called, assignments are given, memorandums read, and debriefing made. Then begins the humiliating degradation by several supervisors, it was a morning ritual that went on religiously, but there was nothing religious about those pricks.

"Okay, listen up! Some of you guys and gals don't know how to write a misbehavior report. I suggest you quit being correction officers and apply for a job at a local McDonalds. Convicts look at your reports and see how stupid you guys are!"

Other supervisors would jump at the chance as well.

"Alright, listen up; I hope you're not parked on the yellow lines out in the parking lot because if you are your vehicles will be towed at your expense."

He turns around and looks at the other supervisors.

"Does anyone else have something to say?"

"Sure," they replied with an expression on their faces, as though they found a bottle of Tylenol while experiencing as massive migraine headache.

"Okay, now listen, some of you guys look like shit! I'm going to warn you this once, start wearing your collar brass and start shining those shoes. What the hell do we pay you a uniform allowance for?" *

Understandably so, supervisors were strict on uniform insignias, (Collar brass). Without it, a uniform just doesn't resemble a uniform.

In Sing-Sing alone, many officers work an entire tour of duty out of uniform, no collar brass, white socks with dark pants, missing buttons, ripped shirts, sneakers instead of shoes, stained, dirty and wrinkled uniforms. Some do this as a form of protest or retaliation against a supervisor. Others do it for lack of morale, low self-esteem or just plain lazy, while some just possess a pig style mentality. In today's Sing-Sing, many young officers with a street thug mentality wear their uniform pants almost to their knees and shirts bulging out of their pants like a sack of testicles. Others refused to remove their dual earrings while on duty. "The up most professionalism in appearance breed's intimation and demands respect. An officer in any given department when viewed by the public does not only represent the department as a whole, but represents dignity, pride, courage and self-respect. Uniform appearance, in my opinion, make up for fifty percent of an officer's morale, while the appearance of a dirty and sloppy uniform, projects the lifestyle you lead."

STORY CONT:

The lineup room speeches continued.

"It has come to my attention that some of you officers don't like me or don't like how I do my job as your lieutenant? Well, that's too bad. If you have anything to say about it, then say it now?"

Actually, to my surprise, several officers raised their hands.

"Yeah, Lou, we have something to say."

Other supervisors, (mostly sergeants) were also surprised and interruptedly replied.

"Well, if you have anything to say, then see me after the lineup!" That angered several guys and they began complaining.

"But the lieutenant just said if we had anything to say, say it now?"

The officers were then given direct orders by the sergeants to address their matters after the lineup or put their grievances on paper. This was a common practice in Sing-Sing.

Whenever an officer had a reasonable or legitimate complaint during lineup, they were instructed to put their complaints on paper or see them after lineup. The only problem was, when you approached the supervisor after the lineup they would then order you to work. *

Sing-Sing officers are not well-liked by many others throughout the state, especially supervisors who transfer in from other prisons with an unconfirmed belief that all who work Sing-Sing are somehow corrupt or lacking the qualities of culture and learning. I'll admit this much, there are a lot of screw ups in Sing-Sing and in the prison pipeline of communications; word gets around fast. Unfortunately, until the supervisor gets to know the officer on a personal and professional level or work with the officer and get to know their reputation, all are treated as such. Except for the very few supervising scum bags I've encountered throughout my career, most supervisors were honorable men and women who never forgot the ethic of reciprocity to, "treat others as you would like to be treated." This simple golden rule is what sets aside those supervisors who were natural-born pricks and those supervisors who saw themselves in your eyes. Many of Sing-Sing lieutenants who I had the honor and great pleasure of working with and working for were. LT. Jeff Finn, also a former Montgomery, NY, police sergeant. He was a small powerhouse with a John McClane attitude from the movie Die Hard, with actor Bruce Willis. He could tackle any obstacle presented in his path with no discrepancies or second thoughts in any of his challenges, yet approachable, fair and willing to step to the plate for an officer. On numerous occasions throughout my career, I submitted applications for a position with the elite correction's emergency response team, but was always turned down by a woman smacking, Mike Tyson looking sergeant called, "The Wiz." Then I became involved in an incident one day involving a convict and Lt Finn at the prison school building. During that incident, I made certain no harm came to the lieutenant. I succeeded in helping to control the convict, placing him in restraints and protecting my supervisor. This action didn't go unnoticed and Lt Finn quickly popped the big question, "Are you in the C.E.R.T, Team," (Corrections Emergency Response Team). "No," I replied, explaining my numerous unsuccessful attempts in trying to enter the team. Lieutenant Finn ordered me to walk with him to the watch-commanders office after the incident where he confronted the sergeant-in-charge of the team applications, (The Wiz) and ordered him to place my application on top of the teams list soon as possible. That was just one of the highlights of my career, and a day engraved in my mind.

Unlike many other lieutenants, who upon appointment to the correction's emergency response team instantly grew chest hairs and began oozing courage, Lt Finn's ability to change rules and techniques had no negative reflection or impact on his officers and most importantly, never sidetracked from his character.

Lieutenant James Holman, he was more of a cool, calm, collective individual and always by book supervisor. He was also approachable, fair and willing to step up to the plate for an officer. Soft spoken on most days, yet could flip the scrip, (take a stand) when presented with a violation of his trust. Respectful, intelligent and a gentleman, Holman could conquer respect with his silence, gain results with his demeanor and most importantly, never sidetracking from his character. One morning while working wall post twelve, which overlooks the Hudson River, the facility entrance and parking lot, I received a call from sergeant Leggy, who was incharge of facility grounds. He apparently didn't like the way I parked my vehicle, (Over the yellow line). Refusing to heed any rational explanation on my part, he ordered a tow truck to remove my vehicle from state property at my expense. He was one of those supervisors mentioned above, who instantly grew chest hairs and began oozing courage upon being appointed to a supervisory position. However, I had a trick up my sleeve; lieutenant Holman. I immediately notified him and he contacted the sergeant and ordered him to stop the removal of my personal vehicle. Of course, sergeant Leggy was very displeased to discover I went over his head. He had to have the last say, "Next time you won't be so lucky." He eventually made it up to the level of captain and was recently forced to retire without a shield. Karma's a bitch I know. I too was a victim of Karma once or twice in my lifetime.

Sergeant Terrance McElroy, he later moved up to the level of lieutenant, captain and deputy superintendent. Cooperative, knowledgeable and habitually energetic, he was a prime example of, "Treat others as you would like to be treated." His lack of favoritism and unfairness is what set him aside from many others. Approachability and willing to step up to the plate for an officer was his principles as well. His unique ability to recognize an officer who may have been experiencing a problem didn't stop there; he'd assist them in their matter and follow through almost always with success.

This instilled in the hearts and minds of many officers that with a simple approach of despair, possibilities for corrective measures and resolutions was one question away. It was this sergeant, who I once approached after my tour of duty and stated, "Hey sergeant I want to buy a home, no one in my family ever owned one before, and I like to be the first. The only way to do this sergeant is to work as much overtime as I possibly can, but I'm not getting any overtime from any other sergeant; can you help me?"

McElroy looked at me and without hesitation or second thoughts, he instantly replied, "No, problem B, (Bermudez) we'll start right now. Go to A-block messhall-bridge and see B-block Trooper John Bishop, tell him you're on his search team." The overtime came nonstop after that and on my days off, I was called in to work. Personal leave slips had to be submitted to break up the monotony and give myself a rest in between. I was leaving for work at five a.m. every morning and returning at one a.m. the following day, only to reawaken at four a.m., and this went on for the next eight months. My body was wearing down, but the goal to own a home was the fuel that kept me going, and nothing was going to prevent me from accomplishing that goal. This was in late 1993, and on September 18, 1994, we moved into our first newly constructed home. The blessing was indeed from God, but it was McElroy, who chose to perform his work, and it was this act of kindness that kept me remembering what honorable men are made of. I once called McElroy from a wall post and who was now a captain and I told him of my sincere appreciation and the respect I had for him. Even today, I don't think he realized the positive impact he made on me and my family.

Lt. R. Patterson, his comportment of family was his coat of arms; his lack of favoritism also set him aside from many others. His approachability, fairness and willing to step up to the plate for an officer was endless. I should know, I witness his battled on my behalf in the United States District Court of New York. My respect for him is limitless and my appreciation immense. He too could conquer respect with his silence, gain results with his demeanor and most importantly, never sidetracking from his character.

Lieutenant Jeff Sarett, photo by Jeff

Lt. Jeff Sarett, what can I say, all the above. Another honorable man, pleasure to work for and would be best described as a down to earth professional, approachable, fair and willing to step to the plate for an officer. His problem-solving techniques were unique and second to none. His ability to shift from lieutenant to a battleground correction officer, in the most extreme out of control circumstances, was instantaneous. Then again, born and raised in the mean streets of East New York, Brooklyn, it shouldn't surprise to anyone. Jeff was a tough Jewish boy from the old neighborhood who was not only knowledgeable in street smarts, but in martial arts as well. As far as we could remember during our career in Sing-Sing, we never had a newly appointed lieutenant approach the officers and officially introduce himself with a handshake as did Jeff Sarett. However, it didn't end there. He conversed with you on a personal level as well. Our first impression of this lieutenant in 1989 was instantly favorable and respect for him was right off the bat. Brooklyn streets have a way of breeding its people, molding their character and forever engendering that identifiable Brooklyn accent, Jeff was no exception.

He had stickball and school yard rumbles written all over him. Lieutenant, Jeff Sarett is now retired and teaches Criminal-justice at Upstate College in New York State. Approaching his 40th year in Martial Arts, he also teaches Karate-Ju-jutsu, which reminds me, if you didn't want to find yourself bent like a New York City pretzel, as seen in the movie; "You don't mess with the Zohan" insubordination would have probably been the wrong approach for this Brooklyn warrior.

STORY CONT:

After degrading and belittling us, the lineup was terminated, and we were sent to do our jobs. We began the walk up the hill to the housing blocks. I was assigned to B-block housing unit which holds a population of six-hundred convicts to approximately twenty-six correction officers. Our first challenge of the day, other than actually showing up to work, was to climb up the endless set of stairs in a poorly lit corridor with water seeping through its eight inch thick concrete walls. Directly below the walls, where it meets the floor follows the entire length of the corridor, are little man-made water ditches, which carry the slow trickling water to local drains. The hundreds of years of wear and tear, and the thousands of paint applications just can't seem to keep the water out. We finally reach the end of the corridor and have two directions in which to travel up to housing block. We can walk through the hospital gates leading to more gates and corridors, or turn right and walk outside where we can view the Hudson River and Rockland Lake State Park Mountains. It was an absurdly simple decision; we turn right, take the one-minute walk outside toward five-building and enjoyed the spectacular view. *

On foggy days, you can see the huge clouds of fog hug the ground surface as it slowly makes its appearance between two mountainsides in the distance, almost resembling the angel of death in the movie, "Ten Commandments." During sunset the sun rays rides the surface of the Hudson River waves, illuminating in a bright orange glow and sparkling like millions of small diamonds. And to think, all you have to do to get this wonderful view is, commit a crime, get arrested, indicted, convicted and sentence to Sing-Sing prison. It's not the greatest place to be, but its natural views are spectacular.

84

STORY CONT:

My job assignment at the time was to run a gallery of convicts, R/W gallery. The galleries were alphabetized, with the first tier being Q/V, R/W, S/X, T/Y, and U/Z. If I'm not mistaken, each of those galleries held approximately one-hundred twenty-two convicts. I dreaded entering those blocks in the mornings for many reasons, mainly because mornings always stunk. When you enter a prison block, the smell is like no other place on earth. Think about it: six-hundred men, half of them passing gas all night, others whose breath could wake the dead, foot odors, sweat, mentally ill who refused to shower and those who used that magical shaving gel that stunk like a batch of rotten eggs. Put it all together and you have an invisible odor that lingered for hours. I reported to the officer-in-charge Officer, E. Mejia and acknowledged my presence. My first responsibility was to get hold of the keys and personal alarm radio, look over my list of confined convicts and up to R/W gallery, I went. The second officer on R/W gallery at the time was a female officer named Hattie Cradle. Her first job responsibility was to go around and ask every convict where they would be that day. This was just in case the convict received a visitor then we could later locate him for his visit. *

Cradle, (aka Mama) was a short African-American woman who was originally from down South. Physically speaking, Mama was not a very attractive woman. She was approximately four feet tall and heavy in weight, but had a heart of gold. A person of great wisdom and ethical principles, she was liked by most correction officers, supervisors and convicts alike. Hattie worked two jobs and cooked one hell of a southern oxtail meal. She also worked endless overtime at the prison while raising her daughter Stephanie Fine, who seems to be heading down the road of entrepreneurship. How in the world, she ever managed to juggle her life responsibilities we'll never know, but for what it's worth, her ability to tackle her obligations and secure her spirit of motherhood was second to none.

STORY CONT:

I took my morning count of living, breathing bodies, making sure there were no escapes from the previous night and no deaths. I turned in my count to the officer in charge then I went back up to the gallery and began making my entries in my logbook. A logbook is where minute by minute activities and unusual incidents are documented. Once that was done it was time to let out the convict porters, messhall workers and those who received morning medication. I then unlocked all the cell doors in preparation for the programs, and morning meal. The cell doors remain closed by a brake bar mechanism until it's manually pulled open by an employee. This brake bar is approximately four inches wide, a quarter inch thick, made of hard steel and runs the entire length of the gallery. It opens and closes all the cell doors simultaneously.

POINT OF INTEREST:

"Many officers at Sing-Sing and other state prisons with a similar brake bar mechanism don't realize the constant months and years of pulling and pushing on the brake bar handles will eventually cause and has caused, countless of long term injuries involving rotator cuff."

The cells that are not turned open with a key will remain locked, even after opening the brake bar. I pulled the brake, and all the convict workers began their exit for work. Once this process was completed, I returned to my office for further logbook entries. The office is a 6x10 cell converted into an office simply by putting a desk inside of it and calling it, an office. As I was making my entry in the log book, a convict porter approached my office.

"Hey, officer, you know something? I can't stand it when a man fucks another man. I mean I hate the sound of that shit."

"I hear you," I said, as I sat there wondering if this convict had a nightmare the night before and was now trying to tell me something.

Then convict continued.

"Good, officer, because my cell number is W-421 and the sound of men fucking men just drives me crazy, you feel me?"

I then understood what he was trying to say.

"You got it, I'll check it out."

The convict then went on his way. I waited several minutes, so as not to make it look as though he just snitched on someone. I made my move and exited my office to area of W-421 cell. I headed halfway down the gallery but decided to walk around the entire gallery instead, so no one could warn others of my impending approach. I quietly removed the chain and lock, opened the north-end gate leading to the area of cell W-421 and slowly made my way there. As I approached, I noticed the cell bars were ninety percent covered with a white bed sheet. I also heard the sounds of moaning and flesh slapping coming from inside. A sheet covering more than fifty percent of the cell bars is clearly a prison violation. I pulled down the sheet and to my surprise; one of my gallery porters was having anal sex with another convict porter who was completely covered in baby oil. The convict on top jumped off and the other convict made-believe he was sleeping. He then surprisingly jumped up.

"Oh, my God, how did you get on top of me like that? I was sound asleep officer Bermudez, and I don't know how he got on top of me like that."

"You actually think I'm going to believe that another man is penetrating you, and you don't feel it? Save me the love story, you're both going to be written up for sex violations."

I locked the cell door with a key and began walking away in search of a supervisor when one of the convicts called me back. "Yo, officer, let me out of here first?"

"Can't do it, I need a supervisor to witness this first."

By this time, R/W gallery convicts were called on standby for the morning meal via loud speakers. This was unfortunate for them, since they were now both locked in the same cell. The convicts were about to be released from their cells, and onto the gallery where they would then wait for the morning meal. As soon as they saw them together in the same cell, they automatically knew some sort of homosexual activity had taken place, and these two were caught in the act. I released the convicts on R/W gallery, and you could instantly hear the laughter and the tormenting of others.

"Oh, shit dog, you were hitting that, (Having sex)?"

Damn, somebody's getting their salad tossed." (Slang for anal sex) "Yo, officer, you got two bitches locked up in the same cell, and one is shining like a pretty little diamond!"

The block supervisor sergeant Carl Johnson arrived moments later and went down the gallery over to cell W-420 as I was letting the convicts enter onto the bridge which led to the messhall. I returned to cell W-420 and as per the sergeant, I let out the convict who didn't live in the cell and escorted him to his own cell where he remained confined. As I began walking away, he called me back and began to whisper.

"CO, check this out, I'm married, and I don't want my bitch knowing what took place here?"

"It's out of my hands. The disciplinary process will have to run its course."

"Yeah, okay, motherfucker," said the convict in a boisterously and who instantly became a cell gangster. This is common with many convicts who are confined to their cells. They have to project a tough-guy image so that others would think they're hardcore criminals, but in reality, it's to keep away potential extorter's and possible booty bandits from violating them. I left him there in his cell and paid no mind to his offer of wolf tickets, (Slang for tough talk). *

Unfortunately, there's lots of forbidden sexual activity within the prison system, mostly on the night shift since the manpower is less and night sets in leaving only the overhead interior lights to see hundreds of convicts in motion. Unlike during day when daylight is everywhere and the need for the lights is not necessarily required. The housing blocks have extremely large windows, which run the entire length and perimeter of the block walls, so there's enough lighting to see a pin drop. Sing-Sing is an old prison with outdated technology, although many improvements have been recently made. In my opinion, the worst tier in B–block is on the top, U/Z. It's the hottest gallery during the summer and winter. At the end of a hot workday, you can always rest-assure, that you will probably develop some form of disease on U/Z, from sweat bumps on any part of your body, to fungus and ringworms. The ventilation is poor and when convicts shower the humidity lingers the entire day. No matter how many fans were turned on, nothing seems to improve the cooling process or its dampish environment.

STORY CONT:

Once the gallery was in the messhall, I am able to conduct three cell searches, but instead chose to perform a security check. I looked for any unmade beds or stragglers left behind who may not have heard the meal announcement. This is also a crucial time because suicidal convicts like to take their lives during the morning meal, since there's no one left on the gallery to hear or see them commit this act. *

Others, who really don't want to commit suicide, will do it when they see a gallery officer walking in their direction. However, God forbid, if the officer is called away while the convict decides he wants to pretend to hang himself; expecting the officer will be there to cut him down. Chances are, if he doesn't have a plan B, put aside, plan A will definitely be accomplished with success. I've witnessed many hangings throughout my career. Some were successful, and many were not. In all the years I've worked in the prison system, I've learned suicides are increased between the months of November through January, holiday months. Officers usually carry a small two-inch knife in a leather case for this reason. Many also commit suicide after a relationship breakup. I've learned the hard way, when you cut a hanging man down, the potentials for serious injury to yourself are extremely high. It's not easy to hold up a man who's over one hundred fifty pounds of dead weight, while at the same time trying to cut him down. However, you do what you can regardless of his convictions. I can recall a convict who once hung himself inside his cell. The convict was being held up by officer John Bishop. I immediately ran to the cell where the officer was yelling for assistance. As I assisted in holding up the convict, Bishop somehow managed to cut loose the knot on the sheet, grab the convict and place him on the ground. Bishop then ordered me to get help while he proceeded with CPR techniques. His amazing efforts and courage saved the convict's life. Help finally arrived and the convict was placed on a gurney. An officer name Harty, who was also a paramedic on the street, jumped on the gurney and continued CPR. As a result of this incident, heroic commendations came down. Officer, Harty received a commendation for his efforts in helping to save the life of another human being.

Officer Bishop, an African-American male, received nothing and neither did I. Although this was not unusual for Sing-Sing, it never stopped or prevented any one of us from continuing to do our job to the fullest extent and without prejudice. This was my first hands-on suicide encounter, but it was not the first John Bishop. He had several under his belt. John, with many years as a member of the correction's emergency response team, was the officer who broke me in as a rookie officer. He was the officer I would duplicate for many years in the prison environment. What worked for John didn't always work for others, but if it came close, it was good enough for me. Consider this, somewhere in our great nation there are presently five or six response team members equipping themselves in preparation for a cell extraction. Some debriefing and negotiations will be taking place involving a supervisor or two in these extractions. The equipment may involve the following; uniforms, equipment belts, body shields, batons, armor, helmets, boots, video camera, handcuffs, chemical agents and other equipment. The costs are in the hundreds when you consider five uniform officers at thirty-five plus dollars an hour, for several hours; not including the cost of equipment. The point is this; John's philosophy in regard to quelling an isolated potential disturbance was quite simple. John Bishop was a no holds barred correction officer, yet he possessed the natural counseling capabilities that many in law enforcement negotiation teams possess today through training. His interpersonal communication skills and verbal abilities of expression usually resulted in a trusting relationship with his aggressor, yet always keeping in mind, not to let his guards down; John could shift his counselable consultation capabilities to a defensive and protective combatable engagement mentality. Good old-fashioned professionalism like this is now replaced with extraction teams and sometimes hours of negotiations. However, regardless of what methods are being implemented throughout our nation's correctional institutions, officers like John Bishop, who are able to tackle any obstacle presented in their path with no discrepancies or second thoughts, are not recognized or decorated for going beyond the scope of their duty. And not recognized for displaying the bravery that many, even in supervisory levels at Sing-Sing, has yet to discover; from the most eastern Caribbean, Haitian loving captain, to the lowest crippled arm, drunken Vietnam veteran sergeant.

STORY CONT:

After conducting my security check and no discovery of suicide, I headed downstairs to the OIC office where coffee was brewed and where officers congregate. We began to discuss new departmental policies and union matters when officer Mejia approached us and informed me he had a personal matter to attend. He had to leave for several hours and was instructed by the assistant watch-commander to hand over all assigned equipment and job responsibilities to me. He informed me officer Anderson was on his way up to B-block to take my place on R/W gallery while I ran the OIC office. Mejia went back to his office to close out his log book. *

Officer Anderson, also known as Andy, was one hell of guy and unique in his own way. Convicts actually feared this guy, not because he was a muscle-bound man; he's far from that, but because he'd write up a convict in an instant. Andy carried lots of papers in his shirt pocket. Each paper had a handwritten excuse ever heard by Andy from convicts. So if he found a convict loitering on his gallery and the convict came up with an excuse, e.g.
"Oh, sorry officer I didn't see you there."
Andy would then reach in his pocket and pull out a piece of paper with the same excuse.
"Oh, sorry officer I didn't see you there."
Convicts were flabbergasted when this happened and speechless when Andy showed them the written excuses. He would then reach for his rule-book and quote the violations.
"Okay, now let me see home-boy 106.10, out of place, 107.10, interference with an employee."
Convicts knew there was no way around it. They would either surrender their identification card knowing full well they're busted and be issued a misbehavior report, or Andy would just let them off with a warning.
"If I ever see you loitering here again I'll have to write you up on several charges, understand?"
Some convicts would smile at the verbal warning, knowing they were off the hook. They would then apologize never to be seen or heard from again, especially on galleries being operated by officer, Anderson.

Convicts knew who Andy was and word got around the jail quickly of his presences. I can recall one incident while working on R/W gallery where Andy was the escort officer. A convict came down on the gallery and asked if he could get a cigarette from one of his buddies. I said it was okay, just as long as he made it fast and returned to his assigned gallery. The convict took one look down the gallery and stopped in his tracks.

"Officer, Bermudez, who's that officer on the gallery?"

"That's my partner Officer Anderson."

"Oh, shit, never mind officer, I'll get that cigarette during recreation. I'm not messing with that dude."

And the convict was gone in a flash. Lord knows how much I laughed that day, but that was the effect Andy had on convicts, a genuine character no other officer could duplicate.

STORY CONT:

Officer Anderson finally arrived in B-block with his famous greeting, 'Hey, dudes, I'm going to use the bathroom Bermudez, and I'll be right back." I went into the coffee room, poured myself a cup and began conversing with other officers for several minutes when suddenly we heard a loud yell come from the OIC office.

"I'm tired of your shit! Everyday it's the same damn thing with you and regardless of what we do or what we say, you're never satisfied! You're going to piss me off one day, and I'm going to take this baton, stick it in the back of your head and turn you into a toilet plunger, dammit!"

It was OIC Mejia, yelling at a convict. Apparently, the center gate was left open and this particular convict came down as he had always done in the past, to create problems with the officers in the area. Once this convict was in the area it would literally take a negotiator to remove him. I couldn't understand what Mejia meant when he told the convict; he'd turn him into a plunger by sticking a baton into the back of his head until I saw the convict with my own two eyes. The convict was a very tall skinny dark male, with poor hygiene and a pair of, 'extremely large lips.' So large, they look like a couple of canoes being held up to his face in an upside down horizontal position. When I saw that and put together what was said, I laughed so hard I almost pissed on myself.

Others heard it as well, including convicts up on the galleries who were looking down at everyone. They too began laughing to the point of almost coughing their heads off. I can't say this was the proper method in applying a little interpersonal communication technique, but this convict never came down again and never gave anyone else a hard time. *

Mejia had a way of saying things and how he said it in his genuine voice made it all the better. He was an extremely funny individual. Sometimes we all wondered why he never got into the acting comedy business. I can recall one of many funny experiences I had with Mejia on our personal day off. While I was driving down a road in Fort Montgomery, New York, we were approaching a horse farm, and several horses were out doing what horses do, eat grass. One particular horse caught Mejia's attention. There was a white wooden fence and a large horse towering over it and innocently eating its morning meal. Mejia instructed me to stop alongside the fence by the horse.

"Hey, Bermudez, do me a favor and stop by that horse?"

"Stop by the horse, for what?"

"Just stop by the horse. I want to talk to it."

"What! You want to talk to it? You're crazy."

"Come on, B, stop!"

So I stopped in front of the horse as he requested. Mejia opened the passenger-side window and loudly let out what sounded like a loud horse's call. The horse instantly picked up its head, took a look to the right and to the left as though it saw a ghost and ran zero to sixty in two seconds. All I saw was a cloud of dirt and a fat horse's ass flying in the wind. I couldn't believe what I was seeing and thought to myself.

This guy knows how to speak to horses. He actually knows the horse's language.

I was in a complete state of shock.

"Oh, shit, Mejia, what did you say to the horse?"

"You really want to know?"

"Yeah, I want to know," asking in suspense.

"Okay, I asked the horse. Hey, horsy, how would you like me to fuck you in that ass?"

93

I could not believe what I was hearing. I broke out in an uncontrollable laugh and I couldn't breathe. My tears were blinding, and I lost total control and concentration of my driving. I had to get out of the car and almost threw up on the side of the road.

"Take the wheel Emil, take the wheel, I can't do this."

I was laughing too much and couldn't drive. Until this day, I can't recall a day in my life in which I ever laughed so long and so hard. To make matters worse, just fifteen minutes into the same trip and after the horse episode, I had to stop for a coffee at a local Dunkin Donuts. We went inside and ordered two regular coffees with one teaspoon of sugar each. The woman attending to us was a little old lady with extremely thick glasses that magnified her eyeballs to twice the normal size. Her eyes actually look like a couple of billiard balls. She began pouring a lot of sugar into our coffee, and we took notice instantly.

"Ah, man, did you see that Emil. She drowned us with sugar?"

"Yeah, I saw it. Hey, lady, you put enough sugar in there to give all diabetes!"

That was all I needed to hear in one day. I was back into my uncontrollable laughing mood. I knew then my lungs would probably collapse, or suffer heart failure. I think the little old lady behind the counter became more upset about my laughing then what was said. She poured out the coffees and threw us both out. I realized that day it was first time I ever called Mejia by his first name, Emil. It's been that way ever since. Another outrageous moment with Mejia was when we were working in B–block and a convict came down demanding we take him to the facility hospital at once.

"Yo, officer, I need you to give me an escort officer right now?"

"What's the problem?"

"Why do you need to know what my fucking problem is?

"Just take me to the hospital or find me an escort."

"I need to know what's wrong, so I can call the nurse and relay the problem."

"I woke up this morning with a stiff neck, and I can't move it, are you happy now?"

"Hey, we're here to help so save us the attitude problem."

"Man, just get me a fucking escort officer, that's all I need!"

"Okay, I tell you what, when you get to the nurse at the hospital tell her you have a small case of,"... and Mejia whispered into the convict's ear.

"What did you say to him?"

"I can't say Bermudez, it's a medical terminology translation and only between me and the convict."

"Thank you Officer Mejia. I'll let the nurse know what's wrong with me."

And off he went to the hospital with an escort officer as he demanded; compliments of Mejia.

"You can't possibly know what his physical problem might be without the proper medical knowledge."

"Don't worry B, he'll be okay."

One hour later the convict returned with his escort officer, fuming and demanding to see officer Mejia. "I want to talk to the officer who sent me to the hospital!"

"What's the problem now?"

"The officer who sent me to the hospital, that's fucking the problem."

I paged Mejia over the loud speaker, and he showed up with a half smile on his face. The convict instantly became angry and began yelling.

"Yo, what's your problem co, you got a fucking problem; you think you're funny?"

"Hey, leave this area right now."

I instructed the escort officer to take the convict back to his cell and Mejia assisted in the escorted. The phone then began to ring, and I answered it.

"You've reached B-block, officer Bermudez speaking."

"Yes, officer Bermudez, this is Nurse Loony from the emergency room. Did you send a convict here from your block with a neck problem this morning?"

"Yes, Nurse Loony we did."

"Okay, why did you tell the convict he might have a small case of necrophilia?"

"What!" I answered in shock, stuttering and tripping over my tongue. "I'll have to get back to you on that one nurse. It was that damn Mejia."

"I should have known," she replied while laughing and hung up the phone. That was the nature of Mejia's character, full of jokes and unexpected surprises.

He had a way of spicing up the day and momentarily helping us forget where we were for those several minutes or couple of hours. However, not all of Mejia's life experiences and job-related encounters were filled with delectability.

On November 07, 1994, four convicted killers broke out of Shawangunk maximum-security prison. It was the first-time anyone had escaped from the Shawangunk in Ulster County, New York, since it opened in 1986. A fifth man, a convicted kidnapper who had been paroled from another prison in July, was caught just outside the Shawangunk grounds and charged as an accomplice, said Michael Kavanagh, the Ulster County District Attorney. The man was discovered in a wooded area carrying a gun and several maps. Correction officials refused to explain how the killers had slipped away from the prison's "close supervision unit," which houses convicts considered likely to try to escape or assault correction officers. One escapee, Sean Ryan, who is serving six and a half years to life for killing a Manhattan man during a 1977 robbery, had previously escaped from Rikers Island, in NYC. An official of the correction officers union, Ernie Benevento, said that over the last two years, the number of officers at the Shawangunk prison had fallen to 220 from 260, while the number of convicts had remained steady at 540. The escapes, which were discovered by officers at about 7:00 a.m. sent ripples of anxiety throughout Wallkill, the tiny hamlet about sixty miles north of NYC where the prison is nestled in an old farm valley. Before the last convict was caught at 4:12 p.m., mothers gathered anxiously on street corners waiting for their children to step off school buses, while other neighbors congregated on their front lawns as correction officers searched their homes. All the while, two state police helicopters buzzed overhead and sever police dogs sniffed the streets for leads. The manhunt encompassed a twenty-five-mile radius and involved more than 140 state troopers, correction officers and local police officers. But none of the escapees got more than a mile and a half from the prison, the authorities said. Two convicts; Ryan and Keith Hart; were discovered at separate times yesterday afternoon near a water tower less than a half mile from the prison. Both were dazed and bleeding profusely, having been cut by the razor wire attached to the fences that surround the prison. A third escapee, Patrick Proctor, who was also badly cut, was picked up by correction officers at 8:00 a.m. as he walked along Route 208.

And the fourth, John Beuther, was caught at 7:30 a.m. within the prison perimeter but outside his high-risk unit. None of the escapees was armed or resisted arrest. Hart, 34, had been sentenced in 1982 to thirty-eight years to life in the killing of a jewelry store owner on Staten Island, the authorities said. Beuther, 37, was serving twenty-five years to life for a murder in Brooklyn, while Proctor, 29, was serving thirty-two and half years to life for a killing in Queens, the authorities said. The Ulster County District Attorney said that Ryan, 35, had been implicated as a member of the Westies, the gang that terrorized Hell's Kitchen in Manhattan during the 1970s and 1980s. "The Westies are a predominantly Irish American organized crime association operating from the Hell's Kitchen in NYC Westside. They were most influential from 1965 to 1986. During this time period, the NYPD Organized Crime Bureau, the FBI, and other organized crime experts believe that the Westies murdered sixty to one-hundred people, making them one of the most dangerous crime groups in NYC." Ryan was convicted of robbing and then killing a garment-center executive, Harry Kassoff, in his East Side apartment in November 1977. In June 1979, while awaiting transfer from Rikers Island, Ryan escaped from his cell. After burning a hole in a Plexiglas louver window panel, he used a five-inch blade to saw through the panel frame. He then slid out the window and shimmied down a fifteen-foot rope that he had fashioned from a blanket and sheets. Daniel Lynch, 36, was free on parole from the Great Meadow Correctional Facility in Washington County, about ninety miles north of Albany, after serving twelve years of an eight to sixty year sentence for robbery and kidnapping in Suffolk County. Mr. Flateau, New York State Correctional spokesman, would not comment on how the accused accomplice Daniel Lynch, was connected to the escapees, (*Jacques Steinberg, 1994*).

But we later discovered how the accused accomplice Daniel Lynch was connected to the escapees. During the escape at Shawangunk, members of the correctional service's fugitive warrant squad were immediately notified of the escape in progress. Officer Emil Mejia at the time was an active member of that fugitive squad and upon notification of the escape, he courageously sprung into action. In possession of an unmarked state vehicle, he went to Wallkill and began patrolling the prison perimeters and local streets.

During his patrol canvass of the area, officer Mejia notice a suspicious individual, later identified as Daniel Lynch 36, exiting a wooded area while wearing a fanny pack around his waist. Officer, Mejia stepped out of his official vehicle, ordered him to stop and questioned his reason for being there. The ex-con stated he was a hunter from Long Island, NY, who was lost and looking for a way out of the forest. Also a native of Long Island, Mejia became suspicious of the ex-con excuses and of his body language. He noticed the ex-con become anxiously watchful of him and suspected this guy was somehow linked to the escape. His inherent disposition of the ex-cons particular behavior would prove him correct and his ability to exercise his extra-sensory perception would later save his life. The ex-con began to reach into his fanny pack. Officer Mejia immediately reached for his weapon, took a shooting stand and gave the ex-con a verbal command.

"Stop right there or I'll fucking shoot your ass!"

Meantime, Mejia managed to call for backup while keeping close vigilance of the suspect at gunpoint. State Police later arrived at scene and helped in securing the ex-con. In ex-convict Daniel Lynch's fanny pack was a loaded .38 service revolver. Officer Mejia later interrogated Lynch, who revealed his diabolical plan of escape and equipment used. With this information, Mejia later searched the wooded area surrounding the prison and discovered two separate setups in different locations. In one setup, he found a duffle bag containing the following items; a crossbow with approximately two-hundred feet of rope affixed with a steel hook, duct-tape, mechanical restraints and a drawn-out plan outlining the entire Shawangunk prison perimeter. During a court testimony by Daniel Lynch, on May 10, 1995, in Ulster County, NY, he stated he was not aware Emil Mejia was actually a corrections officer.

"If I knew then he was a co, I would have killed that motherfucker. I thought he was a cop."

On this same day May 10, 1995, Officer Emil Mejia, who later moved up the ranks from officer to sergeant, lieutenant and now captain, stopped at the Ulster County courthouse for a brief testimony. He was then taken to Albany, NY, for a ceremony and awarded the Medal of Honor by Commissioner Philip Coombe, Jr., for his efforts and extraordinary courage.

Captain Emil Mejia, photo by Emil

Since 1825, almost two-hundred years of Sing-Sing's history and notoriety existence, no other correction officer has ever received the distinguish Medal of Honor. Emil Mejia was the first, and I'm proud to add, "Latino at that." But that was as far as it went, there was no further recognition. While hundreds of other correction officers are being recognized with Medal of Merits and stories being published on local news media, newspapers, magazines and photos pasted everywhere on the internet, nothing was mentioned on Emil. No mention of it in local news media, the internet, newspapers, local magazines or any other recognized correction's publication. The NYS trooper, who came on the scene and assisted officer Mejia in subduing the ex-con, was later credited for the apprehension and for breaking the case he had no previous knowledge of until Mejia officially and voluntarily relinquished the information. Fact of the matter is; it was Officer Emil Mejia, who witnessed the ex-con exiting the forest, initiated the call for backup while holding the subject at gunpoint and brought to surface the internal facts of the escape. Later revealing it was not an inside job as first thought by local law enforcement authorities and correction officials, but rather an outside job.

But no matter how unethical and unjust this may all seem in his lack of recognition, "Honorable men are not fazed by the ignorance and injustice of others. Their determination is unscarred by the absence of recognition and in Emil Mejia's case, who's now a captain; he is no exception to the rule."

STORY CONT:

I prepared myself for the OIC office. Officer Mejia and I discussed policies and programs not yet implemented in our daily activity. As he closed out the logbook I double checked my equipment making sure of its operation and took a fast but precise count of all my gallery keys and keys transferred by Mejia. Once the equipment transfer slip is signed, there's no turning back, you're responsible for any missing keys and/or equipment. I take a quick count of all the confined convicts in the block. I put my papers in order and double-check the messhall running order. I look at the officer's assignment sheet and make sure to notify them of the staff count. The officer's security count slips are then taken to the sergeant, who sends it to the watch commander's office along with the convict population count. I put my lunch away in a locker and make sure the lock is secured. Not that I don't trust the convicts in the area, it's the officers I'm concerned about. A good home-cooked meal left in open view, is like a four-carat gold diamond ring sitting on public grounds. Officer Andy finally came out of the employee's bathroom, and after a short briefing I gave him my equipment and responsibilities of R/W gallery. Mejia finally left to attend to his business. I was now the officer-in-charge, (OIC) the big cheese. I didn't have to walk up and down the galleries the rest of the day and didn't have to yell my lungs out trying to get convict's attention. I didn't have to worry about my office cell door being opened, closed and locked. I didn't have to worry about locking individual cell doors that were called on visits, went to work or placed on confinement. The OIC office cell door was always left opened, but secured in a sense where the presence of officers was always in the immediate area, and any slight act of suspicion would attract them almost instantly. I now had approximately one hour of relaxation, in which I could just lay back and talk to other officers who were available.

100

Alternatively, I can just simply let my mind travel outside the prison walls before the messhall operation was over and convict programs began. This was now a time when I would subconsciously make premature decisions and get ahead of my work. However, it was also a time when I could just sit back on the office chair while the radio played low in the distance to the sounds of Jazz music. I turned down the headache causing fluorescent lights and begin to reflect back on my life, back to my childhood in Brooklyn, New York. Back to the times when headline news didn't matter, where the responsibilities of rent payments and utility bills were nonexistence in our childhood minds. When the only important and meaningful consequence was to wake up early the next day and meet outside with the neighborhood friends. In a time where, only one brief eye contact with a neighborhood girl would instantly affect the rhythm of your heartbeat, almost always resulting in a romantic and everlasting summer crush. *

Chapter Three

~~~

My Life's Autobiography
To continue with the story, go directly to
STORY CONT:

My life began in 1958. I was born in Cumberland hospital, Brooklyn, NY. The same hospital former heavyweight champion Mike Tyson was born. I was raised in the Marcy housing projects of Bedford Stuyvesant, where Shawn Corey Carter, better known as Jay-Z, was born and raised. I lived for a very short while on the south side of Williamsburg Brooklyn, Coney Island, Bensonhurst, Gravesend and eventually Newburgh, NY. I was the third of seven children. My parents Margarita Morales Pereira, was a stay at home Mom and father Deusdelid Bermudez, a custom tailor. They were both natives of Monte Santo in Vieques, Puerto Rico. My mother later divorce and married Cruz Morales of Culebra, Puerto Rico, a career handyman and cousin to professional wrestler, Pedro Morales. They both exercised regularly at the YMCA on Division Avenue in Williamsburg, Brooklyn. As a child I vacationed with my stepfather Cruz on several occasions during the summer months in Vieques and Culebra, Puerto Rico, where my culture and tradition slowly became part of my family manifestation.

Vieques is a little island just east of the mainland and east of Vieques is another even smaller island called Culebra. I attended P.S. 297, Abraham Stockton School, where I almost got myself suspended on numerous occasions for getting out of my seat every time the fire trucks came out of the firehouse; Engine 230, Ladder 701, on Park Ave. What can I say; I was infatuated by those big red trucks, the yelping horns and screaming sirens. I also attended Mark Hopkins JHS 33, Eastern District HS, and later Abraham Lincoln HS. The New York City Mayor in 1958 was Robert F. Wagner, and New York State Governor was William Averell Harriman. The New York Yankees were scheduled to play the Boston Red Sox on the fifteenth of April. The Brooklyn Dodgers became Los Angeles Dodgers. The first off-duty NYC police officer to die that year of a heart attack was Francis O'Rourke, Detective from the thirty-second squad. The first and only to die on duty was Herman Corn of the fifty-second precinct from an auto accident while on patrol. In Cuba, Fidel Castro's revolutionary army began its attacks on Havana. A brand new 1958 Buick Lesabre sold for $1,495.00, and the average home sold for $30,000.00. A gallon of gas was twenty-four cents, a gallon of milk one dollar, loaf of bread nineteen cents. US stamps were four cents, and of course I had my very first drink of milk.

103

Nostrand Avenue Station 1969

The Brooklyn Rapid Transit traveled over Myrtle Avenue. The trains were dark green in color, and the fare was ten cents. There was also a Broadway Ferry Express Line, which passed every now and then with no side doors, windows or walls. Riders were met with steels rods that ran the entire length of the car, and the exit doors were located in the rear and front of every car. I remember there were times when we would wait on the Nostrand Avenue station where the platforms were two-by-six lumber and when the train came to a stop, the whole station would swing back and forth. I would actually hold on to the steel columns for balance and support. It would terrorize me as a child and I came very close to pissing my pants on several occasions. Many terrible childhood experiences revolved around these stations, from doors opening with no platform to step on, only a railing and pavement below, to suicide jumpers. During one sunny afternoon when I was approximately ten years old, my sister Joanna and I were sent on an errand to a local pharmacy called Ditchek, on Myrtle and Tompkins Avenue. As we walked out an African-American man threw himself from the Myrtle and Tompkins Avenue train station platform to the pavement below and landed directly in front of us.

Myrtle/Tompkins Avenue 1969

He also did this in the presence of his own daughter, who at the time was handicapped and had metal braces on both her legs. I can still remember her as though it was yesterday. She had two ponytails and a long dress with flower designs on it. His head split open from his left eye to the top of his head, oozing out blood and exposing brain matter. I always wondered whatever happened to this girl and how a father could commit such an act directly in front of his child. Our nights after witnessing this suicide were sleepless for many months. I remember watching Eyewitness News Anchormen, Roger Grimsby and Bill Beutel, everyday for weeks on Channel seven, wondering if it would make the news. I can't even begin to imagine what his daughter went through, but I do hope her suffering was short lived somehow. The Nostrand Avenue station was located on the corner of Myrtle and Nostrand Avenues. Directly in front of the station, was a factory that was later abandoned. On a Wednesday, in October 1972, and at approximately six a.m. while we were sleeping, we awoke to an extremely loud explosion. Our mother made us dress immediately and told us to stand by. We all looked out of our windows and could see the neighborhood, and all the surrounding buildings illuminated in a bright orange glow.

It was quite obvious there was a catastrophic fire somewhere, but we couldn't see exactly where it was coming from. My brothers and I quickly ran up two flights onto the rooftop and could see flames reaching high into the sky from the intersection of Myrtle and Nostrand Avenues. The abandon three-story factory and adjacent buildings that once stood there were gone and demolished. We couldn't believe what we were seeing, and the only way for a closer look was to see it from street level. The handball courts to be exact. We asked our mother for permission to head to the scene, but it was still a little too dark outside, and we had to wait several minutes. We were scheduled for school that day and would later walk a mile and a half on Lee Ave to Division Avenue toward Eastern District High School in Williamsburg, Brooklyn. As daylight lit up the morning sky revealing the devastation of the explosion's aftermath, we hurried up with our breakfast and went to the handball courts.

From there we were close to the intersection. There was a police car that may have been parked there during the explosion and was thrown literally into a city bus across the street as a result of the blast. The police officers inside the patrol car were injured, along with some of the passengers from the city bus. The streets were crowded with people who lived nearby. Tenants from the adjacent buildings where the explosion occurred were coming out of the damaged buildings with all sorts of injuries. You could hear the screams of people calling out for their love ones. There were many fire trucks, ambulances and police emergency vehicles everywhere. Just beyond the fence, opposite side of the handball courts and directly across the street, was a grocery store. I remember someone stopped their car to help and left his vehicle unattended with its doors opened and the radio loudly playing the song, Clean up Woman, by singer Betty Wright. A police officer later closed the vehicle door. It's that song that brings to surface the memories of that particular day whenever I hear it. Unbelievably, as massive as the explosion was, no one was killed as far as I know. In all, a total of approximately twenty eight people were injured, and hundreds were left homeless. Minutes before the explosion a man was heard screaming and seen running from the factory. The finalization of the investigation concluded an arsonist was responsible for the explosion and to my knowledge; no arrest has ever been made.

John & Al's Sport's Store Williamsburg, Brooklyn 1973

Barely, three months later in January 1973, another crime of magnitude proportion began to unfold at John and Al's Sporting Store in Williamsburg, Brooklyn. While walking on Flushing Avenue toward Broadway on our way to Tom, Dick and Harry shoe store for a little window shopping, we began hearing police sirens, in the distance. Coming from all directions were scores of patrol cars racing down Broadway, one right after another. Then the unmarked cars with their cherry red lights on top and large emergency police trucks were not far behind. Something was going on, and we began running in the direction of the emergency vehicles. As we approached Broadway and Lewis Avenues, we could see hundreds of flashing lights and emergency vehicles. Then the gunfire, in the distance, and for some ridiculous reason we picked up the running pace toward the sound. As we got closer to scene, we can see there was a police officer down on the ground. He wasn't moving, and we knew then something of magnitude proportion was going on. Officers immediately ordered us to leave the area, and we took off like a bat out of hell, but returned moments later. We can see it involved John and Al's Sport Store. This was an establishment frequented by my father.

107

My brothers and I met with our father every weekend at a luncheonette several doors down, for coffee and those huge cinnamon rolls. Not far from there down the street was Tom, Dick and Harry where we purchased our sneakers. Directly across from the sport store was the bullet-riddled furniture store where my mother's new furniture was placed on layaway and where store credit was a person's word of honor or a firm handshake. As bits and pieces of information were being passed around, we learned a group of radical Muslims went into the sport store and took numerous hostages. Hundreds of people began to gather in every corner and on every tenement window above. Hundreds of police officers can be seen positioned in every nook and cranny of Myrtle-Broadway train station and on nearby rooftops. The following days brought thousands of people and many lowlife spectators who mingled within the crowd to view the siege began yelling and throwing bottles at police.

We couldn't understand the reason behind their actions and police, who previously lost one of their own, were not about to ignore the bottle throwing escapade. Within minutes hundreds of people began running in every direction and as the crowd began to clear, I saw a wall of police officers running in our direction and striking spectators across the heads with their batons. I immediately began running with the crowd, and as I turned around to look behind me, there was a police officer towering over me with a baton raised over his head looking down at me. Quite possibly realizing I was just a teenage kid. He instead struck an adult who was running alongside of me, and I can hear the sound of his body hit the pavement and a loud exhaled as he hit the ground. Seeing a dead officer on the ground unable to be rescued by his comrades, other officers wounded, bottles being thrown at police and people getting struck on the head with batons was more than enough violence for us. At that precise moment, we decided to leave the area and head back home. There's always the news on television or the newspapers at our local grocery stores if we really needed to know the outcome. I was fourteen years old and even at that age felt the emotional pain and sorrow for those officers. I never forgot the confused looks on their faces that would eventually turn to despair and anger. The same pricks that shot them down and the same pricks who threw the bottles, are the first pricks to dial 911 and ask for help when the shoe is on the other foot.

The radical Muslims with their well-thought-out plan and highly educated skills now had nine hostages. They vowed to kill them all and die in a blaze of glory with police. Leaving the hostage unguarded for a moment gave one of the store owners just enough time to gather the hostages and slip them away up to a stairwell to the rooftop where they were met by police who instantly took them away. Discovering they lost the hostages and their bargaining tool, the radical Muslims were now left with two choices, die in a blaze of glory as they said they would or commit suicide? They chose to surrender to police instead, but not before asking to pray before giving themselves up; so much for their faith and blaze of glory. The last I heard New York State had spent thousands in law suits representing these guys who were filing discrimination and civil rights violation lawsuits while in the correctional system. I also heard NYS Parole was considering the release of these lowlifes. It's one of those things I never understood about our criminal-justice system. While many are incarcerated throughout our nation for crimes they didn't commit, and no evidence to prove their guilt, these guys did not only take hostages, but killed a police officer and wounded two others. Let me guess, they all participated in an alternative to violence program, received their GED, (General Equivalency Diploma) participated in a drug and alcohol rehabilitation program, didn't receive any or received minimal misbehavior reports, have no history of fighting others and show no signs of anti-social behavior, (All elements needed for parole). A true career criminal is a person who not only knows the laws of our state and of our correctional system, but one who know how to manipulate the system and all those who are a part of it. The true career criminal enters a correctional system with nothing, and upon his or her release will usually have a bank account worth thousands of dollars and in some cases, hundreds of thousands. Their methods in obtaining these large monetary awards are done by participating in frivolous lawsuits against the state and their employees, either for excessive force, petty violations and/or discrimination claims. These mutts mentioned above are no exceptions to the rule; they are the true manipulative career criminal's society will have to deal with upon their release. The cop I saw lying dead on the street that day was Patrolman Stephen Gilroy, who I'll always remember.

William 'Billy' McKinley, November 1958

As faith would have it, thirty-five years later I learned Stephen Gilroy had a brother name Brian Gilroy—also a patrolman from the 105 squad in Queens, NY, served in the United State Marines and was wounded in battle. William, (Billy) McKinley was my neighbor for many years in Newburgh, NY. He too served at the one-hundred-five squad in Queens and knew Brian well. Billy also served in the Korean War on the Amphibious 877. He later retired from NYPD as a Detective and appeared on the David Letterman show in 2005. The other two patrolmen that were wounded that faithful day survived their assault; they were Officers Frank Carpenter and Jose Adorno. Disastrous and detrimental incidents like this are unfortunately a part of our lives and being witnessed throughout the world by many other children and in greater numbers. It's a never-ending cycle of violence and tragedy with no end or significance. However, there were also good times in those neighborhoods. My first childhood crush was with a girl named Pearl. She lived in the same building on the first floor; I lived on the fifth floor.

We use to walk to school together almost every morning and when no one was looking, we sometimes held hands. We also liked sitting together on the building's front steps. I can once recall sitting on those steps and listening, in the distance, to a song by singer Marvin Gaye, "Mercy, Mercy Me." Even now that song brings back those childhood memories whenever I hear it. We sometimes sat on those steps and chat for hours, or so it seemed. The fall season was always the best time for us, because the nights were cool, and we sport the latest in windbreakers and sweatshirts. When no one was looking, we'd sort of cuddle together side by side, looked up at the windows for potential witnesses and steal a kiss or two, but that's as far as that went. Those were innocent times back then, and it's amazing how memories like this can hibernate in our minds for many years, usually resurfacing in our thirties with a song, a conversation, a photo and even a familiar scent or smell. Pearl was an extremely attractive young girl with a nice complexion and always well dressed. I sometimes wondered whatever happened to her, but as fate would have it, I would learn about her almost thirty plus years later. While working at Downstate facility in Fishkill, NY, I was warned by several supervisors during the lineup about four blood gang members who were brought in the previous night. They were being housed in my unit, and the word around prison was, 'they're looking to slice open an officer's face with a razor as part of an initiation.' As I stood there listening to the announcement, I became angry and couldn't help but plan on what actions to take upon arrival to my unit. I remember thinking to myself.

"They're on my unit and looking to cut one of us, us possibly being me. I'm not having it."

After arriving on my unit and taking my morning count, I made it my business to confront the convicts who were brought in the previous night. I observe their mannerism and learn every detail of their faces. As I passed their cell doors, one convict courageously spoke out.

"Hey, co, are you a white boy from upstate?"

As others laughed, I quickly replied in a form of a question.

"Does it matter whether I'm a White boy from upstate, a Black man from down south or a Latino from Marcy projects?"

Several seconds of silence filled my surroundings and surprised faces stepped up to the cell doors while gazing upon one another.

111

AB Initials done 1974, photo by Braulio Rivera, Jr. 2011

Quite obviously, something I said got their immediate and full attention. Numerous questions concerning Marcy projects were coming from all four gang members who were brought in the previous night. All ears were set on what I had to say. One of the blood members began questioning me, "What do you know about Marcy? You live there, do you know someone there?"

I briefly described my Marcy childhood upbringing, my neighborhood friends and a girl who I liked very much. I also mentioned she lived in the same tenement on the first floor, and her name was Pearl. One young convict with a shattered look muttered his words, "Oh, Shit."

You could almost hear a pin drop, and everyone stopped talking. The largest of the four convicts looked across the floor to another convict at his cell door.

"Yo, isn't that your Mama?"

I looked at the other convict who was being questioned and instantly knew in my heart that young man was Pearl's son. His last name was Stanley.

"Wait a minute, wait a minute, what address did you live in and what floor?"

"I lived in one-twenty-one, on the fifth floor apartment 5-A. Before moving away, I painted my initials, 'AB' outside my bedroom window on the brick wall with a paintbrush. And from what I hear, those initials are still there thirty-five years later."

112

Marcy Projects Softball Park 1969

"Oh, shit; yeah. It's still there. That was you? Ok, it makes sense. Your name is A. Bermudez. So what apartment did my Mother live in?"

"I can't remember, but I do remember the apartment was on the first floor to the left of the incinerator chute and the elevator door. I think it may have been apartment 1-C; if I'm not mistaken."

Stanley gaped.

"Yeah, that's right, co, that's right."

"I know its right. And now that I look at you more, I can see the resemblance to your mom. Your mom was a very pretty young lady. We were friends back in the day, we were around twelve or thirteen years old. By-the-way, how is she doing?"

"Mom passed away while giving birth to me at Woodhull Hospital."

I stood there in shock and felt bad for the young man. With nothing further to say I then dismissed myself.

"I'm sorry to hear that young man. Well, I have some work to do, and I'll see you guys in a few minutes."

As I began walking away the other convicts began antagonizing him.

"Damn, that officer could have been your father, yo."

Another convict deceitfully added his comment.

113

"Could have been... that is his father. Look at them yo, they look alike!"

Other convicts began to laugh, and Stanley put up his defense shield.

"Nah, that co didn't know my Mama, fuck yall. Yo, I'll talk to you Niggas later, I'm going go back to sleep."

I later came back down and ask if they were going to participate in keeplock recreation, since they were all on twenty-three hours disciplinary confinement. All accepted, but Stanley, he refused to go and stood behind. They were eventually picked up for the recreation by an escort officer. While the others were out, Stanley called me down to his cell. As I approached his cell door and looked at him one last time, I was convenience this was indeed Pearl's son. He asked me many questions concerning his mother, what kind of girl she was back then, what school we attended, did we go steady as girlfriend and boyfriend, was I her first crush, how she dressed, how did we break up and did we ever keep in touch. I told him all I could remember concerning his mom. I told him we were kids at the time, just childhood friends, so it wasn't a real relationship and no breakup to brag of. I told him my parents moved from Marcy in 1976, and as a child I didn't have much of a choice. I told him that I would write a book some day, and in that book I would mention my childhood experiences. I also told him to look for it, and he asked, "Will my Mama be in it?" I promised him she would be, and she is, '*Rest in Peace, Pearl*.'

Marcy projects of Bedford Stuyvesant, was also known as junkie's paradise during the 1960s into the early part of the 1970s. At any given time I could look out my fifth floor window facing Marcy Avenue, as I've always done many times before, and see the neighborhood junkies inject themselves on park benches with homemade syringes filled with heroin. Little glass tubes with a baby bottle pacifier tip affixed to it for the pumping of fluids, and rubber-bands holding it in place. A belt was wrapped around their arms while holding it tight with their teeth. At the time, I couldn't understand what they were doing or why, but I did know the end-results would either, put them in a nodding state of mind, or they would huddle together like football players and begin to harmonize and sing songs that are now considered oldies. Songs by groups like the Dells, the Moments and the Whispers.

Marcy Projects Handball Courts 1969

Most of those junkies were Vietnam Vets, victims of a nasty and horrific war, but they were well dressed junkies that set the fashion stage for many others in the Marcy housing projects. Clothing styles included, sharkskin pants, mod koratron pants, checker shirts, polyester suits, bellbottom pants, stitch shirts, knit sweaters, cashmere coats, velour jackets, three-quarter length leather jackets; playboy shoes, high platform shoes also called marshmallows, pro keds and converses. Converses were also becoming available in different colors at ten dollars each, off Marcy Avenue. Many of the hats worn were the; brimmed hats, tam cloches, kangos caps, apple jacks, black fedoras, brown berlesoni and beaver hats with baby oil and different color ribbons. Many of those hats worn in the housing projects were stolen from nearby Jewish neighborhoods in Williamsburg Brooklyn. The Marcy neighborhood crooks would head up Lee Avenue and walk to the Jewish neighborhoods, where they would then watch the neighborhood streets and look for the weakest victim wearing the nicest hat. The much older men were the easiest targets, since they couldn't run after the crooks. However, some criminals were not only limited to stealing hats, they stole plenty of bicycles too. Many who stole them sold it for booze and/or drugs.

115

One brand new bike brought enough cash for a couple of bottles of booze, some cigarettes, heroin, methadone, acid or marijuana. Neighborhood kids not aware the bicycles were stolen had their parents purchase the bikes at very reasonable prices. Police that later patrolled the projects sometime confiscated the bikes and returned them to their rightful owners. The crooks that sold them were nowhere to be found, and if you did find one, he was usually too strung out on drugs to remember. The neighborhood was catching on to the crimes, and the Jewish residents began arming themselves with whistles. Whenever a crime was in progress, no matter how small, the whistles came out and were blown, not only by the victims, but by anyone who had a whistle. This was a successful tactic and one that deterred crime for quite some time. When the crooks began to catch on to the whistle concept, they then began taking the whistle away before fleeing the crime scene. It didn't always work because some people had extra whistles. Those who stole a hat and were caught were lucky to be left alive.

When those Jewish neighborhood people decided it was time to open up a can of whoop-ass, you better believe you were going to get the ass kicking of your life.

I've seen many dudes come from those neighborhoods into the Marcy projects trickling blood while resembling the cartoon character, "The Crusher from Looney Tunes" after an unsuccessful wrestling match with Bugs Bunny. Going to and from Eastern District High, I've walked Lee Avenue into this Jewish neighborhood many times and personally never encountered a problem. On a contrary, coming from the housing projects into those neighborhoods made me realize there were actually other neighborhoods with little to no crime in existence. The environment was pleasant, people were friendly, streets were clean, no graffiti, no loud music. No abandoned cars, no fighting, no drugs and most importantly, no thugs around every street corner or behind every tree waiting to take your lunch money or bus pass. And when you did find yourself in trouble, it was always other kids from adjoining neighborhoods who came into the Jewish neighborhoods for the sole purpose of committing crimes or mischief. Even on those rare occasions when you found yourself in trouble it didn't matter what nationality you were or what neighborhood you were from.

Corner of Marcy/Nostrand Avenues 1969

The Jewish neighborhood people were always there to lend a helping hand. Many times when I did find myself in trouble the residents immediately call police or got involved, and on some occasions escorted me to the neighborhood borderline for my own protection. Bottom-line? If you got yourself a serious beat down in a Jewish neighborhood of Williamsburg Brooklyn, chances are you most definitely earned it. When Marcy's neighborhood crime was at an absence, we played basketball in nearby garbage cans that were chained up to the front railing of the building's entrance or chained up to a fence post. Stoopball was another favorite, the idea behind a double play or a home-run was to make sure you threw that ball as hard as you could and hit the very edge of those steps. Stickball was a favorite too, between residential windows on a brick wall of 113 and 111 Nostrand Avenues. With our chalks, we'd draw a square box between two windows and threw the Spalding ball with its blue or red line directly down the center of that box. Thinking back, I wonder how those residents living in those apartments where we played stickball, could put up with all those hours of constant pounding by the ball. In Marcy, my very first friend was also my next-door neighbor named Jamaal Ashley. We were the same age and attended the same school.

As a member of the Boy Scouts of America, Jamaal went on a lot of camping and recreational trips, but in one of those trips Jamaal never came home. While attending a boy scout camping trip, Jamaal went on a canoe ride, his canoe flipped over and Jamaal drowned in the lake. He lived in apartment 5-B, I lived in 5-A. His mother's cry was piercing and endless. Her pain was felt by everyone at home. For many days and nights, I gazed out of my window and looked over at Jamaal's bedroom window, where he kept a basketball and baseball glove on his windowsill. I always thought he would return and many times saw the window curtains move only to reveal a sad stricken mom that tried in vain to smile back at me as I stared over at her apartment window. He would be the first of many friends who would later die of accidents, suicides, natural causes and murder. My childhood friends were one of a kind, who I still keep in contact with today. There were four Latino families living in the Marcy projects Nostrand side, the Rivera's, Torres', Pagan's Bermudez's and Morales.' The three oldest of the gang were Albert (El Salsero) Rivera, Nick (Intellectual) Torres, and Pete, (College Boy) Pagan. The rest of the gang were Robert Rivera, my brother Deusdelid Bermudez, Braulio Rivera, Johnny Torres, my brother Lee Bermudez, Alfred Rivera, David Torres, Cruz Morales, Derrik Morales, and of course, me. Al Rivera was basically the individual who formally introduced me to Latin music, "Salsa." He also introduced me to my first pompadour at a barbershop off Manhattan Avenue in Brooklyn. He took me on those weekend walk on Graham Avenue and introduced me to the first old-fashion hairspray for men, by Consort. Al Rivera was very much into the salsa scene and was right on top with the latest in Latino music, fashion and entertainment. We had many visits in Al's room where everyone hanged around and listen to his music, admired his latest threats and made plans for the weekends. He was definitely the Spanish version of Saturday Night Fever, Tony Manero, played by John Travolta. I once entered Al's room with a brand new military-style coat and was showing off its quality to the fellas for their fashion approval. I told Al the coat was a special fabric made of fire resistance materials. As Al stood there having his Canadian Club with soda on the rocks, he decided to put my coat to the test and lit a match to it. The coat instantly went up in flames like dry brush in a forest. A sudden overwhelming fear came upon me, and we immediately turned it off.

118

Ft Greene Park Myrtle Avenue Brooklyn 1969

I couldn't believe what just happened; Al Rivera of course, began laughing his head off with everyone else after the initial shock.

"Oh, shit, Bro. I thought it was fireproof?"

The coat went back to the Army and Navy store a week later, and I got my money refunded—so much for the 1970s military fire retardant coats. As far as I can remember in Al's room, the first three salsa songs that attracted my attention was Ismael Rivera's, El Nazareno; Ray Barretto's, Vive y Vacila; and Ismael Miranda's, Asi se Compone un Son. Those were great moments in time. My first park experience and first walk in the park were with Nick Torres and my brother Deusdelid, (Duce). With mom's permission and without our knowledge, Nick and Duce schemed up a plan one day and took all the young neighborhood kids by surprise by giving us an entire day at Fort Greene Park. The same park where during school hours, my sister Joanna helped patch up a puppy love breakup between two neighborhood lovebirds, Angie Pagan and Irving Rodriguez. They later married and are still husband and wife today after all these years. I'm sure those two remember it very well. There were good times in that park, but even now after all these years I sometimes wonder if Nick and Duce did this out of the goodness of their hearts, or they just wanted to stimulate their eyes by watching all those attractive looking Latinas that walked the park.

119

Nick always had a nonchalant candor way about him and was good in conversing with the ladies. Regardless of their reasons for taking us to Ft Greene Park, those were great memorable moments. Another neighborhood friend was Pedro (Pete) Pagan, who would later become my brother-in-law. Pete attended college, worked at a local supermarket and was a good dresser. Mild mannered, Pete always made time to hang with the fellas; he was the first in the group to sport an Afro, was an excellent artist and smarter than most. He was also the only one in the neighborhood with three young sophisticated sisters Angie, Connie and Nydia. The other sophisticated young ladies were Nick's sister Judy Torres, my sisters Joanna Bermudez, and Milagros (Millie) Morales. These were the Latino families in our neighborhood of Marcy projects on the Nostrand Avenue side during the late 1960s and mid 1970s. Other Latino families later moved into Marcy, but no matter how many other friends we made, none could compare with the childhood friendship that would eventually conform into characteristics of a family. As I think back at those times I can't help but also remember the honorable stay at-home moms, who made this all possible for every one of us; my mother, Margarita Morales Pereira, Benita Torres, Minin Rivera, Guillermina Pagan, Carmen Medina Velez, y Maria Cruz.

'Gracias Señoras, por darnos todo los instrumentos necesarios en la vida para tener éxito, por hacernos miembros productivos de la sociedad y decente ser humanos. Todos sabemos que sin ustedes, esto no habría sido posible. Hay muchas mujeres honorables en este mundo, pero honorabilidad combinado con valor y inexorable sacrificios para el amor de su familia, va más allá de lo que las palabras pueden describir, Dios la Bendiga todas,'

(Thank you ladies, for giving us all the tools needed in life to succeed, for making us productive members of society and descent human beings. We all know that without you, it would not have been possible. There are many honorable women in this world, but honorableness combined with courage and unrelenting scarifies for the love of your family, goes beyond what words can describe, God Bless you all).

We played many different games and sports in Marcy. Handball was extremely popular with the gang if not the most favorite. We played at the handball courts off Nostrand Avenue. The adults filled up the handball courts on the weekends and my stepfather Cruz Morales, Sr, was the man to beat. Many of the adults who came to play placed their cold bottles of booze on the ground along the fence line. The most popular booze was Boones Farm Strawberry Hill, followed by Swiss Up with Kool–Aid and Wild Irish Rose. Listening to music was a must while playing handball, but also very limited. Back in those days we didn't have much of radio station selections. There was no FM radio, only AM. The song "I'll Be There" by The Jackson Five played precisely every twenty minutes, right on schedule. There were no boom boxes with large speakers, and eight-track tapes were not popular yet. And when they were popular, once you played an entire tape or two, you better hope to have extra batteries; those eight-track tape players were energy guzzlers. Double Dutch was another popular activity we didn't participate, but sure like to watch those girls jump rope in those short skirts.

When one of the girls jumping rope would make the eye contact, I would let out a great big smile, and she would too. If I blew away her concentration, and she screwed up her jump competition, I knew I would get to know her by the end of the day. Many of the African-American girls of Marcy housing projects were some of the most beautiful girls in Brooklyn. Although I must admit I do remember there was one girl named Ruby, who no one would talk to, and if you were seen chatting with her, others would make fun of you and torment you in school. She was uglier than most girls, wore thick glasses and was very poor. That didn't matter to me though, I actually felt a little sorry for her. I was once walking to school one morning on Ellery Street, between Marcy and Tompkins Avenue, and she was sitting on a building stoop.
I stopped to chat with her and others began to notice, but I didn't care, and we instantly became friends. We walked to school more often after that, and I began liking her more with each passing day. Other kids would try to make fun of me, and I had to stand up to them. I pretty much got my little ass kicked most of the times, since I was alone and there were several of them.

That would eventually change as I got older and gradually began building a small reputation for myself. After getting to know Ruby I discovered she was a kind-hearted person. She began looking prettier to me as time passed. I don't know if it was because I saw her more often, or if she was physically changing. The last time I saw Ruby she was in her teens and was slowly blooming. I don't know whatever happened to her, but I do know wherever she may have gone, she blossomed into the flower she was meant to be. Putting aside all the crime and problematic circumstances, the housing project's way of life had its great moments, from scraping cans on the cement sidewalks for the Johnny pump spray on a hot summer day, to playing Hot Peas and Butter. That's a game where one kid hides a belt without allowing others to see where it's hidden, then yells out to the other kids,

"Hot peas and butter, come and get your supper!"

The other kids have to find the hidden belt. The closer a kid comes to the belt, the warmer he or she becomes. The further away from the belt, the colder they become. Once a kid got close to the hidden belt, then you would have to yell out the kids name and the words warm or hot. The further away, then you would yell out the kids name and the words cold or freezing. By yelling hot or cold, or warm or cool; it gives other kids a sense of direction. Once the belt is found, the finder of the belt has to hit everyone around them with the belt before they make it back to their assigned home base, then the whole process starts over again with hiding the belt. There were many different kinds of games in Brooklyn, Spin the bottle, Coco leevio, Johnny on the pony, Tag, Hide and seek, Scully, Knuckles, Stealing the old man's bundle, Duncan yo-yo, Spinning tops, Card flipping, Hot wheels racing, Comic book collecting, Baseball card swapping and many others, even hooky set parties. Throwing a pair of tied sneakers on trees or street cables was a game we once played too, but not very popular. A lot of those games were changing with time and game boards were becoming popular. Like the electric vibrating boards with plastic football player figures bouncing on top and the electric race cars that always seem to find the floor rather than stay on its track. Fashion was gradually changing, and windbreakers were coming in style with shoulder zippers, and pleated pants with long rope watches fixed to the waist belt and carried in the pocket.

The ever popular silky hot pants were fading out, and more psychedelic clothing was starting to appear. All that street acapella singing eventually gave way to park disk jockeys. Graffiti was beginning to show up on city buses, trains, buildings and hallways. One of the most seen and memorable graffiti names for me at those times was, "Super Strut." It was seen throughout the five boroughs and outside of NYC limits. Sideburns became extremely popular too. Short leather jackets, and shirt collars as wide as a hand glider, was coming in style. The Spanish boys and I used to head over to Graham Avenue, now known as La Avenida del los Puertorriqueños (Avenue of the Puerto Ricans). Willie Colon was the most popular *Salsero* known to mankind, with his long and wide sideburns. He was one hell of a dresser and inspired many of us to dress like him. Some of us tried in vain to grow sideburns just like Willie and those who couldn't, well; there wasn't anything in mom's cosmetic drawer or pocketbook that couldn't solve our temporary manhood dilemma. Mom's eye pencils were the way to go. It always came up missing and by the end of the month, and she would ask us in Spanish.

"Oye que sucedio con todos mis lápices de ojos negro," (*What happened with all my black eye pencils*)?

"Don't know Mom," we always answered back.

We'd get together on weekends and head to the corners of Graham Avenue, where we would watch and smile at the girls as they walked past. As children we learned about Graham Avenue when our mother would take us to Valencia Bakery on Flushing Avenue just off Broadway. Almost every weekend religiously, she would head up there for those wonderful pastries and fabulous pineapple cakes. The local marqueta de verduras (vegetable market) was another must stop location as well, especially para las Navidades, (for the holidays). Graham Avenue was also the place where we sold toys during the cold holiday months and sold ice cream from a Mister Softee truck with owner Eddie Candelaria during the summer months. As time went on and we gradually matured, we stood tall on Graham Avenue while sporting the latest in threads, but we were a bunch of imitation Salseros.

Although I must admit we were up to date on all the latest Salsa music and entertainment. With latest artists, Latin percussions, percussionists, musicians and entertainers like; Willie Colon, Symphony Sid, Hector LaVoe, Ray Barretto, The Palmieri Brothers, Ralphy Mercado, Ismael Miranda, Tito Allen, Ray De La Paz, Joe Bataan, El Gran Combo, Celia Cruz, Roberto Chucky Roena, Cheo Feliciano, Johnny Pacheco, Pete El Conde Rodriguez, Joe Cuba, La Fania, Chamaco Ramirez, Yomo Toro, Mongo Santamaria and the Jewish Salseros, Andy Harlow, Larry Harlow and Barry Rogers the trombone player. We even knew all about Izzy Sanabria's Latin New York Magazine and his incredible album cover designs. I can recall a heated conversation in the prison lineup room concerning a Salsero entertainer, Izzy Sanabria. Some officers swear Izzy Sanabria was a Latin Percussionist. Others swore Sanabria was a musician of Mexican descent, while others were sure, he was a local Politician. This was a conversation I knew a little about and was ready to put my two cents in.

"Hey, fellas listen up. Let me tell you a little on who Izzy Sanabria is."

Officers gazed at me with precarious looks on their faces.

"What, now you're some sort of managing editor for Univision or something," sarcastically replied an officer.

"No, he's a managing editor for El Gordo y la Flaca," (A Spanish talk show). Several officers laughed hysterically.

"Come on fellas, come on; give me a break. I use to work at a Manhattan building complex as a security officer off Lexington Avenue where Izzy Sanabria was a resident."

Now all the ears were set upon me, all talking stopped and everything became silent. All the gatos de yarda, (Alley cats) were now paying attention to what I had to say.

L to R: Al Bermudez and Izzy Sanabria, 1982

"Izzy Sanabria, (aka Mr. Salsa) is not only an actor and entertainer; he also hosts the La Fania at Madison Square Garden and many other concert halls around the world. He's an author, a publisher and artist. He's responsible for many of the creations and designs of the music album covers that you guys probably own. Another of his most famous piece was the Latin New York Magazine and the two skyscrapers playing percussion instruments. Anyone remembers that?"

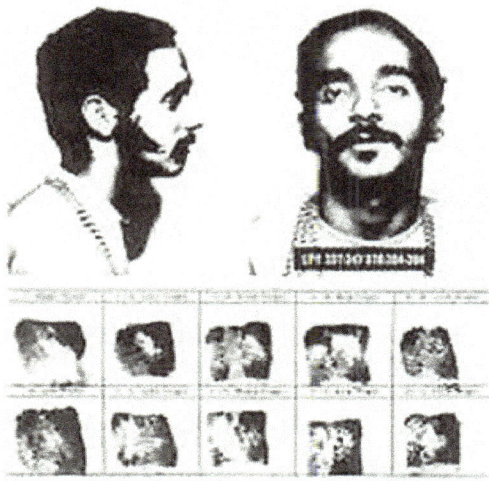

Album designed by Izzy Sanabria, 1971

Everyone spoke up at once, acknowledging the Latin New York Magazine and the percussionist art pieces as though it was a symbolic trademark for all Latinos around the globe. Some began speaking highly of Izzy Sanabria and remembering his monumental existence.

"Yeah, I remember. Without a doubt ese tipo un hombre de caliber, (That guy is a man of caliber).

"Dignified and distinctive in his own right, I remember him now," said another officer.

I continued my brief and knowledgeable description of Izzy or what little I knew about him, but they didn't know that, and I wallowed in my attention.

"Does anyone here remember the ever popular black-and-white Willie Colon record album cover, 'Wanted by the FBI,' where Colon had a mug shot, and profile placed on it?"

Again, an abundance of replies filled the air with personal past encounters, experiences and unforgettable moments associated with the album cover and its songs.

"Yes, we remember that album, what about it," asked several officers.

"Well, that album cover was created by Izzy Sanabria, and although he created hundreds of other album covers, this particular cover was probably his most important and controversial piece. It somehow got the attention of the, Federal Bureau of Investigation."

"I never heard that before. Was it because of the mug shots," asked an officer?

"I don't know if the mug shots alone had anything to do with it. I think it was a combination of things. The words, 'Wanted by the FBI,' combined with the photo mug shots and fingerprints layout. It probably looked too official for the Feds. Not to mention even Willie Colon's own mother thought he was a wanted man when she discovered similar posters being posted on every street corner."

Popularized in the 1960s, 70s and 80s, Mr. Sanabria, did not only touch thousands of people throughout this country with his artistic talents and unquestionable entertainment capabilities, he sported some of the unique male fashion trends for many years, inspiring many of us growing up within the five boroughs of New York City and abroad. I remember attending a Salsa concert in New York City's Madison Square Garden during the 1970s. We had very good seats, just three rows from the stage. There were six of us, four teenagers and two adults. We thought we were the gift to all Latina women, and why not? We were in our teens, extremely young, energetic, good-looking and considered ourselves to be the new Latino generation walking the newly paved road constructed for us by important stylistic entertainers like, Izzy Sanabria, Larry Harlow, Willie Colon, Johnny Pacheco, Pete, "El Conde" Rodriguez and many more. We were convinced in our minds, although we were not celebrities up on stage—that we were the ones who would pave the road for those little Latinos and potential Salseros yet to be conceived. We'd looked at one another from time to time confirming the quality of our looks and of our treads.

We knotted our heads in contentment knowing we were up to date with the latest in Latino fashion. That is until Izzy Sanabria walked out on stage sporting bellbottom slacks, a thin sport jacket under a wide collar shirt and a small shaggy Afro. Still sporting our Kango hats, stitch shirts and sharkskin pants, we knew we were heading down the road of fashion disaster. We looked at one-another and all agreed, 'Bathroom.' We ran to the bathroom like football players rushing to a huddle with only seconds left in the finalization of a football game. We got in and immediately put a plan in motion. The hats had to go, and off they came. Jackets were swapped to match the others treads. Shirts were unbuttoned on top and collars came out. I remember running the sink faucet and adding little sprinkles of water to the hair for that frizzy, Izzy shaggy look. If it was close to an afro, that was good enough for me. We were done and went back to our seats. People in the immediate area took notice of our changes. Now that I look back thirty plus years later, I don't know if they're attention toward us was one of impression, or they thought we were a bunch of little LSD, (Psychedelic drug) induced teenage freaks. Either way, they were positive and memorable moments that will last a lifetime. Today, my personal friend and legendary Mr. Izzy Sanabria continue his entertainment, showing no signs of letting up and still sporting the latest in Latino fashion. He's the gentleman seen sporting a red suit in the beginning of the 2007 movie, 'El Cantante,' the life of Hector LaVoe with superstar celebrities Marc Anthony and Jennifer Lopez.

My brief description of Izzy Sanabria earned me celebrity status among my peers almost instantly. The conversations and questions concerning Latino celebrities and musicians went on. It's was a never-ending topic brought up every morning. However, regardless of all this musical knowledge, we were still too young for the club scene, like The Cheetah or the Marion Manor in Brooklyn. My God, how we loved Women's Lib Day at the clubs. We would dress to the max, head over to the club and stand across the street to get a glimpse of those Latinas entering the club. We'd cross our fingers hoping the women would arrive early, since we had to be back home by ten p.m., and when all that eye stimulation was over, it was back to reality at the housing projects.

Where every now and then I would look out my window and witness, a fight or an assault in progress, caused by gunshots, stabbing or baseball bat fights. As soon as mom heard a gunshot, she would run into the room and made sure we were not at the window. We already knew this, and we would clear the window before she entered the room. The New York City police wore dark uniforms with a round patch on their arm and a shield. The rookie officers wore gray uniform shirts and patrolled with a regular officer. The police cars were white, black, and green. It had a very large single red light on top and a chrome siren right in front of it. The siren was loud and by the time it stopped yelping, the crime scene investigation was completed. Inside the patrol cars were huge black telephones used for communication.

We eventually left the Marcy projects in the mid-1970s and moved to Coney Island, Carey Garden housing projects. It was no better than Marcy. I went from living on the fifth floor in Marcy to living on the sixteenth floor in the crime infested Carey Gardens. Where my view of criminal activity covered much more ground and gave me much more viewing enjoyment. The Verrazano Bridge was always in view. On a good day, we could see the Statue of Liberty and on a very clear day we could actually see the two red and white petroleum tanks from Williamsburg Brooklyn. I remember one early morning while chatting with my mother and sitting by the window on my first day of school, a large human-like object flew past our window and made a loud bang seconds later. We looked at one another.

'What the heck was that?'

I cautiously opened the window and slowly looked up toward the roof then look down. It was a nude African-American woman who was apparently thrown off the rooftop. Seventeen stories high to be exact and she landed on the cement pavement below. The force of her body bent an entire section of a chain-link fence below. We could see the trickle of blood leading from her body to a nearby drain. Some neighbors began screaming and the next thing I knew many windows were opened with spectators and potential witnesses. The perpetrator was apprehended somewhere on a lower floor by two housing police officers that coincidentally enough, were walking up the stairs on their daily morning patrol as the perpetrator was running down from the crime scene.

In another incident, I was once waiting on an elevator that would never come, it was out of order. I was running late for work, so I decided to make a quick run sixteen flights down. I quickly opened the door leading to the stairwell and slipped on a large pool of foamed up, contaminated blood. Apparently, a couple of nights before, some guy had his throat slashed in the stairwell. His street name was Snake, and he survived the attack. I later befriended Snake in the projects and later began working construction together in NYC, Soho. He actually turned out to be an excellent worker who constantly worked overtime. His famous excuse for working constant overtime was, "Gotta feed the kids or the kids need milk." Snake had the look of a murderer or an ex–con. He was a slim African-American man who stood six feet tall and was black as night. He always wore a rag on his head and the new large scar across his neck only added to his dark side. But if you personally knew Snake, you would know he was one of the nicest guys you'd ever want to meet.

Carey Gardens consist of three buildings, two directly across from one another on 23rd street between Mermaid and Surf Avenues. The third building was between Mermaid and Neptune Avenues. All three buildings were riddled with crime and notorious criminals. Several floors below us, was a young twenty-one year old mother who took her newborn baby daughter after giving birth, walked down the hall and threw her down a garbage chute while she was still alive. The babies' lifeless body was found in the garbage chute by a housing employee. The mother was later charged with the murder of her newborn daughter after the medical examiner discovered blunt trauma to the head and neck. In another incident, an eighteen year old disturbed individual became enraged when he was told by his mother to leave the apartment because of his verbal insults toward his family. The little prick grabbed a kitchen knife instead, went to his mother and began stabbing her. Then he decided he wanted no witnesses, so he went into a bedroom and began stabbing his twelve-year-old sister, and her twelve-year-old friend who was visiting, he killed all three.

Another who lived in the same building was a man who served ten years in state prison. He was released and committed numerous other crimes before being arrested for the rape of a local woman. He should have never been released from prison in the first place.

130

I've personally dealt with this lowlife prick on the streets and in the prison system. He burned down a Waldbaum's supermarket in 1978, which caused the lives of six NYC firefighters when the roof collapsed on them. On another floor were two crooks that were responsible for committing over sixty burglaries throughout Coney Island and Brighton Beach. In their burglaries, twelve of those became robberies when victims came home or woke up during the crime. These crimes were just a drop in the bucket. Crime in Coney Island surpassed all the crimes I've ever seen in Brooklyn's Bedford-Stuyvesant section. In this next crime, I was listening to a police scanner with my brother Cruz, who was a NYC police officer and off-duty at the time. The call came in as a person down and in need of medical attention on West 20th Street. We arrived just minutes after the radio transmission, where a small crowd of onlookers and several children on bicycles were gathered. There was a woman on the ground face down, wearing a coat and hat while still holding a small plastic bag containing what appeared to be VHS videotape cartridges. A little boy standing by her side told us it was his mother, and she just fell to the ground. We didn't see any signs of blood and suspected she may have suffered a heart attack. The day was cold and there was a light drizzle. We didn't want to disturb the preservation of evidence and waited for police to arrive.

After police arrived, we spoke for several minutes and went home. The following day the newspapers posted a large photo on its front page showing the crime scene and the children on their bicycles looking at the body. Those same children just minutes before arriving at the scene on their bicycles, were on a rooftop two blocks away on 20th Street and Surf Avenue with a high-powered scope rifle. They wanted to test fire the rifle and test their marksmanship using the woman as their target. They shot the rifle several times missing their intended target. They finally found their target and shot her from the back. The bullet pierced her heart killing her almost instantly. We saw those kids at the crime scene when we arrived and just before we left. I can't begin to say how natural they all appeared, even moments after murdering another human being. Coney Island is basically three streets, which ran parallel to one another, Surf, Mermaid, and Neptune Avenues. Surf Avenue became known for its prostitution from West 8th Street to the 30s.

131

Many outsiders and travelers used Surf Avenue as their main point of entry to and from Coney Island and Sea Gate. Neptune was the least traveled and in my opinion, the road with the weirdest people at night. During the day, it was filled with people heading to Mark Twain Park for picnics and sports, but at night, many people were found dead for reasons unknown. Mermaid was the most popular and crowded, of course not including the amusement park of Surf Avenue. Mermaid Avenue had many different stores, supermarkets, post office, restaurants, shops, apartments, prostitutes and drug dealers. Guys with new cars would race up and down Mermaid with their music blasting and motorcycles defying the laws of speed. There were many accidents and homicides on Mermaid. On any given day, you could walk down the Avenue and witness a death of some sort or its aftermath. Mermaid had its share of corruption as well. I remember during the 1970s, a Hispanic cop that patrolled most of Mermaid Avenue constantly attracted small crowds. He also worked in a grocery store at the corner of W.16th Street. He would stand at a building entrance between West 23rd and 24th Streets, wait for crooks to walk up and precariously exchange stolen goods. I also saw these transactions take place on numerous occasions through binoculars from my sixteenth floor window. I once brought it to my mother's attention who in turn told me to mind my business. One day my curiosity got the best of me, and I went to this location. I approached an individual who walked up to cop and completed a transaction.

"Excuse me, what's up with the cop, what is he buying?"

The thug looked at me with a puzzled look. He was unsure of what to make of me.

"Why you wanna know, are you a snitch or something? Are you working for the fucking man?"

"No, I'm too young to work for the man and what would I snitch about?"

"Then you have something to sell?"

I didn't know what to say, but since he mentioned the word sell an idea instantly popped into my head.

"Yeah, I have something to sell. I have a new car radio."

"Man, he (the cop) only buys gold. He's not going to be interested in any car radios!"

The thug brushed me off and walked away. I knew then this cop was no good. I also knew if I ever found myself in trouble on the streets of Coney Island, he would be the last guy I'd go to. However, he was not the only corrupt cop, there were many cops that were heroin users and frequent visitors of 28th Street where they purchased heroin in uniform. Others parked in housing project parking lots for the sole purpose of having sex with their prostitutes in the back of their patrol cars.

Another corrupt officer was a tall Afro-American cop named Ronnie. He was obviously a body builder and rode on a police motorcycle. He also patrolled at night. I witnessed this cop beat and slap numerous people on Surf Avenue. He once ran over a guy with his patrol motorcycle and broke the guy's leg. Several years later I learned he had an investment in Surf Avenue prostitution. I also learned that most of the beatings I witnessed on the streets by this cop were being done to those who didn't pay their protection dues on time or came up short. This was the same officer who patrolled Abraham Lincoln High School and received numerous complaints from parents for slapping high school students across their faces and throwing others down school stairwells. Police officers that drove by the school use to yell out to him from their patrol car microphone.

"He's six feet tall and meanest of them all, big Ron!"

Well, six feet tall meanest of them all Ron's career didn't last twenty years. Last I heard his corrupt scheme was finally discovered, and he was either forced to resign, or was fired from the force. The third cop I distrusted was a red-headed cop with a handlebar mustache. He was always inside of his RMP, (Radio motor patrol). Everywhere this character saw me—he would refer to me as "motherfucker." The strange thing about these encounters was, I didn't know this cop, and I had never seen him before. My first of many encounters with him was on 28th Street after visiting my girlfriend from work in 1978. As I was walking toward Mermaid Avenue on my way home, a patrol car pulled up alongside of me. The driver-side window gradually opened revealing the red handlebar mustache than the familiar voice.

"Hey, motherfucker, where did you just come from and where the fuck are you going?"

After telling him I was returning from my girlfriend's house and confirming the address, he became agitated.

"You're a fucking liar. You know what—you see that junkyard? I want you to run through that junkyard motherfucker, before I get out of my patrol car?"

Sensing I was being set up for an arrest or a possible bullet to the back, I refused to run through the junkyard.

"What the fuck you said, you're not running?"

He immediately exited his patrol car, pulled out his service revolver, and I ran my little narrow Spanish ass across that junkyard so fast I burned a path that others used as a shortcut for weeks to come.

I began disliking this cop more and more with every encounter. I told myself, if I ever became a criminal and had nothing to live for; I would search for him and pay him a visit he'll never forget. These were just some of the very few bad apples in a barrel found in every walk of life. The NYC police department as a whole is one of the most prestigious and professional police forces in the country. I've had and continue to have many family members and friends on the force, from street patrol to horseback. Labeling an entire department for the few pricks, I had the privilege of knowing during my lifetime would be unjust and unfair to all who serve.

However, with all the police corruption and crime, there was one trusted cop that I personally knew, along with many others in Coney Island. This was a cop that residents could depend on and who walked the beat for thirty-two years. He wasn't six feet tall, wasn't muscle bound or didn't intimidate local residents for kicks. His by the book attitude, fairness and consistent display of professionalism got him the respect he deserved. He was a cop that carried two or three firearms on his waist side and a white handkerchief around his collar on a hot summer day. His name was John Innacone, aka, 'The Lone Wolf,' from the 61st precinct.

Brooklyn's 60th Pct, photo by Bermudez

His unique ability to do his job as a cop also came with the trust and respect of his supervisors, fellow officers and the general public. In all the years, I resided in Coney Island, I had many positive brief encounters and conversations with John Innacone, who always advised me to stay out of trouble and seek a career in civil service. John was the only cop I trusted and the only cop I knew who was a straight arrow and clean as a whistle. I've witnessed many gang members being chased by other gang members down Mermaid Avenue, who ran directly to John's post knowing he would be there to save their ass. Many of them, who were wanted or had rotten reputations, avoided at any cost being seen by John. Others attempted to disguise themselves by growing beards, cutting or coloring their hair, wearing clothing not affiliated with gangs and any other change in appearance you can think of. But John knew them all on a personal and professional level. One small verbal description given to John Innacone by a victim of a suspect was like typing an alias on a detective's computer in today's modern times. His mind went to work in seeking a mug shot and almost 100 percent of the time, his compulsory disclosure revealed the suspect in question.

Of course, there are other cops like him, and when I think of John Innacone; I can't help but to think of story of a former New York City police officer named Jose M. Sanchez Picon. Honorableness, dedication, courageousness and professionalism are the words I can think of to best describe this individual, who I had the privilege of knowing at Sing-Sing maximum-security prison.

Drafted in 1965, the outspoken Joe Sanchez did not only patriotically serve his country, like many others in our military. He fought the war in Vietnam, lost many close friends in the process and was wounded in battle, receiving a purple heart from the United States Army. After returning home from war, Joe later applied for and became a New York City ambulance driver, dedicating himself in the efforts of helping others, while always remembering the travesty and friends he left behind at Vietnam. However, his story doesn't end there.

In 1971, Joe Sanchez successfully applied for and became a New York Port Authority police officer and although his career went far beyond his expectations, his heart was set in becoming a New York City police officer. Joe Sanchez was a man of action and NYC streets never lacked the abundance of what Joe was interested in, 'extinguishing criminality.' Unfortunately for Joe, he had a couple of strikes going against him; he was Latino and one quarter inch under the height requirement of five feet seven inches. But Joe was far from being discouraged. He continued his efforts in trying to enter the NYC police department and after several years of constant battling, Joe won the war, becoming a NYC police officer in 1973.

Joe's career included countless of arrest with successful indictments and convictions. In one of seven gun battles on the streets of New York City during the 1970s and 80s, Joe's then partner Susanne Mecicis, was the first NYC policewoman ever to receive the Combat Cross and later inducted into the New York City Police Museum. Joe was relentless in his dedication, serving and protecting the citizens of New York State was his passion. Regardless of whether he was wearing a uniform on duty or wearing civilian clothing off-duty, if Joe witnessed a violation of law, he would make the collar, (arrest). However, this dedication came with a price, and many enemies were made, not only between criminals, but within the department as well.

Joe Sanchez Picon, Courtesy: BlueWallNYPD.com

Joe was an extremely outspoken person and a cop, who with countless of arrest, was racking up hours of overtime. Not an advisable thing to do during the 1970s and early 1980s. This was catching the attention of the brass, (supervisors) enemies within the department and the stage was set to take down a good cop; a cop labeled as,

"A Super Cop in 1987, by New York Daily News staff writer, John Marzulli."

While on his official capacity inside a patrol car, Joe and his partner Herman Velez, observed a suspicious individual sporting a white cowboy hat enter a building complex known for drug activity. In hot pursuit, both officers followed the male up to a set of stairs to an apartment where the suspect knocked on the door requesting drugs. They then observed a male tenant open the door while brandishing a firearm. Both officers gave the order to drop the gun and immediately rushed the door in an attempt to subdue the suspect with the gun and the drug buyer.

137

The suspect with the gun resisted while trying to shut the door and screaming to others inside, "La policia, la policia" (The police, the police)! Officers Joe and Herman again gave the command to drop the gun and the suspect finally complied dropping the weapon on the floor. The suspect was then immediately subdued by Herman, who also retrieved the weapon while Joe Sanchez held the suspect at gunpoint and transmitted a 10-13, (Code to assist) via radio to central command. All procedures were followed in accordance with departmental rules, and the arrest of all involved was made. Confiscation and preservation of all evidence in relations to the incident were also followed, and no lives were lost or injured. Without a doubt, a successful and courageous arrest, or was it? What should have resulted in the commendations of both arresting officers, instead turned into an indictment and miscarriage of justice for one decorated cop. All the criminals involved somehow got together with the powers that be, in this case the departmental brass, and formulated an erroneous scheme to take down officer, Joe Sanchez.

Like in the movie Serpico, played by actor Al Pacino, the story of an honest cop Frank Serpico, who was faced with the dilemma of working within a corrupted police department, Joe was also an honest cop, who despised criminality, but foremost despised corruption. Before his indictment, Joe was introduced to a lieutenant during a coworker's softball game. Fully aware of the lieutenant's corrupted reputation, Joe wanted nothing to do with his companionship and strictly kept his distance and conversation to a minimal. The lieutenant knew this—he had a reputation for bagging money from local businesses, drug dealers and taking nude photos of underage children from the Dominican Republic. His next encounter with this Lieutenant took place at a police stationhouse. Although Joe walked into the station on time, he was distracted by a fellow officer who required his presences on an official capacity, thus causing Joe to miss the roll call. Joe was later confronted by the lieutenant and was verbally threatened with a write up, (Disciplinary action). Being the outspoken person that he was, Joe didn't take to the threat lightly. He informed the lieutenant he would not only expose his corrupted activities, but would expose his possession of child pornography. The lieutenant now concerned with Joe's statement, approached his superior, a captain who also a corrupt bagman.

The captain then approached Joe and threatened him with insubordination and disciplinary action. Joe knew the stage was set and followed through with exposing the lieutenant's corrupted activities and child pornography. But just as the house of cards was about to collapse for the lieutenant, Joe was informed that his previous arrest at the building complex concerning the drug dealers was unjustifiable. He was then indicted, arrested and charged with numerous counts of grand larceny, burglary and assault. His partner Herman Velez was not mentioned in any indictment. Thomas Duffy, the then appointed Special State prosecutor and his assistant ADA Joe Hester, offered and insisted that Joe cop a plea. Joe wasn't having it. A new special state Prosecutor, Charlie Joe Hynes, would later exonerate Joe of all charges. While criminals are given the right through the United States Constitution, Amendment VI, to be confronted with witnesses against them and a trial by an impartial jury of the state and district wherein the crime has been committed; Joe was not allowed that rightful opportunity. Nor was he allowed in submitting his testimony to any grand jury, simply because it was a sealed secret indictment. Tooth and nail, Joe who was no stranger to battle. He fought and successfully had all of his charges eventually dropped. It was quite obvious to the Appellate Court there was more to this injustice than the NYC police department, and the special prosecutor's office was willing to admit.

An official document handed down by the Appellate Court, clearly said it best.

"The actions of the then special state prosecutor, (In this case Thomas Duffy) in prosecuting a jurisdictionally defective criminal proceeding, especially where that special prosecutor had full knowledge that petitioner had transactional immunity, can only be described as 'outrageous' and the petitioner, especially given his past exemplarity service with the department, should not have been made to suffer any prejudice in connection with his improper prosecutorial conduct and certainly not automatic termination from civil-service position without a hearing," (*Supreme Court of the State of New York, Appellate Court Division 2nd Judicial District*).

In a recent NY Daily News article, dated July 16, 2008, written by John Marzulli and titled.

"Fired NYPD cop writes gritty book to set record straight." Joe Sanchez story was told. More than two decades after he was terminated from the police department, the highly-decorated supercop that terrorized bad guys in Washington Heights still loves the job despite everything. Everything includes getting double-crossed by the Internal Affairs Division, which wired him up to catch a crooked lieutenant and captain; then his arrest on the allegations of a drug dealer; a conviction for assault that was overturned and an unsuccessful bid for reinstatement. Joe eventually went as far as to Commissioner, Benjamin Ward in an attempt to regain his job. However, the damage was done and the bridge was burned. Joe violated the most sacred trust of the NYC police department; he broke the 'Blue Wall Code of Silence.'

He did not only turn over another cop, he turned over a police lieutenant and Benjamin Ward wasn't having it. Reinstatement was denied. Joe was not deterred; he later applied for and became a United States Postal worker, where he worked for several years before applying for and becoming a New York State correction officer. During his career as a correction officer, Joe was assaulted on several occasions by convicts he arrested in NYC, and in one incident, an attempt was made on his life. He sustained numerous injuries during the course of his career. Joe later retired from New York state corrections and recently became an established published Author of, "Latin Blues" and "True Blue, A Tale of the Enemy Within." The book, True Blue, A Tale of the Enemy Within, is a made for movie book that specifically and in graphic detail describes all he endured throughout his lifetime as a New York City police officer and as a human being. Persistence and determination are an understatement in describing Mr. Joe Manuel Sanchez Picon. I'm not only proud to have met this gentleman during my lifetime, but also proud to know that he is a, "Positive and unique representation to all honest Latino officers around the globe."

Joe's partner Herman Velez went on to retired as an aircraft pilot. He and another retired New York City police officer, Ernie Sierra are members of the famous 1950s, Doo Wop group, 'The Eternals.'

**L-R: Fred Hodge, Alex Miranda, Anibal Torres, Ernie Sierra &
Carlos Girona, The Original Eternals**

In the summer of 1956, five Latinos of Puerto Rican descent
from the Freeman Street section of the Bronx met while in Junior
High School 40, (JHS 40). Ernie Sierra, (Founder) Anibar Torres
and Alex Miranda formed a vocal group after hearing Frankie
Lyman, and the Teenagers perform at the Freeman Theater in the
Bronx. They called themselves; The Starlites. All three were
school friends who attended JHS 40. Ernie's brother Richie had his
own group 'The Trells,' who were being groomed by a manager
name Bill Martin. After singing three-part harmony for a while,
the boys decided a fourth voice was needed.

141

**L-R: George Villanueva, Ernie Sierra, Fred Clavel,
Herman Velez/George Santiago, photo by Herman**

Aldo Acosta soon joined the group, and they later won a talent contest in JHS 40. In 1957, Carlos, (Charlie Girona) replaced Aldo Acosta in the Starlites and then renamed them, 'The Gleamers.' It appeared that Carlos had tried to join the Trells, but they had sufficient personnel and was referred to Ernie Sierra by Richie. The Gleamers now consisted of Ernie Sierra, Carlos Girona, Alex Miranda and Anibar Torres. A friend, (Ray Rivera) referred Fred Hodge, (Pineapple) in 1957, and the first quintet was formed. The members of this quintet included were: with the lowest part in harmonic singing and bass: Alex Miranda, having the compass voice of a baritone; Anibal Torres, the extraordinary lead voice of Carlos Girona, and the intermediates between bass and alto capabilities of first tenor Fred Hodge, and second tenor; Ernie Sierra. Although they emulated The Flamingos, The Spaniels and The Heartbeats, it was two novelty Latin-flavored tunes that would eventually put them on top of the Rock 'N Roll charts. During a rehearsal, The Gleamers were approached by a noted vocal group manager and dancer, Bill Martin. Extremely impressed with the young teenage groups' capabilities and performance Bill Martin later became their manager. He coached the group and when their sound was distinct and polished, he brought them to the owner of Melba Records, Morty Craft.

Lead singer Carlos Girona wrote a seasonal tune entitled, "Christmas in the Jungle," it was this song, which brought them to the famous Beltone Studios of New York City in late spring of 1959. The lyrics were later revised by Carlos Girona to accommodate a post-holiday season release, thus, 'Christmas in the Jungle' became 'Rockin in the Jungle' and released on Hollywood Records Label; not only hitting New York City radio waves and becoming a favorite with New Yorkers, but climbing its way to the eleventh spot and seventy eighth on the National Billboard charts. With this new-found fame also came a new name for the teenage group. With the suggestion of their manager Bill Martin, and based upon a passage from the bible, "The Gleamers," thus were dubbed, "The Eternals." Their next release on Morty Craft's Warwick Records label was "Blind Date," and featured George Villanueva with, 'Today.' Their second recording, "Babalu's Wedding Day," another spirited novelty rocker, featured Girona's bouncy Latin lead, Alex Miranda's incomparable bass and a hot sax solo by King Curtis made it to number fourteen on the hit charts. Its flipside, 'My Girl' was written and led by Ernie Sierra, and was a personal dedicational song to his girlfriend of three years, who he would eventually marry for twenty-seven years.

But all this would come to a halt as a result of inappropriate recording transactions and without Manager, Bill Martin's knowledge and approval of two recorded songs, 'Blind Date and Today.' A law suit ensued on behalf of Bill Martin and resulted in a stoppage to a great-sounding group. Seeing the group's progress halted, first tenor Fred (Pineapple) Hodge left The Eternals. In 1960, Fred joined The United States Army and was later replaced by George Villanueva, (From the Bronx Rialtos). The group changed personnel as Carlos Girona left for California. Sammy Marrero from the Rialtos then came in. Unfortunately, it was too late. Though a number of demos were ready for release, the legal wrangling prevented Eternals from reaching the charts again. From then on, personnel changes were occurring up until the 1970s when the nucleus of today's Eternals began forming. Ernie, now a NYC policeman, was joined by three more NYC policemen, Herman Velez, Ray Figueroa and Mike Rivas. With the help of Artie Ramos, (Side Street fame) the group began performing again and evolved into today's Eternals.

143

Personnel changes and the passing of Alex Miranda in 1967, eventually brought in new members to The Eternals; George, 'Tito' Santiago and Hector Garcia. There were few and infrequent engagements, but no new releases. Family and occupational responsibilities slowed things down for the group until the early 1970s. The Eternals reformed with Ernie Sierra steering the group; along with George Santiago and Herman Velez, (The Hemlocks) providing the nucleus of the present-day Eternals. Fred (Fefe) Clavel joined as bass and the return of George Villanueva provide the longest lasting aggregation of The Eternals. The Eternals have remained a, 'Class Act' and have been on stage with the best of the ever shrinking great original Doo Wop groups. The Eternals have released The Eternals' CD "Through the Years" and recorded a Ronnie I Clifton Records release entitled "The Eternals, Today." Through the years, The Eternals have performed at such notable venues as New York's Radio City Music Hall, Westbury's Music Fair, the Pittsburgh Oldies Record Collectors Club, The UGHA shows and many more. They have endeavored to stay true to their original sound and have been successful through the efforts of founder, Ernie Sierra and through the talents and spirit of this unique vocal quintet, The Eternals. However, it was never an easy road for The Eternals. As it presently stands for The Eternals, they continue their non-stop entertainment in the music industry and show no signs of ever slowing down, "Que Viva Para Siempre Los Eternals," (*Ernie Serria, Herman Velez, George Santiago, Fred Hodge, 2009*).

Getting back to Coney Island's bad cops and problematic circumstance that plagued the small island, one good thing came out of it for me that forever changed my life and led me in a positive path of responsible mannerism, my wife Lydia. One summer night in April 1976, while hanging around the neighborhood off 27th Street and Surf Avenue, I saw a female who caught my attention. I've seen her several times before and felt an attraction toward her. I decided to analyst her for a bit as she mingled and conversed with others. I realized this would be the perfect time to become acquainted with one another, so the move was made. Looks and smiles were exchanged, then the approach, and official introduction. After a long conversation, some jokes and a little laughter, it was quite obvious the chemistry was there, and in no time we were partners in love.

Al and Lydia (Smiley) Bermudez, 1976

So much so, we once kissed on a set of stairwells in a housing project for two hours, ignoring everyone who may have walked past us. We then later tried breaking the kissing record on a wooden bench under an oak tree in New York City Central Park. We were both wearing white bellbottom jeans with an embroidered rainbow on our legs. Crochet shoes with rope braided soles and listening in the background to an Andy Gibb song titled, 'I just want to be your everything.' But the two-hour attempt was short-lived, and although we failed to succeed in breaking the record, we didn't mind. We knew there would soon be more future occasions in which to try again. We spent many special moments together and many hours on the phone. I also remember spending many days at the famous Nathan's of Coney Island where she worked during the 1970s; waiting on her lunch break. I have to admit she looked good in that Nathan's uniform, and their hot dogs weren't the only one cooking on a grill.

145

Lovers in love, we were once on cloud nine, holding hands, making promises and walking gingerly across Mermaid Avenue on 28th Street toward Surf Avenue when something momentarily brought us back to reality. There was a Latino couple around our age walking in our direction and also holding hands. As they passed alongside of us heading in the opposite direction, they smiled, and we naturally returned the smiles. As they made their way across the street, a shirtless young Latino male appeared directly in front of us brandishing a two-foot machete with a look of murder upon his face. He screamed out the girls name and bolted in their direction. We saw the couple run across the street and spilt in different directions. Her companion ran toward 29th street, and she ran toward a grocery store. As she made her way to the grocery store entrance, she managed to grab a fruit and vegetable display and drop it to the floor in an attempt to either stop her attacker or delay the attack. It was unsuccessful; he went inside the store immediately after her. Seconds later customers ran out screaming, and he emerged from the store with both arms extended up to the sky while brandishing the machete over his head and screaming the words, "I don't give a fuck!" The machete was stained in her blood and so was his chest as it trickled down to his stomach. He began running in our direction with the blood stain machete in hand and for a split second, I thought we were next. He ran past us and into a building tenement where he then disappeared. We later learned she was his former girlfriend, and he was upset about their recent breakup. She miraculously survived the attack. Several weeks later her brothers saw her attacker and cornered him in the lobby of the same tenement he disappeared into. They shot him fourteen times and he too miraculously survived the attack. He was later arrest, convicted and sent to prison where I would eventually see him. Witnessing this encounter we vowed never to hurt one another or to think something that horrific could ever be imagined inside our heads. We married one year later in 1979, and had two sons. Our marriage, although not perfect to any extent, had its good memorable moments and survived many downfalls. Like most people, we discovered no marriage on earth is perfect, and if it is, it will inevitably end in death. Through all the hell and high waters of our lives, we also discovered that love, trust, respect and forgiveness, are the four most important elements in keeping a marriage alive.

146

Marriage life throws us all many curve balls. Temptation, which hovers ever so endlessly above everyone's lives; midlife crisis constant deception plaguing and corrupting our minds; and last but not least, those lowlife snakes who lurk within our lawns, patiently waiting for those moments of uncertainty and vulnerability. But through it all, thirty-three plus years later who would've thought we still be married. I'm content enough to say we've had a good life together, and I personally wouldn't change a thing with my Latina woman. A woman who's sentimental, caring, kind, forgiving, hardworking, thoughtful and sincere as she; is a woman is sacred to me. I have been one of the luckiest men to have married such a woman in my life. So in that sense, Coney Island with its riddled crime and poverty-stricken environment produce a diamond in a ruff for me. We later left Coney Island, and I entered the corrections academy in 1985. Our academy session in New York's Harriman Training Academy was like the American television sitcom, F-Troop. To say we were clumsy, ridiculous and unprofessional in our performance would be an understatement. Although I must admit we had fun in the process. There were many clumsy injuries among the cadets, resignations and verbal disputes during our academic session, including a squad leader whose military cadence was, 'Olianna.' Olianna when we marched morning, noon, night, and every day for three agonizing months. One cadet became so enraged with the Olianna cadence that he invited the squad leader to a fist fight outside academy grounds because in his words.

'I can't take this Olianna shit anymore dammit!'

My first unusual experience at the Academy was with a small North American mammal that decided to enter the academy building one early evening while everyone was studying. Being a New York City native, I was not familiar with its smell and continued my studies until it became too potent, and my eyes began irritating. I heard yells coming from other rooms to evacuate the building and without any hesitation I did. Not understanding what was taking place, I saw recruits throwing mattresses out of their windows. I somehow thought there was a fire, and the recruits were trying to save the building by eliminating as much furniture as possible. I ran back inside and was preparing to throw my mattress out the window as well, along with my bags and a piece of furniture I accidentally damaged.

Just as I was about to throw out a piece of furniture a recruit entered the room and ask what I was doing. I courageously stated I was going to throw some furniture out of the window to prevent the escalation of fire.

"Fire, what fire? There's a skunk in the building dummy!" Apparently, the recruits who were throwing their mattresses out of the windows were doing so to have something to sleep on, just in case they were not able to return into the building. The skunk was eventually removed, and we all returned to our quarters an hour later. I was then sent to the sergeant's office and was reprimanded for destruction of state property during the course of my courageous EFR, (emergency furniture rescue).

In another encounter, we were all performing physical defensive tactics in the academy gymnasium. On one side of the gym cadets were striking a heavy punching bag with their coco-bolo batons. On the other side cadets were on their knees with arms bent at the elbows and open palms facing forward. The concept behind this position was to drop to the floor on your forearms and hands while turning your face just before your forearms hit the floor. While kneeling on the floor and waiting for our verbal command, we were observing other cadets striking the heavy punching bags. The next cadet was a female officer from Buffalo, NY, named Hall. She was standing like a pro runner, while holding her baton in a crossed combat position. It was quite obvious she was tough and eager to pounce on the heavy bag with her cocobolo. The command of attack was given by an instructor, and she ran toward the bag striking it with fierce force. The baton instantly bounced off the bag and struck her on the forehead opening a large gash. She turned around crossed eye, wobbled from the waist up and blood trickling down her face. She was immediately placed in a state van and taken to a local hospital. Although I know I shouldn't have laughed, I couldn't help myself and was ordered by an instructor not to do it again. A half hour later we were on our knees and waiting for our next command. The command came, "drop!" We all dropped and turned our faces just before hitting the floor with our forearms, but one very tall and clumsy cadet didn't. He went down and hit the parquet floor nose first. He too got up crossed eye, wobbled from the waist up and blood trickling down from his nose. He was also immediately taken to a local hospital. I was later sent to the sergeant's office and was reprimanded for laughing again.

148

Our next training was firearms, with the Colt AR-15 rifle to be exact. After several hours of shooting at one-hundred yards we all pass the training course. It was now time for a little celebration, and celebrate we did, at a local Harriman bar called, 'Shot in the Dark.' We had a good time and didn't realize how fast time had passed. The academy had strict rules, and if you were found violating those rules, reprimand was not far behind. We were allowed to leave academy grounds, but had to return no later than eleven p.m. We left Shot in the Dark in a taxi cab arriving at the academy at exactly one minute passed eleven. The instructors were furious and escorted us to our rooms. Apology was not accepted and all exercises the following day were doubled. One-hundred pushups, went up to two-hundred, seventy-five sit-ups went up to one-hundred-fifty and so on. Everyone in the class was subjected to the same rigorous exercise, there were no exceptions. We were all exhausted by eight a.m. but managed to complete our exercises with success. We eventually went back to our rooms, showered, had our breakfast and I was again sent to the sergeant's office for reprimand. Only this time the sergeant, who looked identical to actor Archie Bunker from the sitcom; 'All in the Family,' threaten to get several convicts released from a nearby prison, have them come onto academy grounds and in his words, "rip me a new asshole." I didn't take to it lightly and stated the idea of bringing over convicts didn't scare me. He became furious and yelled, "Get the fuck out of my office and if I see you in here again it will be your last visit!" It wasn't my last brush with the sergeant. I was again ordered to his office when I failed a law exam, only this time my agitating presence was welcomed with a different sort of tone.

"You again, what is it with you, why don't you resign. Don't we treat you good at this academy?"

I felt as though I broke the sergeant down and brought him to his knees. I didn't; he would eventually have the last laugh. Days before the graduation ceremony we were all called to the academy auditorium for briefing, last minute ceremony preparations and photographs. I was instructed to sit in the front row of the auditorium with the graduation class. Graduation was finally here; just days away and we would soon be returning home as full fledged sworn correction officers. The sergeant stepped out onto the stage and verbally demanded everyone's attention.

"Alright listen up, congratulations to all on your successful completion of this academy," (Applauses).

"You should be proud. We take pride in our commitment and past that pride and commitment to you. I hope we have accomplished our goal in making you proud women and men of a great and professional paramilitary law enforcement organization. You have chosen a tough career, and we wish you all the best. Now—where's the recruit named, Al Bermudez?"

Naïve and unaware of what would come next, I raised my hand, as though I was a recipient for a Medal of Merit Award.

"Now young man, you're not going to graduate with the rest of this academy class. You will instead remediate one week, so please do us all a favor and get the fuck out of my auditorium!"

I knew then what it felt like to be broken and brought down to my knees. I also knew my failure to perform as expected in the academy came back to haunt me. Although my intentions were not to hurt the sergeant or anyone else, for that matter, I knew I had to bite the bullet. The following week I watched the graduation ceremony from my room window. It was a complete mess, and I was glad for that moment, I wasn't a part of it. Squad leaders were instructing the marching cadets to turn left, but others turned right, causing a catastrophe. Another squad leader continued with his military cadence, 'Olianna.' And to add insult to injury, a single black cloud hovered above the ceremony for five minutes before dropping a load of rain, thunder and lighting. When I returned the following week, I wanted to find the sergeant and tell him how glad I was not to have participated in the graduation ceremony the previous week, but decided to leave it alone instead and bring no further attention to myself. I remediated the week and scored 100 percent on both my law exams. I met with the sergeant one final time, but on good terms, this time around. I took the oath and later had a long conversation with him. I told him his actions at the auditorium opened my eyes and somehow made me a better person. I also apologized and assured him my actions were not intended to cause anyone harm. Apology accepted. I saw him again during the 1990s, he was now a lieutenant. I asked him if he remembered me, and he stated, "We have hundreds of recruits come through our academy in just one year and you're asking me if I remember you from five years ago. How can I forget officer Bermudez, you were in my office more then you were attending the damn academy." END OF AUTOBIOGRAPHY

150

STORY CONT:

I finally woke from my life's reflection, and here I now sat in an OIC office within the confines of what was once one of the most notorious prisons in the United States, Sing-Sing maximum-security prison, where 2,250 plus prisoners are confined, and six-hundred-thirteen were electrocuted. Where celebrities like James Cagney, Robert DeNiro, Peter Falk, Billy Crystal and Spencer Tracy, were involved in great movies. And musicians like BB King, Joan Baez, and Salsa musicians like Eddie Palmieri and Larry Harlow all performed during the 1970s. *

Yep, Sing-Sing Prison in Ossining, New York. Where it was once said, neighborhood residential lights would flicker during the electrocution of prisoners on old Sparky, (Electric chair). Where many nightshift officers insist, you can sometimes hear the moans and groans of those who perished the death house from wall post six, situated directly behind the death house. Good Old Sparky was a scary and ugly looking chair with those wires and straps hanging from it. The leather straps were worn, dirty and greasy looking. The adjustable clamps were also old, and the steel floor brackets were rusted. The seat was ripped, padded and had a slight tilt to it. It wasn't designed for comfort that's for sure. The human body is not much of a resistor; it's actually a good conductor of electricity because the fluids in our bodies are solutions of salts and ions, which readily enable electricity to flow freely throughout. When voltage and current are sufficient, the electric flow through the body can fatally interrupt the electrical circuitry of the heart in addition to burning us alive. I was once tasered by Lake County Sheriff's deputies during a training exercise for five seconds with over fifty-thousand volts. As I stood there paralyzed, I thought of many things and for some unknown reason, I briefly thought of those electrocuted at the prison. It made me wonder what was going through their minds, or if they were able to think at all. Sing-Sing was notorious for many things and were not only limited to electrocutions, there were many other forms of punishments and torture. Sing-Sing Prison also had women convicts confined during the mid 1800s. Brief encounters with male convicts caused many impregnations and prison officials couldn't figure out how in the world it was happening, since they were kept separate.

151

Many babies born dead and unclaimed by family members in Sing-Sing, were buried outside the chapel building presently marked with white stones in the shape of a cross on its lawn; old Jewish bibles are also buried in this area. Prisoner bodies that were buried in Sing-Sing were mixed with lime for a faster decomposition process just outside of wall post fourteen, now a parking lot. We called it the dress up lot since many women visitor's take their revealing clothes off while in their vehicles and changed to more acceptable clothing before entering the prison visitors area. This was the same parking lot where lowlife serial killer Albert Fish was buried. He was the prick that raped and kidnapped children off the streets of New York City during the early 1900s. He would take them home or to other locations, tie them up for several days, torture them and spank them continuously. The concept behind this hideous act was to tenderize their human flesh. Many of his victims were roasted in the oven and others were made into a stew mixed with herbs, onions, and vegetables. He was such a severe mental case that he deliberately embedded needles into his groin which he later removed. Some needles became so embedded deep inside of him, they were impossible to remove and remained there until his death. He also repeatedly hit himself with a wooden paddle which had many nails protruding through it. Some would attribute his crimes to his family who also suffered from a history of mental illness and beatings he often received as a child during his stay at an orphanage. The more he was beaten, the more he began liking it; to the point of getting an erection. A total of six children were tortured, murdered and eaten. In a letter written to one of his victim's families and later traced by police, this is what he wrote:

"Dear Mrs. Budd.
In 1894 a friend of mine shipped as a deck hand on the Steamer Tacoma, Capt. John Davis. They sailed from San Francisco for Hong Kong, China. On arriving there he and two others went ashore and got drunk. When they returned the boat was gone. At that time there was famine in China. Meat of any kind was from $1-3 per pound. So great was the suffering among the very poor that all children under 12 were sold for food in order to keep others from starving. A boy or girl under 14 was not safe in the street. You could go in any shop and ask for steak chops or stew meat. Part of the naked body of a boy or girl would be brought out and just what you wanted cut from it.

A boy or girl's behind which is the sweetest part of the body and sold as veal cutlet brought the highest price. John staid [sic] there so long he acquired a taste for human flesh. On his return to N.Y. he stole two boys, one 7 and one 11. Took them to his home stripped them naked tied them in a closet. Then burned everything they had on. Several times every day and night he spanked them tortured them to make their meat good and tender. First he killed the 11 year old boy, because he had the fattest ass and of course the most meat on it. Every part of his body was cooked and eaten except the head bones and guts.

He was roasted in the oven (all of his ass), boiled, broiled, fried and stewed. The little boy was next, went the same way. At that time, I was living at 409 E 100 St. near right side. He told me so often how good human flesh was I made up my mind to taste it. On Sunday June the 3, 1928 I called on you at 406 W 15 St. brought you pot cheese strawberries. We had lunch. Grace sat in my lap and kissed me. I made up my mind to eat her. On the pretense of taking her to a party, you said yes she could go. I took her to an empty house in Westchester I had already picked out. When we got there, I told her to remain outside. She picked wildflowers. I went upstairs and stripped all my clothes off.

I knew if I did not I would get her blood on them. When all was ready I went to the window and called her. Then I hid in a closet until she was in the room. When she saw me all naked she began to cry and tried to run down the stairs. I grabbed her and she said she would tell her mamma. First I stripped her naked. How she did kick bite and scratch. I choked her to death, and then cut her in small pieces so I could take my meat to my rooms. Cook and eat it. How sweet and tender her little ass was roasted in the oven. It took me 9 days to eat her entire body. I did not fuck her though I could of had I wished."

She died a virgin.

STORY CONT:

As I sat there on my office chair, another loud scream from one of the above galleries startled me and got our immediate attention. I turned up the lights, ran out my office and was joined by numerous other officers with batons in hand who heard the screams. The scream was coming from a convict on R- gallery. We immediately ran up and saw officer Cradle standing in front of a cell, extremely upset and yelling back at a convict. With a little assistance from fellow officers, we calmed her down and escorted her away from the cell. I then went back to the cell with a couple of officers and questioned the convict as to why he was screaming at Cradle.

"Yo, officer, I was sleeping, and I kept hearing this voice asking me where I am going to be the rest of the day. Then I woke up and saw that little ugly ass officer standing in front of my cell and thought the devil came to get me."

I thought I had heard it all. This was an original and as much as I respect Mama, I couldn't hold this one back. I walked away from the cell with the other officers, and we began to laugh uncontrollably. We even laughed the next day and following weeks after that. I must admit, although there are convicts who are total morons—others are naturally funny, and this character was no exception. We all went back downstairs to the OIC area where we were met by a fuming and a furious female correction officer.

"I'm writing that ass up for interference and whatever else I can write him up on!"

"I'll be a witness if you like?"

"Witness...you're laughing at what that ass said to me, and you want to be a witness? No, thank you, I'll do this one by myself!"

Mama was a lovable and kind person, but angering her would instantly turn her into a little human Tasmanian devil. She left and took with her several misbehavior reports. It was quite obvious she was going to write up the convict and who can blame her. No one wants to be screamed upon so early in the morning, especially by a convict who thought you were the grim reaper sent from hell to take him away for all his committed sins. The messhall run was coming to an end and back to the office I went in preparation for other programs spread throughout the prison. *

These programs included the old death house where six-hundred-thirteen convicts were once electrocuted. It was converted into a vocational building where convicts could learn job trades like fire and safety, small engine repairs, plumbing, electrical and basic carpentry. It was also a good place for turning worthless pieces of steel, plastics or aluminum scraps into homemade knives or shanks. The last gallery of convicts was now entering their cells, and officers began securing the galleries. All assigned escort officers then came down to the OIC office for further reassignments, but only after their morning sip of coffee of course. Some officers would be assigned to the school area, others to the gym and yard recreation while others stood by for last minute emergency escorts.

154

All escort officers return to their assigned blocks or housing units for the eleven a.m. count. The process repeats itself again for the afternoon messhall and program activities. I then enter the officer's names on the employee's assignment sheet and their work destination or location, in addition to entering the completion of the messhall run. As escort officers come down, they check the assignment sheet; some complain about their new assigned post. Others complain simply because they like to complain. Those assigned to the yard complain of the cold and when it's summertime, they complain of the heat. Others don't like the gym because it stinks too much and others don't like the idea of being enclosed in a gym where there are two hundred fifty plus convicts to three officers at any given time. Prison has a way of intimidating people, regardless of where you work or who you are. I can recall working in wall post three, on overtime detail and hearing several Latino convicts call an officer in Spanish *puta,* (whore).

She was a Latina officer who happened to work a different shift and was walking in a direction away from convicts who were standing on the railroad bridge overpass leading to the school area, also known as the tunnel. They didn't like the idea of her not paying any attention to them, not to mention she was an extremely attractive woman. Convicts would use this tactic as a form of intimidation in hopes of breaking down an officer's spirit. Sometimes an officer gives in to prevent any further and future harassment. The convicts didn't know wall post three, was manned. I was watching them through a pair of binoculars and could easily identify who they were. I stepped out onto the wall tower catwalk and instructed the officer not to pay attention to them.

"They don't bother me Bermudez, I'm going home. My shift is done and I'll be going to NYPD real soon, anyway."

She eventually left Sing-Sing several months later and became a police officer. I know she'll do extremely well as a cop, probably better than most male coworkers I know. In the meantime, I notified the escort officer via landline and pointed out those involved in the harassment. I wrote them up, they were then escorted back to their housing unit, (HBA) and each confined to their cells.

'*Who's laughing now, dummies,*' I quietly asked myself as I saw them being escorted back.

155

They looked over to my wall post, surprised and unaware this wall post was manned during their verbal torment. As an officer or civilian, if you haven't developed a method to ignore these kinds of verbal harassments or torments, chances are you'll give in and become stressed to the point of calling in sick or become corrupt in every sense of the word.

STORY CONT:

All the escort officers were now done with their morning conversations and with drinking their coffee. Sergeants were in their office, and convicts were all locked in until the programs and recreation was released. The facility count was now completed, and the announcement was made via radio transmission.

"Sing-Sing base to all radio holders, the count is clear...I repeat the count is now clear. All Sing-Sing radio holders respond?"

All radio holders, including myself, responded. It was now time to make sure all other areas of the facility were prepared and ready to accept convict movement. Clearance with other areas must be made to prevent hundreds of convicts from one housing unit approach an area that may already have hundreds of other convicts from other locations. This prevention cuts down on the possibility of assaults, contraband swapping, extortion, and any messages being passed on from one convict to another. B-block has many transient convicts who are either, waiting to be transferred to other blocks and correctional facilities up north, or waiting to be released into society. A-block has convicts who are serving anywhere from three years to natural life. Before dropping any programs, I like to step out of the office, look up to the galleries and make sure I can see the gallery officers. I also like to make sure there are no convict stragglers whom someone may have missed or forgotten to lock in. As I'm standing there observing the galleries above, a sudden voice from behind startled me momentarily.

"Yo, co, I've been hit up." (stabbed).

I turned around and observed a short Latino convict in his early twenties standing there with blood sprinkling from different parts of his body, almost like a standing water fountain.

I couldn't believe how calm this convict was and for that second I had no idea how to stop the bleeding from so many wounds. After several seconds instincts naturally kicked in and I immediately yelled out for a blanket and several convict porters. Officer, Dobbins in command of Q/V gallery ran up moments later with a blanket, and we wrapped it around the convict like a pig in a blanket. We then had him lay on a medical stretcher where four convict porters and an officer carried him to the facility hospital. The distance to the facility hospital was equivalent to three city blocks approximately. The convict later identified his attacker and stated he was stabbed because he refused to give up his morning breakfast, 'French toast with syrup.' With this information, officers gathered up, went to the cell and conducted an immediate search. The attacker was placed in handcuffs, questioned by supervisors, read his Miranda Rights and escorted to a special housing unit, (SHU). I noticed there were a lot of unusual incidents taking place so I got together with other officers before dropping the programs.

Then I popped the big question correction officer's dread to know the answer to: "Was there a full moon last night?" *

There somehow seems to be a connection with a full moon the night before and criminal behavior the following day. For some unexplained reason, when there's a full moon the night before I can almost guarantee there will be an increase in unusual incidents. Is it a myth, or a fact that the moon is somehow responsible? After speaking with several officers from different law enforcement departments and other states, they all seem to agree with this fact. I once read that the moon's powerful gravitational pull, "woman handles" the oceans, creating two high tides and two low tides daily. All sorts of sea creature's mate when the moon is new or full and many humans report an urge to merge. Hospital workers swear obstetric wards are busier on a full moon night, a result some say, of the lunar tug on the womb's fluid. Western science insists these "biological tides" are all in our head, but individual scientists disagree. Robert A. Millikan, a Nobel Prize winner and former chairman of the California Institute of Technology, once stated, "If man is not affected in some way by the planets, sun and moon, he is the only thing on Earth that isn't."

This reminds me of one particular transportation incident. It was a sunny morning in July. I asked my partner if there was a full moon the night before; he couldn't remember. We had a transportation trip, and I knew a full moon the night before would probably result in a bad transportation experience. Unfortunately, there was a full moon and quite naturally the moon did affect our day. As a transportation officer, I received a transporting itinerary authorization form, signed by a sergeant. We were to report to Westchester County courthouse by eight-thirty a.m. with two convicts who had a history of assault on security staff. The procedure in obtaining all documents relating to the convicts and transportation was complete. We now had custody of both convicts and were exiting Sing-Sing's eighteen grounds sally-port. The trip to the courthouse was normal, and both convicts appeared to be engaged in their own conversation, although while en route several antagonizing comments were made toward my partner, but none was considered to be a threat or concern. We arrived at the courthouse, parked our state vehicle and entered the correction's security side of the courthouse with our prisoners.

Upon verification with Westchester County correction officers and a brief description of their rules, keys to an upstairs holding room were given to us. We entered an elevator and went up to the twelfth floor. The mechanical restrains were then removed from both convicts. They were led inside the holding area, and room was secured with its key. I then exchanged court information with state court officers, and they returned to their assigned location outside of our area. After conversing with my partner, we both decided a cup of coffee wouldn't be a bad idea. We notified court and correction officers of our decision to get coffee. I waited for the elevator and was later taken downstairs by a county officer, while my partner stood behind with the convict's locked in their room. As I entered the courthouse lobby, I was amazed by the detail construction and architectural designs. I saw a stationary store located in the lobby. I approached the vender and ordered two coffees. While receiving the change from the vendor an alarm sounded off. Court officers from every direction began running toward the elevator doors. I immediately stopped one of the responding officers and asked what floor was the alarm being activated from the twelfth floor he replied.

158

I threw the coffees in a nearby garbage can and ran toward the elevators with the officers. I informed them it was the same floor where my partner was stationed with two convicts from Sing-Sing. The elevator arrived and we all packed inside like sardines in a can. You could hear the hard breathing and feel the tension among the officers. It was one of the longest elevator rides I have ever been on. Just before the elevator doors opened the officers did something I've never seen before and something that impressed me even today. They positioned themselves by facing one another with their backs to the elevator walls and leaving open approximately a two foot-isle. I later learned this unusual, but impressive maneuver, was to prevent any possible direct center of mass gunfire by a suspect who may have been armed and positioned outside the elevator door. This was an advantage to any element of surprise. As the elevator reached the twelfth floor, we could hear banging and screaming. The doors opened revealing my partner standing away from the holding room while the convicts were screaming and kicking the door.

The observation glass to the room was now cracked, and the convicts were out of control. I ordered them to cease their violent behavior, or they would be placed on mechanical restraints. They comply with the instructions; the situation was finally under control, and all responding officers eventually left the area. I question my partner as to what led to this disruption, and he didn't know. After several minutes, I left the area again and went over to the court officer's room. We compared notes on the convicts, and they informed me the judge was in. I then walked over to the water fountain and began drinking when another alarm was activated from the twelfth floor holding area again. I ran over to the entrance door and could hear the screams and banging coming from the other side. I immediately made an entry and found my partner frozen in time with his back to the wall as the disruptive convicts continued their violent outburst. This time my verbal commands and threat of mechanical restraints were not being adhered to. I removed my revolver from my holster, open the cylinder and handed the weapon over to my partner. I didn't have much of a choice; I had to enter the holding room with mechanical restraints and attempt to secure both convicts.

It was quite obvious to me my partner was not cut out for the job. I was alone on this one. I knew it, and the convicts knew it. I then instructed my partner to stay at the ready when I entered to room. I pulled out my baton from its holder and ordered the convicts to step away from the door. At that precise moment, the elevator doors opened and a sign of relief made its presence known. A Green Haven, officer named R. Strother stepped out. He saw and heard the commotion in progress and quickly stepped up to the plate. I knew then I was in the company of a correction officer and not a coward. I also knew he possessed the courage needed in helping me to subdue them and place them both in mechanical restraints. We stepped inside the holding room, and Strother did just that. One particular convict, (the aggressor) was restrained a little more securely than the other. Unfortunately, his little fingertips were turning slightly blue. Their disruptive and out of control behavior finally came to a stop. Like two little children, convicts 0964 and 7130, sat in their holding rooms quietly. The convicts periodically got up and look out the door window for any signs of officer Strother, who would then answer back with a smile.

"Yeah, we're still here."

The convict was finally called into the court room, and the court officers arrived for the escort. I refused to remove the restraints and informed them of the convict's disruptive and violent behavior. The convict was brought into the court room, and the presiding judge became outraged.

"Wait a minute, who is responsible for allowing this prisoner to enter my courtroom in full restraints like this?"

The convict interrupted.

"Your honor; look at me, this is cruel and unusual punishment. Look at my hands and my fingers, its turning blue."

A court officer interrupted.

"Your honor the transporting officer is responsible for the restraints."

"Well, bring that officer into my courtroom right now."

I was standing just outside the courtroom entrance and heard the judge's request. I also heard the convict's mercy plea concerning his ten little blue fingers. I walked over to the bench and announced myself.

"I'm the transporting officer your honor."

"Why is this prisoner in my courtroom wearing shackles?"

"Your honor; the convict is in shackles because he left me no other alternative. His behavior became violent and he began destroying court property,"

The convict interrupted again.

"Your honor; look at me, this is cruel and unusual punishment," the Judge interrupted.

"Shut up! You destroyed my property of the court, and now you want to discuss cruel and unusual punishment? My advice to you is to keep quiet and sit there, or we'll hold this hearing without you!"

The Judge looked over to me.

"What's your name officer?"

"Sorry your honor; I'm officer Bermudez from Sing-Sing."

"Nice to meet you officer Bermudez, I now understand the nature of the restraints, and it will remain on the prisoner. You can leave or have a seat which ever you prefer."

"*Damn she's tough,*" I thought to myself as I left the courtroom. I didn't see her name plate on the bench and decided to ask a court officer.

"What's the judge's name?"

"Jeanine Pirro, you'll hear more of her. She's running for Westchester County District Attorney."

"Is that right, I tell you what, NYS corrections can use a commissioner like her."

Jeanine Pirro was the first woman county judge to serve on the bench and first District Attorney of Westchester County, New York. As a prosecutor she never lost a felony trial. She is one of the most influential and innovative figures in the American criminal-justice system.

We were done with the hearing. The convicts were checked out from the courthouse, and we were on our way back to the prison with no further incidents during our return trip. We entered Sing-Sing's sally-port, eighteen-grounds, verified our information and drove inside the prison. I informed my partner and the convict that I would be taking the mechanical restraints off. I also told him he was free to do whatever he liked upon removal of those restraints.

"Ok tough-guy, I'm taking the restraints off and we'll see how upset you really are?"

161

The restraints came off, and I passed it over to my partner, who immediately left area while saying,

"I have to turn in the paperwork at the watch-commanders office, I'll see you inside."

I then focused my attention toward the convict.

"What's the problem, why are you looking at me like that?"

"What's the problem, you're the problem. You gave me a hard time today, and now I like to see how tough you really are."

"Well, you take the first swing?"

"I take the first swing? You mean to tell me you acted like a fool the entire day. You wanted to fight and project a tough-guy image, now you have your chance and you want me to swing?"

"Yeah, you swing first."

"I tell you what; get the fuck out of my face."

"Yeah, whatever," said the convict.

The batterer of elderly women walked off. A hardcore convict, or any man for that matter, would have stepped up at the invite. Convict 0964, began shaking like a little wet dog on a cold day, and I knew then this confrontation would not go any further than where it was. This was not my first encounter with a prick convicted of beating, shooting and robbing elderly women, there were many during my career. But I must say it was the first and last time I've ever worked with a partner who was, not only a coward who fell asleep on every transportation trip, but disgraceful to the extent where I couldn't refer to 'Pigpen as an officer' during the writing of this article.

STORY CONT:

So we all confirmed it, there was a full moon the night before. It was quite obvious we were definitely in for a long and busy tour. With this fact now into play, all the officers reported to their post and kept more vigilance then they would have on an ordinary day. Before I released the convicts for the programs, the sergeants, and I agreed to post extra officers on galleries to monitor convict movement from above and below. We hoped the extra presence would deter any further violence. Once they were all in place and the areas of travel were cleared, we then began to release the convict population.

I first released those who attended school, then the workers, and finally the gym and yard recreation was released. Once they were all gone the only convicts left in the block are those confined to their cells twenty-three hours a day, known as keeplocks. If they agreed to attend recreation, an officer assigned to keeplock recreation detail will release them individually. They would then be monitored as they walked down and pat frisked for contraband or weapons by other officers assigned to keeplock recreation. Keeplock convicts are allowed one hour of recreation on a daily basis and can refuse to attend. They are convicts who, for disciplinary reasons, are confined to their cells. Reasons for their confinement can range from having sex with other convicts, fighting, stealing, contraband possession, violating departmental rules and so on. Today, thirty plus convicts on keeplock status want to participate in recreation, an unusually high amount. On any normal day, ten to fifteen convicts attend recreation. Extra officers have to be assigned for this reason, bringing the total from two to three officers. I assigned a rookie officer from up north, who always appreciate doing his job, regardless of what it was. All the programs and recreation were now gone, and we had the entire block to ourselves, except for one convict who came running up to the north gate while yelling, he missed his school escort. I stepped out of the office and asked him why he missed his group.

"I was taking a fucking shit, if you really want to know."

"Okay, just as well, go finish taking your shit and forget school. You missed the escort anyway."

"Yo, what's up officer? Are you denying me my education because you're sorry GED ass doesn't have a real diploma? You uneducated motherfuckers think you're better than us. You think you're above us because we're convicts. The difference between you and us is that we got caught, and you didn't!"

I knew I was in for a battle with this guy. The hostile manner in his approach started getting the best of me.

"Are you done?"

"Yeah, I'm done co, what now?"

I remembered an old Readers Digest I once read. It was an article quoting a statement made by actor Andy Garcia. Adding a few words of my own for good measure, I applied a little philosophy and interpersonal communication skills.

163

"You're wrong, the difference between you and us is, you're a convicted criminal, and we're not. Let me tell you something. I believe a man's social status is in no way a measure of his worth. Just because you consider yourself on a higher level of a social structure doesn't necessarily mean you have more dignity or character then some gentleman serving you at a dinner table. The uniform I wear, the shield in my pocket and the equipment worn around my belt doesn't confirm my manhood or who I am, you understand?"

Looking impressed and puzzled by what was said and while trying to make out the name on my nametag, the convict replied, "I hear you officer."

I radioed the school escort officer who was still waiting in the corridor on clearance for school movement. I informed him he had a school straggler being released from the block as the convict continued rambling.

"Hey, officer, what school you went to?"

"Doesn't matter, go catch up to the others in the corridor, they're still there."

"Thanks co, you're alright and my apologies."

"Don't worry about it. Go to school and absorb some knowledge and implement what you learn in a positive manner."

The conversation ended as the convict made his quick exit. To say the convict was impressed would be an understatement; so was I. I'm not a good talker, never have been and a public speech or interview on my part would probably be disastrous. My gift is in my hands, outside of that I don't have a prayer. Keeplock recreation was now gone, and the only ones left were a few convicts who stood behind and refused to leave their cells for whatever reason. Some slept the entire day, read books, or wrote letters to friends and family.

Others were writers who later became bestselling authors, as did former convict and artist Anthony Papa, his book was titled, 'Fifteen Years to Life.' Another was Dewey Bozella, who received a Bachelor's and Master's degree, the Arthur Ashe Courage Award and won his professional boxing debut at the Staple Center in Los Angeles, but not before receiving a telephone call from President Barack Obama who reportedly wished him luck. It came as no surprise—these individuals were extremely talented and well mannered. Dewey's trademark was that red and white Everlast professional boxing robe, which hung in his cell for years.

164

I took advantage of this time to make notations in my logbook and to catch up on work, since it had been a rather busy morning to say the least. I then walked over to the movement and control office located right next to OIC office. *

Movement and Control is an office which contains hundreds of photographs, names, cell locations and state identification numbers of every convict confined in B–block. A state identification number, (DIN) is issued by the state upon conviction. Examples of Din numbers are as follows; 05–A–1234. The first set of numbers 05, is the year the convict was convicted, 2005. The letter A, in this case, represents the processing facility, Attica; it can also be other facilities. The remaining four numbers 1234, represents the 1,234[th] person convicted that year, in this case 2005. Other letters are also used, G, for example, is given to women who enter the state correctional system. All other identifying numbers are the same as that of a male. We sometimes looked through all six-hundred-thirteen photos. In most cases, we come across convicts who we grew up with as friends, others we've seen in neighborhoods and even family members that went missing. Other photographs we identified through newspapers articles or public news media stories. One convict was a former New York City housing police officer that hammered his wife to death.

Another was a convict from Long Island, who killed his wife on Christmas Eve, reported her missing and helped local police in their search efforts the following day, Christmas. Another convict who caught my attention was a preppy rich boy from New York City Central Park area, who killed his girl, then blamed it on a rough sexual encounter that got out of control. The stories connected to the photos are an endless cycle of madness, curiosity and bullshit. I discovered during my career that many criminals actually believe in their minds that society is at fault for their downfall and incarceration. Alternatively, the victims should have been more cautious or alert of their surroundings. In other words; don't blame the criminal, its society's fault and the criminal-justice system for the dismemberment and mutilation of another human being during the act of their crime. A crime initiated by the perpetrator in the first place and in some cases in the comfort and tranquility of the victim's home.

Some people in our society actually believe in accusing victims for crimes committed against them, is this for real? A good example was a lowlife convict in Green Haven state prison that was made the chapel trustee by a trusting liberal preacher, (prison chaplain). The convict was convicted of abducting a woman, taking her to a wooded area, raping her, flinging her body into tree trunks, ramming sticks into her mouth and other parts of her body, burning her with cigarettes, biting her nipples off, biting her face open, biting her nose, slashed her throat and finally stomped her to death. This was just one of the four victims killed by this lowlife prick. One of those victims was a female NYS correction officer who he also mutilated and murdered before placing her body in a garbage bag and dumping her into a state-owned sanitation truck at the prison. Her body was later discovered at a nearby county landfill. This is the real world we live in, and as long as we have those bleeding-heart liberals out there who somehow are convinced criminals can be converted to productive members of society with the turn of three Bible pages, then we as a society will continue to witness and become victims of ruthless and senseless criminal violence. When I was a rookie officer in 1985 and working a gallery, I experimented with convicts and with my job performance for six days.

On the first day, I worked on a gallery and gave convicts whatever they were entitled to, from toilet paper to toothpaste. I let them out early for recreation and waited for them to step in their cells for the morning and afternoon counts without ordering them to do so. By the third day of my experiment, I had a gallery out of control, convicts refusing to lock in and some even called me a fucking asshole. I went on my two days off exhausted, but vowed to return. After returning from my days off fully re-energized, I then experimented with the same gallery and same convicts for three days as a no-holds barred and by-the-book correction officer. This time, whenever a convict asked me for anything they were entitled to, I wasn't giving it up. I refused to play the role of a restaurant waiter for anyone. I would tell them I didn't have it or tell them they would have to get it on the next shift. When it was time to release them for recreation, it was done not one minute sooner and sometimes even later. When it was time for the morning and afternoon count, it was time to lock in their cells or physically get put in.

166

By the third day, I couldn't believe how easy it was to run a gallery—it literally ran itself. My days off were pleasurable to say the least. It was obvious through my experiment that my kindness and fairness were mistaken for weakness and abused to the fullest extent by ninety-nine percent of the convicts. While my tough and by-the-book attitude got me the respect, the fear and cooperation, I didn't expect. I knew then what I needed to do to make my job and career as comfortable for me as possible, and in the words of the great professional boxing referee Joe Cortez, 'be fair but firm.'

This kind of abusive behavior by convict's breeds hatred among the officers and changes a gentleman into a hardcore son of a bitch. During a conversation concerning criminal activity and abusive behavior, someone once asked me.

"Dealing with these criminals on a daily basis and being verbally abused like that, does it hinder your opinion on the death penalty?" I immediately answered.

"No, I don't believe in a death penalty without the shadow of a doubt that factual evidence exists."

My answer often puzzled many, especially my fellow officers, and almost always, it's followed with another question, why?

I answer with a true story of two former corrupt attorneys and one innocently convicted man.

Chapter Four

~~~

To clearly state my story, and the facts of this case, let me begin with a news story made public, concerning two attorneys our family hired to represent my brother Lee Bermudez in a criminal trial—attorneys Martin Light, (aka Mighty-Light) and Stanley Meyer.

"He was expected we do the right thing." That was Attorney Martin Light's description of the simple code he followed during his fifteen years as an attorney for the Mafia. And what exactly was the right thing? Counseling mobsters to perjure themselves; take the Fifth Amendment and destroy evidence? Helping them to intimidate witnesses and jurors? Paying off judges, prosecutors, and police officials and even fingering clients as suspected informants? "To do the right thing means to protect the family, explained Light; it's a way of life." When Light, 50, appeared before the President's Commission on Organized Crime in Washington, he became the first lawyer gone bad, in the parlance of law enforcement officials, to give public testimony to the Federal Government. Appearing under heavy security, as well as a grant of immunity from prosecution, the dapper former attorney, who is serving a fifteen year sentence for heroin possession, fielded questions with a sometimes nonchalant candor during a two-hour session. According to Light, he was one of twenty to thirty attorneys formally servicing the mob in New York City, and he claimed that other such lawyers operated in more than half a dozen major American cities. He contended that the Mafia has infiltrated "legitimate businesses" in New York, including a fuel oil distributor and a school bus company that has obtained a lucrative contract from the city's public schools.

Light told the commission that he began hobnobbing with mobsters at an early age. Growing up Jewish in a predominantly Italian neighborhood in Brooklyn, Light hung around his grandfather's bathhouse, which was also frequented by members of the notorious Murder, Incorporated. Upon graduating from Brooklyn Law School in 1962 and going to work as an assistant district attorney, he began to moonlight as legal counsel for some of his acquaintances from the neighborhood. When the district attorney ordered him to abandon his private practice in 1969, Light instead quit so he can work full time for the Cosa Nostra. He said he received eighty to ninety percent of his fees in cash," the best way to get paid."

The Mafia lawyer worked closely with reputed Colombo family lieutenant Gregory Scarpa, tipping off the mobsters about clients of his who he thought might be cooperating with federal authorities. The penalty for informing: execution. Said Light of Scarpa,

"He could have dinner with you, then when it comes time for dessert, he could kill you."

Light also testified that he won an acquittal for Billy "Wild Bill" Cutola, a Teamsters Union official who, he said, shot a suspected informant in the head. According to Light, the victim was stuffed into a fifty-five gallon drum, which Cutola then dumped into the East River. As Light tells it, the body's gases caused the drum to rise to the surface.

"Next time I'll know better," a jocular Cutola reportedly told Light after he was cleared of the murder charge. "I'll cut his stomach open."

Martin Light's arrest for heroin trafficking occurred, he maintains, while he was delivering two grams of "junk" for a friend, but other public documented information states the trafficking was also from the Middle East. At his 1984 trial, NYC prosecutors contended that the dope was part of a much larger quantity that Light was dealing. Federal authorities declined to say what kind of deal Light may have cut with the Government in return for his story. When Deputy Commission Counsel Stephen Ryan asked Light, "Would [the Mafia] kill you for what you're doing today?" He replied soberly, 'Without a doubt' (*Milligan, 1986*).

During those undercover investigations by federal and local law enforcement officials, attorneys Martin Light and Stanley Meyer were representing my brother Lee, in a murder trial. I attended many of those hearings and at times notice an increase in the absence on Light's behalf. Other than the absences, no other indications led us to believe any of the attorneys were involved in serious criminal activities or misconduct. When we questioned Stanley Meyer of those absences, and he stated,

"There were other cases of high profile status, which demanded Light's immediate and full attention."

After months of trial hearings, Lee was subsequently convicted and sentence to a term of fifteen years to life. Can you imagine if we had the death penalty? During this lengthily trial Stanley Meyer stated he had no knowledge of any criminal activity on Martin's behalf and therefore, could not disclose any information. After Lee's conviction and incarceration, I began conducting legal research on his behalf. I later discovered attorney Martin Light was arrested, indicted, convicted and sentence to fifteen years in prison. In addition to my discovery, I also learned through newspaper articles in 1994 that Stanley Meyer claimed to have information regarding Light's criminal activities. In April 1998, Meyer was disbarred, but that didn't stop him. His willful disobedience of the lawful mandate of the court came to surface when he appeared in the Supreme Court of Kings County, on February 4, 1999, in the matter of People v. Muchnik. He was held for criminal contempt of court. Every attempt on my brother's behalf in appealing or overturning his conviction was subsequently denied. The appellant courts and court of appeals, ignorantly and inconsiderately refused to acknowledge the miscarriage of justice, the ineffective assistance of trial counsel, the existence of concededly meritorious constitutional violation and the fraudulent behavior. Lee's trial quite obviously constituted extraordinary circumstances, either for a new trial or dismissal. A consequent obligation of a lawyer is to maintain the highest standards of ethical conduct. Obviously, Martin Light and Stanley Martin Meyer failed to demonstrate this in every sense of the word. Their lack of representation and criminal activities only helped to send an innocent man to prison. Who knows how many others fell through the cracks? My mother clearly stated to, Martin Light, "Please, don't lose this case with my son. He's innocent Mr. Light."

170

Don't worry; I haven't lost a case yet," he replied.

Naturally, I took this case very personal and decided to do a little footwork-investigating of my own. I later discovered the culprit responsible for the death in which Lee was subsequently convicted. Canvassing neighborhoods, conducting interviews and questioning people on the streets led one name to surface. A Latino man, who went by the street name T, was identified as the actual shooter. Word on the street was, T, had a brother named Jap. I knew the name…I've heard of him and seen him on several occasions walking the avenues of Coney Island in Brooklyn. Jap and T were both residents of Brighton Beach. I didn't know what T, looked like, but I knew what Jap looked like. I vigorously began patrolling the streets of Coney Island and Brighton Beach looking for Jap. Nothing panned out after several weeks of canvassing the neighborhoods. But as luck would have it, that would soon change. I became a correction officer a couple of years later and while conducting a security check on R/W gallery in Sing-Sing Prison, lo and behold, I saw Jap in a cell. That explained why I couldn't track him down on the streets of Brooklyn. I confronted this individual at his cell, and these were the words we exchanged.

"You look familiar. Aren't you from Coney Island in Brooklyn?"

"Yeah, I'm from CI. I thought you looked familiar too officer."

"I don't know you personally, but I know of you. I have seen you around the neighborhood. They call you Jap, and you have a brother named T, right?"

"Yeah, that's me. I had a feeling you were from Coney Island."

"That's right, I'm from 23rd Street off Surf Avenue. My first name is Al, and my last name is Bermudez. You ever heard of the name?"

"Bermudez, the name does sound familiar."

"Yeah, it should sound familiar, to you and your brother."

"Why is that?"

"Because my brother is doing a fifteen-year sentence for a homicide you're fucking brother committed in Brighton Beach. Now you remember the name?"

"Yo, co, I have no clue of what you're talking about man. I don't have any brothers."

"Oh, so now you don't have a brother named T?"

"Nah, I don't and I don't know what you're talking about."

"Well, relay this message to the brother you say you don't have. You tell your brother T, that my brother is in prison for his sorry ass, and he had better make good for it. You can also tell him I said he had better start sending my brother a little compensation for all the hell and high waters, he put my brother and family through."

"Like I said officer, I don't know what you're talking about."

"Yeah, well, I'm sure the message will get across," and the conversation ended. After that encounter whenever Jap saw me in the prison corridors he'd make all efforts to avoid me. I later learned his last name was Suarez. I obtained all of his information from the movement and control office and notified the Brooklyn's District Attorney's office. In a show of support, my brother Cruz and I visited the Court of Appeals. I went in a full correction's uniform, and he went in full police uniform. Although a judge appeared impressed and stated, "Your brother Lee is well represented" our attempts to prove his innocents still fell on deaf ears, repeatedly. The last I heard on the streets and in prison, both brothers Jap and T, may have died from the AIDS virus, although that's still unconfirmed. Meantime, Lee Bermudez continued attending parole board hearings every two years in an attempt to gain his freedom and every two years he denies any involvement in the death. Many parole officials see this as a denial of their responsibilities in relation to the crime, so ninety-nine percent of the time, convicts will be denied parole. Unfortunately, two additional years are added to their sentence. During a telephone conversation with my brother from a correctional facility, he stated he would tell the parole board committee, he committed the crime in hopes of gaining his freedom. I couldn't tell him not to. It has been twenty-three years of a fifteen-year sentence. I wished him luck and said a prayer on his behalf, but that too backfired and he was hit with an additional two years for a total of twenty-five years. It sort of reminded me of the prison movie, "Shawshank Redemption."

Every time the prisoner told parole officials the truth, he was denied release. When he finally couldn't take it and told them to stop wasting his time, they approved his release.

172

If you ever wonder where those movie directors get their ideas from, I can tell you they get them from actual prison life circumstances. Our beloved mother Margarita Pereira Morales since passed on in 2003, after a long battle with cancer. She never saw the release of her son—thanks to what, in my opinion, were a couple of lowlife prick attorneys from Brooklyn, who helped condemn a man before he could ever get a chance to a fair trial. I think those rat bastards have more things to worry about then the mob fitting them with a pair of cement shoes, and thanks to the two lowlife pricks Jap and T Suarez, from Brighton Beach Brooklyn, who without a doubt managed to beat the criminal-justice system and get away with murder.

To say they are a disgrace to an entire Latino race would be an understatement. Growing up in the ghetto and seeing firsthand how unfair the criminal-justice system can be toward the poor and less fortunate, is just one of many reasons for not believing in the death penalty or an impartial criminal-justice system.

1. Incarcerating people for the sake of closing a case or earning the rank of detective is not my idea of justice.

2. Allowing without a doubt, a guilty criminal to cop-a-plead for the purpose of receiving a lesser sentence, and saving the state time and money, is not my idea of justice.

3. Giving a maximum sentence to those who choose to go to trial because they know without a shadow of a doubt, they're innocent as charged, is not my idea of justice.

4. Allowing a guilty criminal to receive a lesser charge or avoid a death sentence for reasons of cooperation in revealing the location of a corpse is not my idea of a fair and impartial criminal-justice system.

In my opinion, a flaw within the NYS criminal-justice system is a crumbling legal bureaucracy with backlogged cases and judges who will delay or postpone cases for the sake of not finding themselves late for a holiday weekend up in the Catskills of New York State with their girlfriends, wives, boyfriends or both. Ignoring miscarriages of justice, the ineffective assistance of trial counsels; the existence of a constitutional violation of trial and fraudulent behavior; constitutes extraordinary circumstances for a new trial and not continued incarceration or guilty verdicts.

I seriously wonder if our criminal-justice system and its methods of implementing and executing its law procedures and convictions could somehow use the public's help in recommending it for an, "Extreme Makeover: Justice Edition." As it presently stands for my brother Lee, I published my first book in December 2006, "Sing-Sing State Prison, One Day; One Lifetime." The book, (Like this book) depicted in detail the circumstances behind his case and conviction. Ironically and coincidently enough, I'm pleased to say his parole was approved in January 2007, after serving twenty-five years of a fifteen-year sentence. Against all odds, I'm also proud to say he has been successful in seeking and obtaining employment, received his driver's license, purchased a vehicle and now a productive and law abiding member of society, but this comes as no surprise to us. Our sincere heartfelt thanks and appreciation go out to those from the New York State Division of Parole, who were responsible for his release. However, let us not forget there are many others who are confined in our prison system throughout our nation with similar circumstances. The only problem is, knowing who's telling the truth and who's not.

STORY CONT:

I left the movement and control office and noticed the entire area was now secure. No convicts hanging around, or up on the galleries, and no ringing of the office telephones. I decided to take a walk up to R/W gallery on the W side of the gallery. The windows there face the yard and gave me a good view of all the convicts and any possible unusual activity. While standing there overlooking the yard through the windows, I noticed a convict constantly looking in the direction of the officers. The convict appeared to be looking for something in the ground while using his foot. The officer in charge of the yard was Angel Torres, (aka Bloodhound). This was a Latino officer who had a natural ability to know where the homemade razors, ice picks, shanks and drugs were kept hidden in the yard. Whenever the Bloodhound stepped out of the yard office booth, you can rest-assure convicts who knowingly were standing near any form of contraband, would immediately disburse the area, no questions asked. I called Torres via radio, informed him of the unusual activity I was observing from the block gallery, and gave him the convict's description.

He continued to observe the convict's activity before making his exit and approach. Although I couldn't see his office booth from where I was standing, I knew he was in motion and was making his way to that location. Convicts immediately began walking away like little roaches after a burst of Raid, Ant and Roach Killer. Some were pretending not to see Torres's impending arrival and pretended to be part of a softball game while slowly leaving the area and walking onto the softball field. Others took off straight to the handball courts. I finally had Officer Torres in view. I could see him pointing at the convict, ordering him to stay where he was and face the wall for a pat frisk.

After a quick search of his immediate area, Torres pulled out what was later identified as a six-inch homemade shank with a taped handle and a string attached. Convicts tie a string on a shank or razor for easy and quick accessibility. Sometimes they color the string with a magic marker for camouflaging purposes and insert the shank into the ground where it blends with the natural earth surroundings, always remembering where it's kept. Others hide their weapons under stones, fence post, cracks in walls, floors, benches, tables, behind and under televisions, wooden planks, telephones, in baseball gloves, sport uniforms and just about anywhere you can think of in a prison yard, including their anal cavity. The convict was escorted back to his housing location and eventually taken to a special housing unit where he would be confined twenty-three hours a day, put through the disciplinary process and not released until the expiration of his sentence, in addition to losing possible privileges, e.g. commissary, telephone calls and packages. *

Working with Torres was always a day filled with unpredictable adventure. One day while working with Torres, the sun was shining and four hundred plus convicted felons were out and about in the prison yard. On the east side of the yard, sitting on a picnic table while playing cards were the Italian convicts with their Jesus Christ tattoos, pompadour hair and a complete lack of trust for all others around them. On the southeast, are the shirtless Latino convicts playing handball off the prison wall. The older men played dominoes with their backs to the wall and eyeballing everyone who looks suspicious.

On the north side by the bocce ball courts were the much younger black convicts glued to the television watching their rap videos, while others play basketball on the south side of the yard convinced they would be the next Michael Jordan. The northerner Caucasian convicts, with their brotherhood tattoos walked around the yard in groups of four keeping close vigilance on everyone, including themselves. The Mexican and South American convicts were at the center of the yard, running like jack rabbits while playing futbol, (Soccer). All the want-to-be Arnold Schwarzenegger's were pumping their iron then walking around the yard after every set while swinging their arms back and forth as though it was lifeless and made of concrete.

The mentally ill convicts were everywhere in the yard begging for cigarettes, food and picking up cigarette buds from the ground while holding long conversations with themselves. The homosexual convicts with their pink little sneakers, petroleum jelly filled faces and tight green uniform pants were walking the yard shaking their asses like women in extreme heat and approaching everyone like a Politian running for office. Officer Torres and I were conducting a visual observation from the north-side of the yard in front of the officers' booth while other officers are patrolling the yard and stationed at the north and south end gates. We notice several convicts looking up to sky momentarily, and we wondered what was going on.

"Hey, Bermudez, you see what I see?"

"No, what do you see?" Torres pointed up to the sky.

"There's a balloon up in the air, and it appears to be coming down into the prison yard."

I looked up and saw what appeared to be a red balloon,

"Hey, let's see where it lands, maybe it's a message sent to a convict, or maybe it contains drugs inside?"

We kept a close vigilant on the balloon and on the convicts in the yard. One particular convict caught our attention. He somehow managed to keep all other convicts away from the incoming balloon and was closely monitoring its every move. The balloon was now approximately twenty-five feet off the ground, and we slowly began making our way in direction and vicinity of the balloon. The convicts consent vigilance on the balloon gave us an advantage to get close without him knowing of our impending approach.

176

"He's getting closer Torres," I said, while preparing for the takedown.

Officer Angel Torres turned around in my direction.

"As soon as he grabs it, we'll grab him."

The grab is made; the convict popped the red balloon, removed its inner contents, quickly put it in his pocket and began walking away. Officer Torres and I made our move toward the convict. We gave him a direct order to remain where he was, but the convict picked up the pace. We rushed him and together took him down to the ground. Torres instructed the convict not to resist. We got him up, escorted him to a nearby wall and began conducting a pat frisk. He reached into the convict's pocket and pulled out what appeared to be a well folded sheet of paper. It appeared to be an elementary-school experiment. The letter was eventually turned over to the facility watch commander, and a Connecticut school was immediately notified of its successful experiment. They insured prison officials this kind of experiment will never happen again at their school. This was just one of many different occurrences involving the prison yard with Officer Torres in which I had a distinctive privilege and honor in being a part of. Before surrendering the letter we opened it and the writing revealed the following.

Dear Balloon Finder:

My name is Jane Doe, and I'm 11 years old. The letter you found in the red balloon is a school experiment, and if you found this letter, please call the school and ask for Mrs. Jane W. Doe, 203-123-2345. We would like to know where it was found, how if was found, who found it and when it was found? If you like to bring the letter to school, please feel free do so. Or if you prefer to bring in person to my home, please call our home at: 203-123-1234,

Sincerely,

Jane Doe and Mrs. Jane W. D.

Elementary School 23. Danbury, CT. 06810

Yard incidents like this, or any other unusual incident, must be documented. A memorandum containing a detailed description of the incident should be written and submitted to a superior officer for review and placed in a file for future use.

"It is highly recommended and advised by all departments to make a personal copy and keep all documentation in reference to any incident, whether unusual, medical or otherwise, for possible future legality and recollection."

Circumstances involving unusual incidents, particularly use of force, have a funny way of resurfacing numerous years after an incident. I was once subpoenaed by New York State Attorney General's Office, nine years later on a case where I was assaulted by a convict and he in turn, filed a cause of action against me in the amount of 2.3 million dollars for excessive force. It was one of many incidents I would never forget. I was assigned to the OIC office one busy day, and the telephone was ringing continuously.

It was a reverend name Harmony, who was also a former police officer. He was calling from the facility chapel and requesting information on a convict.

"Good day, officer Bermudez, this is Reverend Harmony, can you please tell me who locks in cell V-365?"

I gave him the information, and we confirmed it was the convict in question.

"Officer Bermudez, do you personally know of this convict?"

"No, Sir, but I can tell you this convict is on keeplock status, and he should be in his cell. He refused to participate in keeplock recreation this morning."

"Well, I'm going to need this convict escorted to the chapel with a couple of officers if you don't mind?"

"A couple of officers," finding it unusual he would ask for two officers.

"Yes, officer, I have extremely bad news for this convict. It appears as though this convict's brother and sister, who have been missing for quite some time, were found dead and dismembered in plastic garbage bags. I don't expect this convict will take this news lightly, and I don't want to get hurt as a result of any uncontrollable behavior."

"Sure, Reverend," I replied.

I immediately related the information to the sergeants. Unfortunately, cases like this are all too common with criminal activity, although not in all cases.

When you take under consideration convicted felons who lived their lives mingling in criminal activities, while burning their bridges along the way, chances are retaliation for unpaid debts will come to haunt them in one form or another. In this case, the tragic deaths of his loved ones were the cost of his debts. I took two of my best officers from their post, Rolando "The Gonzo" Gonzales from the center gates and former college football player David "Big D" Fentress from the front gate. I informed both officers of the circumstances surrounding the convict from cell V-365. Once the convict was released from the cell, they then escorted him out of B–block and brought him over to Reverend Harmony in the chapel. We were now short two officers who would normally control the convict movement in and around the OIC area. The OIC office is located between four gates, north and front gates control by Officer Fentress and south and center gate's control by officer Gonzales.

Nevertheless, as long as other officers do their jobs, and I do mine, there should be no traffic or stragglers wandering about. I was now responsible for Q gallery north, south and its gates. After making the daily entry into my logbook, I exited the OIC office en route to Q gallery with the area keys, but left my personal radio on the office desk since all other area of the OIC was secured, a decision I later would regret. My job now was to secure the convicts on Q gallery until the regular officers returned from the escort. I figured that shouldn't be a problem, two minutes at most. As I approached the gallery, I notice a convict standing outside a cell. I verbally ordered the convict from the gallery to lock in his cell, enter the gym or go out to the yard for his recreation. The convict ignored my instructions and continued his conversation with another convict who was already in his cell. This time I yelled out the verbal order a little louder.

"Hey, you, if you lock on the gallery, then you must step in your cell, go to the gym or yard recreation!"

I got no reply from the convict. I noticed an officer named George Rest, standing outside the gym gate. He was closer to the convict then I was, but he was not assisting in helping to secure the gallery. I decided to make my way down the gallery and confront the convict.

"Excuse me; do you have a cell on this gallery?"

"Yeah, I have a cell here, why?"

"You will have to either step into your cell or attend a recreational program." He began walking away and stopped directly in front of cell number Q-18.

"This is my cell. You want me to step in—open it!"

I immediately sensed this convict was problematic, but he kept both his hands in his pockets, so I didn't see any reason to suspect anything more than an attitude problem.

"Your cell is open, so step inside."

Again, no reply, I then gave him yet another verbal direct order to open his cell and step inside. As the order was being given, I could see through my peripheral vision Officer George Rest, open the gym gate. He stepped inside the gym leaving me alone with the convict. In that instance, the convict saw the same thing I saw and became boisterous with a boost of self-confidence.

"Fuck you, you want me inside the cell then you open the fucking cell door!"

Apparently, the convict knew the officer turned his back on me. I then opened the cell door and ordered the convict to step inside while informing him he would receive a misbehavior report. He became enraged.

"Fuck it, I don't care motherfucker!"

I pushed closed the cell door and went over to the brake bar to close all the cell doors simultaneously, but the convict slightly opened his cell door just enough to prevent the brake bar from fully closing. I walked down the gallery again, only this time I would turn the key in his cell door cylinder, and he would remain keeplocked. As I approached his cell, the convict stepped out and began his verbal assault.

"What! You little motherfucker, I'll beat your faggot ass!"

Standing there in shock I ordered the convict back into his cell, but he continued to refuse the verbal orders and continue yelling while using threading gestures.

"Fuck you, little bitch faggot, you put me in!"

For that fraction of a second, just as I took my eyes off the convict to look down the gallery for possible assistance, the convict began his physical assault.

Al in B-block Q-gallery, photo by Wolpinsky 1990

First, was a direct punch to the nose, shattering my nasal septum and bridge. After this first hit, I was dazed and wasn't sure what happened. I felt as though I wasn't conscious enough to realize I have just been hit. Then he struck a second time, and I still couldn't make heads or tail of the situation. Somehow after the third hit I finally realized I was being assaulted. I also realized I had blood pouring from my nose and onto my uniform shirt. A fourth punch connected, directly to the jaw, and I immediately grabbed the convict with my left arm placing him in a headlock and squeezing him as hard as I possibly could. As I held him there in a lock, the fifth punch came; an overhand left and connected directly to the mouth taking out one of my front teeth. I finally realized this convict was not going to stop his attack. While still holding him in my headlock, I pivoted slightly with my right foot and began continuously punching the left side of his ribcage. The convict then reached behind my legs, picked me up and slammed me onto the cement pavement. I could hear the baton hitting the floor, and I immediately got up, but couldn't find it. By this time, all the other convicts who were in their cells stepped out for the show and formed a human circle around us.

I knew I wasn't getting out of this without a fight, so I got up from the floor, took up a boxer's stand, and I remember clearly saying to myself,

"Okay, motherfucker, you want some of this, let's finish it off."

The convict looked at me with rage, let out a scream and lowered his sense of gravity. He managed to lift me up a second time and slam me to the floor. This time while I was down and rumbling on the floor with him, I felt other convicts stomp me with their boots about the neck and head. During the struggle we stood up. The convict then reached for something and came toward me with it. It was a stainless steel mop ringer. Fortunately, several Latino convicts stepped in and stopped the convict from using it against me. They pulled it away from him, and I remember them saying.

"Nah, man, you're not going to hit this cool officer with that, this is a one-on-one fair and square."

I remember thinking to myself.

"Yes, now this is my turn, and I'm not going down this time."

I knew many of the young convicts who stepped in and pulled the mop ringer away from the other convict. Some were from Brooklyn, Bronx, Manhattan and Coney Island. Others I met within the prison system, mostly in B-block. We've spoken on numerous occasions, and some had fathers who knew me from local neighborhoods. The courageous Latino convicts I can't thank enough were; Nelson from Coney Island, son of green eyes Tito, GQ and Pizo from the Bronx, Playita and Indio from Manhattan, Pipo and crazy Louie from Brooklyn.

Their act of courage gave me the second wind I needed and the opportunity to finish off the fight. The convict then saw my baton on the floor and tired reaching for it, but I managed to pick it up first and throw it over the crowd who gathered. I was hoping the distinct sound of the baton hitting the concrete floor would get the attention of fellow officers in the area, or from the galleries above. I took a boxer's stance again and was much angrier as a result of all the dirty stomps I received while I was down. It started again and this time I began throwing jabs and overhand rights. Nothing in this brawl pertained to anything I've ever learned in the Academy. On contrary, it had everything to do with what was learned on the streets. Survival doesn't wait for sight-alignment, baton jabs, and breathe control.

182

For some-odd-reason as we were brawling, I began thinking of my sons and wondering how they would go on without me—should this convict succeed in killing me. Then I realized these thoughts would only hinder my concentration. As we were standing there like two toe-to-toe boxers in a professional ring, I faked a right punch and just like I planned, he went for it. He leaned over to his right in an attempt to avoid what he thought would be a right punch, but it would never come. As he bent at the waist to his right, I released an uppercut left, chest high. It connected over his right eye and directly on the eyebrow. I could instantly see the blood pouring from his head covering his face, blinding him. I now knew the tables were turned. The convict realized he was hurt, "Okay, co, you got it. You got it!"

However, that wasn't enough for me. I could hear the voices inside my head.

"Give this motherfucker one more, give him one more."

And I did. I gave him one left to the jaw and saw him drop like a towering pine tree in a forest. That's when I was sure, the assault was finally over and in between all this chaos, fifteen minutes had lapsed. We both went down to the floor once more. I was tired, winded and felt as though I was about to collapse from lack of oxygen and stamina.

I could hear the sound of music in the background.

"Officer down—officer down!"

It was two courageous one-to-nine shift officers, Arthur Stamp and David Stansfield, who were entering the block and heard the sound of the baton hit the floor moments before. They looked around, saw the struggle and without any hesitation immediately responded to the incident and helped restrain the convict. I ordered all the other convicts back into their cells and told them the show was over, but not before approaching those who I suspected of stomping me while I was down. I promised them I would be back and would deal with them at a later date, and that I did. Officer George Rest from 2nd Avenue in Manhattan; the coward who turned his back on me and quietly stepped into the gym, left Sing-Sing and became a NYC police officer. Now, nine years later after this incident I found myself in a federal courtroom being sued for excessive force by the convict who initiated the assault in the first place. He had received several bruises and a small cut above his right eye that required four sutures to close.

I sustained multiple abrasions with subcutaneous hemorrhage of the face, neck and chest. Two herniated cervical discs, one bulging lumbar disc, closed head trauma, loss of a front tooth, a broken nose, permanent facial disfigurement and reconstructive surgery. After a long and lengthy trial at the Federal Courthouse, the jury went into their chambers for deliberation. I went downstairs, and outside the courthouse where I began chatting with several US Deputy Marshals and within fifteen minutes, the verdict was returned: not guilty. Out of the 2.3 million he sued the state for the prick didn't receive a penny. In that instant, my faith in the criminal-justice system was somewhat restored. When I think of the attorneys who represented me in this case from the State Attorney General's Office in New York, Alan Kusinitz and Richard Rubinstein, I can't help but think of their professionalism, determination and respect at its best. These are the kind of lawyers who without a doubt bring to surface the best in people when circumstances are at their worst. An introduction to a formal document that serves to explain its purpose from Cornell School of Law describes it best.

"Law so grounded makes justice possible; for only through such law does the dignity of the individual attain respect and protection. Without it, individual rights become subject to unrestrained power, respect for law is destroyed, and rational self-government is impossible."

Lawyers, as guardians of the law, play a vital role in the preservation of society. The fulfillment of this role requires an understanding by lawyers of their relationship with and function in our legal system. A consequent obligation of lawyers is to maintain the highest standards of ethical conduct as unceasingly demonstrated by Attorneys, Alan Kusinitz and Richard Rubinstein. In fulfilling professional responsibilities, a lawyer necessarily assumes various roles that require the performance of many difficult tasks. Not every situation the lawyer may encounter can be foreseen. Fundamental ethical principles are always present for guidance. Within the framework of these principles, a lawyer must go forward with courage and foresight and be able and ready to shape the body of the law to the ever-changing relationships of society. It was a privilege, not only to be represented by such professionals like Alan Kusinitz and Richard Rubinstein, but to witness firsthand the process of professionalism and honorableness.

184

However, they were not the only one responsible in making this a successful and interesting trial. Officers Arthur Stamp and David Stansfield were the other professional and honorable men who played an important part in this entire episode. A former military policeman with the US Army Security Agency, Arthur Stamp continues his career as a correction officer. He received a General Commendation Medal and Certificate for located escape and evasion plans in a NATO post, ninety miles from the Soviet Union. Working since the rightful age of seventeen, David Stansfield has since retired from corrections. During his career, he sustained numerous injuries requiring several surgical operations.

"The quality of mind or spirit that enables a person to face difficulty during danger, pain without fear and with an extended amount of bravery, is a person who represents the true meaning of the word courage. These two men were not only my protectors, but the saviors of my wellbeing. They too as guardians of the law, play a vital role in the preservation of our society. And although many correction officers like them are not recognized throughout our correctional institutions or by the general public, unethical and unjust recognition does not faze those who are driven by integrity and honorableness."

I never understood why this convict assaulted me like he did, until I was told the nature of his conviction by other convicts and an Assistant District Attorney. Apparently, what happened, the convict who assaulted me was in the gym watching television when a local news brief suddenly appeared to disclose his case and showed his photo. Officer George Rest, released him from the gym and allowed him to loiter on the gallery. The convict was from Yonkers NY, in Westchester County. He was arrested in 1989, convicted and sentence to state prison in 1990, for committing numerous sexual acts against a ten-year-old-girl. He did this in her apartment, on the rooftop of her residential complex and in nearby neighborhood parks. He assaulted her physically, forcibly inserting his penis in her anus on numerous occasions, forcibly penetrated her vagina and forcibly penetrated her orally. Many of these sexual attacks occurred in the presents of her younger brothers. In an attempt to keep them quiet, the convict struck and beat her younger brothers with a stick on numerous occasions and wrapped an electrical wire around the neck of one of them, almost choking him to death.

185

The children were in constant fear and couldn't take it anymore. He, (the convict) was their uncle. His nine year old nephew finally got up the courage and told his mom, (the convict's sister). Understandably so, she lost control of herself when she heard what her children have been going through. She grabbed a kitchen knife in an attempt to stab him, but he managed to take it away from her and stabbed her several times instead. Convicts in the gym who were gathered around the television watching this news brief looked at him and recognized who he was. He then quietly got up and walked away; leaving the gym and finding himself back on Q-gallery.

In this case, the convict was now left with three choices:

(1) He could go back to his cell, lock in and hope others won't try to hurt or kill him;

(2) He could report to the sergeant's office and request voluntary protective custody; or

(3) He could go out with a bang. Assault an officer, be confined to a special housing unit and build up a tough-guy reputation that takes no orders from security staff.

Unfortunately, for him, three was his choice. Such assaults against staff were just one of many methods and tactics used by convicts in order to remove themselves from harm's way. Especially, those convicted of rape, molestation and child murder. Although convicts don't approve of women being raped, many don't see it as a death sentence.

I realized during my career that convicts convicted of rape and child molestation are always the pricks who give an officer the hardest time. They have to, in order to camouflage the nature of their conviction and project a tough-guy image. Now he was safe and secure in a special housing unit away from convict population and any possibility of harm being committed against him. The last I heard of convict 4906, he continues his assaults on officers. He has to, it's the only way to avoid the general population and make others think he's one bad gangster, but a little punk pussy is more of his description. Thanks to memorandums and written documentation, which I kept throughout the years, I was able to reflect on it and refresh my mind to the point of precise recollection. I've also discovered in this entire episode, if you sustain a convict related injury, the facility administration will back you up one-hundred percent of the time.

However, once it's discovered you're seeking psychotherapy or some form of psychiatric care, they automatically assume you're seeking a disability retirement, and you're left to fend for yourself. For some unknown reason, it's almost common practice for the prison administration to reverse an approved compensation claim to a controvertible status. Correction officers on a daily basis are assaulted throughout the state and country. I've personally seen many officers throughout the years sustained serious physical and mental injuries. Unfortunately, there are many who tried to milk the system with bogus compensation claims resulting in many other claims being labeled as such.

In Sing-Sing alone, I've seen a rookie officer sustained numerous bites and twenty-one stab wounds to the head, neck and back with a screwdriver by a convict suffering from AIDS. Other officers slashed with razors across their faces, heads, arms and necks requiring many sutures. I've witnessed feces and urine thrown at an officer face, and within minutes, his face swelled to twice the normal size as a result of a hepatitis infected convict. I witnessed a convict intentionally ram an officer's head against his cell bars, resulting in massive multiple head injuries; a convict physically attack a female officer in an attempt to rape her. Another officer knocked unconscious and brutality stomped resulting in the officer's mental disability and inability to ever speak normal again.

These are just some of many incidents, which take place on a daily basis in our correctional institutions throughout the United States, and never make the local news as would a police officer that sustained similar injuries. These attacks are not only done on security staff, it's also committed upon civilian staff members as well, but at a lower rate. When I was the OIC officer in Sing-Sing's B-block, I had the opportunity and privilege of meeting countless correction officers from all walks of life. Many were assigned permanently and others later left to different law enforcement agencies throughout the country. Most were temporary officers from northern upstate waiting on transfers to other prisons. Many of the officers I've seen enter the department, are people of good moral character, decent men and women who came on the job for employment stability and family health benefits and competitive wages.

Others didn't mind the pay since the cost of living up north was less than that of New York City region. After several years, I could see the changes in many of the officers that enter the prison system. Many unfortunately were hitting the bottle, washing away their sorrows and eventually becoming alcoholics. Some officers became downright nasty in their demeanor and bringing the problems home to their families. Others were getting divorced after fifteen plus years of marriage. Some officers turned to a life of crime, while others used drugs and corruption as a form of relief. Suicide was high there and continues to be a big factor in prison among correction officers today. In Sing-Sing, a rookie officer, that I had the privilege of knowing, threw himself off a seven-story building to his death. Several others shot themselves in the head. In one prison upstate, I was told seven correction officers committed suicide all within a one-year period. In July 2004, a fellow officer and friend from Downstate, who just recently transferred to Upstate facility, tried unsuccessfully to commit suicide by driving his official state vehicle in the path of an oncoming truck, while on duty. When that didn't work he simply walked away from the accident scene into a nearby wooded area, pulled out his state issued service revolver and shot himself once in the head, resulting in his death. According to several sources, the average life span after retirement for a correction officer is five years. I didn't believe those statistics until an employee from the State Insurance Fund of White Plains, New York, told me during a telephone conversation.

"We advise if anyone is going to close a compensation case, the award will only be based on a five year life expectancy."

"Unfortunately, correction officers are much less studied than police officers throughout the US. There is some evidence that correction officers suffer reduced life expectancy, higher divorce rates and greater rates of alcoholism than any other law enforcement officers. Correction officers are three times more likely to commit suicide than to be killed on the job. Studies of a multivariate logistic regression analysis indicate that the risk of suicide among correction officers is thirty-nine percent higher than that of the rest of the working age population," (*Ericson 97*).

STORY CONT:

I returned to the OIC office from W gallery, having completed my good deed of the day with Officer Torres, and made my entry in the logbook. I was now able to relax for a couple of hours until the programs were terminated, and all the convicts returned to their respective locking locations for the afternoon count. Then the whole process will repeat itself all over again. *

There are numerous counts conducted throughout the day by all correctional facilities at every state, county and local level. This is how correctional institutions make sure there are no missing convicts, and no escape has taken place. Should a convict come up missing, a second, third and quite possibly a fourth count could be performed. All efforts will be exhausted in conducting a thorough search before an official alarm and alert of an escape are determined. In the approximate thirteen years, I was a correction officer at Sing-Sing, I can remember several escapes and attempts. The most talked about escape was on April 13, 1941, where correction officer John Hartye and Ossining police officer, James Fagan were both shot and killed by escape convicts Charles McGale and Joe Riordan. The most memorable escape for me personally, was that of a disabled crippled convict who was wheelchair bound for several years. He was always in and out of hospitals, but little did everyone know his disability was just a bluff and a plan that would unfold catching everyone by complete surprise, from Sing-Sing's administrators to hospital doctors and Albany Command Center. He was convicted murders and one day taken to Helen Hayes hospital in Rockland County, NY, by Sing-Sing transporting officers. Sometime during the course of the day while in a hospital elevator and sitting on his wheelchair with crutches on his side for support, the disabled crippled convict stood up from his wheelchair. He proceeded to strike the officer on the head with his crutches and overpowered him, successfully grabbing his service revolver. These were just some of the words the convict said and told to me by the officer.

"The convict hit me with the crushes, dropping me to the floor. He took my gun and said, stay down motherfucker. Now, give me a fucking reason why I shouldn't kill you? I told him, please don't kill me, it's not worth it."

189

The doors to the elevator opened at that precise moment and the disabled crippled convict ran out of Helen Hayes hospital like a steroid induced athletic track star in search of an Olympic gold medal. The convict preceded to pistol whip a woman out in the hospital parking lot and carjacked her vehicle. While driving down a town road the convict realized he was traveling in the wrong direction and decided to make an illegal u–turn when he was spotted by a local police officer on patrol. Unaware he was an escaped murderer who just assaulted a correction officer, pistol whipped and carjacked a woman, the police officer gave chase. After several miles of being pursued the car driven by the escapee ran out of gas. He again ran like a bat out of hell, but was later found hiding in someone's backyard shed and was apprehended by state police. Several years later, this same cripple convict was stabbed to death by another convict at an upstate maximum security prison, 'Karma's a bitch.' During an autopsy conducted by local medical examiners, it was discovered the convict had swallowed numerous balloons filled with heroin, which was sitting at the bottom of his stomach.

Another Sing-Sing escape I remembered was from the prison school building. The school is located directly in front of the Metro North railroad tracks, used by thousands of New York and Connecticut commuters daily. Three convicts managed to slip down a bathroom window, cut out a hole in a fence adjacent to the railroad tracks, and jump down approximately twenty-feet below onto the tracks. Homemade smoke bombs for distraction and a thirty-foot rope braided from shoelaces enabled them to escape. One convict sprained or broke his ankle during his landing, but was still successful in hopping away like a wounded little bunny rabbit. He was probably a pro in hopscotch during his adolescent years. They didn't get very far though; all three were recaptured within forty-eight hours. Officers found one hiding in a neighborhood boat on someone's property. Another was found in a nearby parked vehicle as a result of the windows condensation. He was without a shirt and apparently freezing his little balls off. The sprained hopper was found hopping along with a one hundred dollar bill trying to hail a neighborhood taxi cab back to Brooklyn. When officers discovered the escape in progress, they ran into the bathroom where the escape initially took place and were met with lots of mayonnaise poured onto the floor.

New York State Correction Emergency Response Team

The concept behind the mayonnaise was to make it easier to slip through the window bars and caused the first responding officers to slip and fall as they quickly entered the school's bathroom. They all planned a good escape, but forgot to plan their getaway. I can only imagine what ex-convict and escape artist Willie Sutton of the 1930s would have said about their well planned and thought-out escape. He probably would have written Sing-Sing's warden a letter requesting to push the Old Sparky button, (electric chair) on all three. Then I'm sure he would have told the state correction officials to keep the fifty dollars paid to executioners during the early 1900s.

"No thank you. This one is on me fellas."

For prison escapes and unusual situations like this, Sing-Sing correctional facility has an elite team that springs into action every time. This unit is called the Corrections Emergency Response Team, (CERT). These officers are highly trained in prison disturbances, riot control, escapes, road blocks, vehicles searches, firearms, chemical agents, extractions, fire combating, rescues and many other tactical procedures needed for bringing stabilization and security to an unstable environment.

191

They are also known as, "The Orange Crush." As part of their exercise, these team members are made to enter clouds of chemical agents, better known to the public as tear gas. The idea is to get used to its effects while limiting any chances of injuries to themselves or others. Total control and concentration during an uncontrollable situation is what they live for. While other law enforcement trains for gun battles on an individual basis using state of the art mechanical devices, the response team trains for physical battles. These combats are sometimes against one hundred to six hundred plus convicted felons, using batons, chemical agents, common sense and a prayer. They're dedicated, honorable, brave men and women correction officers of New York State Department of Correctional Services, who I personally had the privilege and honor of being a part of for many years. When you take under consideration the state correction officers' pay and all the responsibilities that come with being a public servant in state prison, you can't help but wonder why they do it? I can personally think of several words: bravery, courage, loyalty and commitment. Some would say they're crazy, while others think it's just a waste of too much personal time. However, when you're being held hostage, involved in a riot or need stability in your correctional facility, these are the guys you want to see coming through the doors and reaching down to pull you out. During the terrorist attacks of 9-11, the NYS correction emergency response team was positioned throughout New York State guarding vulnerable structures of great significance, like the Indian Point Nuclear Energy Center. The NYC correction's emergency response team was responsible for the loading and unloading of human body parts from refrigerated trucks. Hoorah!

STORY CONT:

All programs and recreation were now terminated for the facility count. All convicts were reporting back to their housing units for the afternoon count. Gallery officers opened the cells, and everyone took their post to monitor convict movement. Yard officer Torres took a position just inside the block's rear doorway, along with other officers and began a random pat frisk for any weapons or contraband. Another officer took a position outside the gym door and followed the same routine.

192

What was a quiet housing block for the last three hours now became a place where hundreds of men were talking, yelling, stomping feet, and slamming cell doors. Officers were also slamming steel brake bar handles, a common method use to let convicts know their cells are opened, and it's time to lock in. The noise is unlike any other place on earth and just like in a baseball stadium, it's almost impossible to hear yourself speak. Like clockwork, came the questions that should have been asked to gallery officers prior to the release of any programs.

"Yo, co;

"Can I get a toilet paper before I lock in?"

"You forgot to open my cell!"

"Did I get a visit?"

"Did you search my cell?"

"My toilet doesn't flush!"

"Can I get a tooth paste?"

"Cell number R-122 is empty can I swap my mattress?"

"What's for chow this afternoon?"

Yo, co this and yo, co that. It goes on and on with no end to the questions until those familiar words are verbally announced, 'on the count' then all questions cease. Through all the chaos, gallery officers finally secured their galleries, and it was time to let the keeplocks in from recreation before the actual count officially commenced. Officers were on standby and extra officers stood on the galleries to monitor the movement as they came up. Many of the keeplocks like to run onto other galleries, either to look for trouble or receive items from other convicts. I stepped out the office and instructed other officers to let the keeplocks in. They began entering the block and for some-odd reason began hanging around the OIC area. I quickly responded by asking officers to lock them in.

"Hey, fellas, let's get these guys back to their galleries and into their cells for the count!"

Several convicts yelled out.

"Hell no, we ain't locking in!"

I didn't take that statement seriously simply because there's not a day that goes by without one convict saying those same exact words. I instructed the convicts to find their cells.

"Alright, guys, let's get back upstairs and find your cells."

"Fuck that!"

Another convict yelled as he punched a fellow convict in the face. Then all hell broke loose. Four convicts began fighting among themselves, another climbed over the south gate leading to Q-gallery in search of a convict he fought with earlier in the week. We had thirty convicts in the area, and half were out of control, fighting, running from the officers and others refusing to lock in. Officers began responding from every direction to assist. Hearing all the commotion, the rookie officer ran inside from the corridor and immediately got involved. Just as he reached in an attempt to grab a convict, another convict reached into his waistband, pulled out a steel shank and while attempting to stab another convict, he instead stabbed the rookie officer clear through his hand exiting the other side.

"Oh, shit, officer Bermudez, I've been stabbed!"

I immediately chased the convict who stabbed the officer. The convict ran over to V-gallery, and before I could apprehend him another convict who for reasons unknown, punched him square in the face causing him to drop the shank. Seeing this, I ceased the moment and took the assaulted convict to the floor. As I was attempting to restrain him, other officers saw I was involved in a fierce struggle and jumped in to help. Alarms were being activated, and chaos was breaking out in every direction. Officers from other housing units and the messhall were responding to our alarms. We finally subdued the convict who stabbed the rookie officer and removed him from the area. As I stood up and my adrenalin subsided, I felt a slight pain throughout my back and chest. I quickly looked at myself for any signs of blood, but instead noticed many footprints on my uniform shirt caused by my fellow officers who somehow thought I was some little German roach on their living room floor. "Damn!" I yelled out, feeling the pain. "Who's the bad guy here?" After the thirty-minute melee, the block was finally under control, and convicts were subdued. All this chaos caused by one convict out in the yard who dared them to do so. Many of those involved were taken to the special housing unit. Some were put in their cells, and others were taken to the facility hospital for observation. I thanked all the officers who helped and showed their endless and flawless courage as they left the housing block. It was later discovered Officer Robert Bermudez, (no relations) was the German roach stomping officer who left his size seven shoe tattooed on my uniform shirt and in my soul.

194

The count was now in progress, and we had to conduct it. All the officers were heated and could be heard yelling on the galleries, 'On the count!'

Angry gallery officers were now walking the galleries with their escorts counting the convicts and telling a few to shut up. Incidents like this can get an officer's blood pumping, and the absence of fear takes over rational thinking and common sense decisions. *

Counts are the most important part of the day and regardless of how big of a melee, it must be conducted. Procedures for a count are as follows: Those who will remain in other locations (Outside of blocks) will be considered an out count and carried by the officers at that location. Other locations include work details, outside hospitals, other housing units, courts, trips and so on. Transportation officer call in the counts to the facility watch commander, (lieutenant) and verbally confirm custody of the convicts. The same applies for those officers on outside work details, including but not limited to construction workers. Block officers take the count and transfer the information onto a count slip. They in turn hand it over to an area sergeant who then verifies it and has it sent to the watch commander's office along with the security staff count. If any discrepancies are discovered, the count will be sent back to its original location for correction. Sometimes an incorrect count could result in a write-up by a supervisor.

STORY CONT:

I finally called the count in and verbally verified it with the watch-commander. We sat back and began talking about the keeplock incident. Officers appeared to be getting fed up with the keeplock s and their refusal to always lock in after recreation. Some were even willing to start escorting them back to their cell three at a time to prevent further incidents like this from reoccurring. As we were in the office debating policies and procedures, a fairly new gallery officer came down to the OIC office with some news about a convict up on his gallery.

"Hey, officer Bermudez, can we talk? There's a convict on my gallery that is seriously hated by other convicts."

"That's nothing new, but why is that?"

"Well, the convict has several photos on his locker that can be seen by other convicts and... I interrupted him.

"What's wrong with having photos on your locker, most convicts have photos on lockers?"

"Well, that's true, but these photos are of his family members. His father appears to be a captain and in full NYC police uniform. His two brothers in NYC police uniform and one sister in State Troopers uniform."

"Shit, this is unheard of, what cell number is he in?"

"He's on S/X gallery, cell, S-200."

"Let's go up there."

I approached the convict's cell and asked him very quietly to approach the bars.

"Why are those photos being displayed on your locker like that?"

"That's my family—my pop, my bros and my sister."

"I understand, but having photos of family members in law enforcement uniforms is a no-no in prison, don't you know that? Other convicts don't like that and may label you a snitch."

"I don't give a shit what other convicts think, this is my family. Unlike them, I'm a criminal not a cop."

"Well, I just thought I'd give you a piece of advice and make you aware of the possibilities of retaliation by other convicts who hate law enforcement."

"I'm not worried about them officer."

I instructed the officer to keep a close watch of the convict and of his cell. *

Although Sing-Sing had many convicted former law enforcement people mingling in general population, their past professions or family photos were not advertised or made available to other convicts. In B-block's movement and control office, we had a convict clerk who was a former NYC housing police officer. He apparently hammered his wife to death in a jealous rage, and although he tried to cover his tracks, forensics eventually caught up to him. Many convicts in Sing-Sing were considered high-profile cases and others celebrity killers. Another convict was a former police officer from Westchester County, who executed an Afro-American man by shooting him several times in the back as he lay on a parking lot floor.

196

This guy was a real character and arrogant. I can recall informing him he had a family visit while he was playing handball with other convicts at Downstate facility. I guess he felt as though his family visit wasn't as important as his game. He continued playing and after several more minutes the game was over. He then went back to his cell and decided to take a shower. Unfortunately for him, the facility count was called and he now had to wait for the count's verification before he could be taken to his visit. He became agitated and angry at the delay, and this was our short conversation.

"Hey, officer, what's the holdup on the visit escort?"

"The count is now in progress, and you'll have to wait for its verification."

"You mean to tell me my people are going to sit in the visit room without me for the next hour or so?"

"Yep, I'm afraid so."

"What kind of shit is that, what if they decide not to wait?"

"You know what; you should have thought about that and thought about them when you were out there playing handball with the other convicts. I have to get back to work. I'll let you out for the visit when the count verification is announced."

"Now I see why you hacks can't become police officers."

"I'm not the one doing twenty-five years to life for murder you are," and the conversation ended.

I couldn't believe this guy was once a police officer, then again, looking back on his conviction, why shouldn't I? During my short tenure as a transportation officer, I traveled to many facilities throughout New York State, from Attica State Prison to Brooklyn's house of detention. I came across and guarded countless of convicted former law enforcement officers, police officers, correction officers, deputy sheriffs, state troopers and even a former commission of correction's employee who was responsible for creating departmental directives. One prisoner I remembered breaking in at Sing-Sing as a rookie officer in 1987. He was convicted of having sex with his twelve-year old daughter. Another correction officer had his testicle sack sliced wide open with a metal can lid by a convict he was anally penetrating.

Another individual I guarded was a young former NYC police officer. His neighbor requested that he counseled their daughter for her wild behavior. He had done the same with another daughter who was previously on the wrong track. When their older eighteen-year-old daughter arrived home one day, she questioned the whereabouts of her younger sister. Her parents informed her she was being schooled by the neighbor police officer. She became upset and stated the neighbor police officer had raped her over a six-year period. She then stated her sexual assaults were taking place on the building's rooftop. They all ran up to the rooftop and found their neighbor police officer having sexual intercourse with their eleven-year-old daughter. I've guarded and seen convicts who were considered special monitoring cases or criminal celebrities as they're called and considered by many in the public media. Among them were Son of Sam killer of six, Happy Land club killer of eighty-seven, Brooklyn Zodiac killer of three, Central Park preppy killer of one, Amityville killer of six, Park Plaza Hotel killer of nine, Christmas Eve Long Island wife killer, who once sued an officer for allegedly, mentioning his case in the presence of other convicts.

Another was a convict who was responsible for the contract death of Brian Rooney, a NYS parole officer. In 1986, while assigned to R/W gallery in B-block, I took notice of many convicts and officers engaged in stares and conversations concerning one particular convict. The conversation seems to glorify or idealize this individual who they referred to as 'Fat-Cat.' I've seen the convict on numerous occasions, never had a problem with him and never suspected he would be a drug kingpin on the streets of NY. Then again, keeping a low profile is the best method in deterring noticeability by law enforcement. There were many convicts in prison with so-call street reputation and fifteen minutes of public media fame. The reputation and glorification by his fellow convicts and narrow minded correction officers didn't matter to me; on a contrary, now he get my attention and not in a good way. I was approached by an officer who with highly gratifying feelings told me.

"You see that guy, (Fat-Cat) he's worth millions and millions on the streets. You and I could never make in a lifetime what he's made in a year."

I looked at him and wondered how easy it would probably be to pay this mutt off with a couple thousands; then I replied with a question.

"What good are millions and millions when you have to spend the rest of your life in prison and the millions you made are confiscated by the government? I think I'll stick with the forty thousand plus salary a year, keep my freedom and get to go home to my family every night."

That was twenty-one years ago. No need to wonder even now, whose better off. I think we all know the answer to that. I was angry to discover state parole officer, Brian Rooney, was never mentioned honorably in their discussion or glorified by those correction officers who glorified the convict like some prophet sent down from heaven. It was quite obvious this celebrity status was going to have a damaging effect on my ability to perform my job. I needed to put a stop to the glorification, put the pressure on the convicts and bring this escapade back to normalcy. My first step was to remove those who posed the problem in the first place, the convicts who came onto the gallery without authorization. Then report those officers who left their assigned post. I spoke with the block sergeant and informed him of the problems we were having on R/W gallery. I began requesting that all officers who were not assigned to the gallery take their recreational visits elsewhere, since all they wanted was to see Fat-Cat, and glorify his existence. Convicts who I found loitering on the gallery were issued misbehavior reports and in some cases confined to their cells.

The pressure was building and some were labeling me a racist, but the gallery environment was soon tranquil and the constant traffic of observers was gone from both sides. What soon followed subconsciously augmented my sense of dislike toward this so call Fat-Cat and dislike for those officers. Television news reported a NYC police officer named Edward "Eddie" R. Byrne was killed while on duty and members of Fat-Cat's gang were somehow involved in his execution. Listening to the news report and feeling the anger, I remember one night preparing for work for the following day. My sights were set on either losing my job or losing my life, but regardless of what the outcome would be, I was going to be the next tainted celebrity. As I drove to work the following day I thought of officer, Eddie Byrne, who was just twenty-two.

I also wondered about my own brother who was a NYC police officer. I finally reached the prison and found myself on R/W gallery. I asked the nightshift officer how was his tour.

"The night was quiet, no problems."

"What about that Fat Cat convict?"

"He's gone. Officers and supervisors came here early this morning and took him away."

"What…where did they take him?"

"I have no idea. All I know is, he's was gone in a matter of seconds."

That was the last I saw or ever heard of Fat Cat. Many roomers made its way around the prison. Some said he was shipped out during the night in a helicopter just outside of eighteen grounds. Others said he turned state's evidence and testified against others for a lighter sentence. Some said correction and police officers from the New York City region wanted to do him harm through prison contracts and was therefore moved for his own protection. We definitely believed the last roomer simply because many officers felt this way. An officer later pointed out a Thorazine induced convict named Pappy, who actually killed officer Eddie Byrne and not Fat-Cat as previously thought. Nevertheless, these are just some of the so-call celebrity killers I've encountered or guarded throughout my career. Another so-call celebrity killer was the NYS lottery killer, a millionaire who won 17.5 million dollars. He killed his pregnant lover, a married woman with whom he claimed to have fathered a child, but was only convicted for killing her father instead, a wealthy real estate entrepreneur. Others were the killer of our first NYS woman correction officer, attempted killer of nine NYC police officers, (who is now deceased) the Long Island Railroad killer of six, Malcolm X killer, West Coast rapper convicted of rape and the Palm Sunday Massacre killer of ten, who I personally had an interesting encounter with. In 1985, while working as a rookie correction officer at Downstate correctional facility, I entered a complex and informed the officers, I was ready to strut my stuff and show those old timers this young buck was no buff and no pushover. I was born and raised in Brooklyn, NY. Bottom-line, Downstate facility and Fishkill, NY, wasn't ready for this gun-ho. Paperwork, direct orders or verbal commands were out of the question.

I was ready to rumble the convicts and show them what New York City society has made of me. I've seen many of Muhammad Ali's fights and seen The Rumble in the Jungle. I've fought many fights out on the streets of Brooklyn, and I lost just as much. Acceptance of those loses wasn't a problem for me. I entered the bubble, (an enclosed office) and was met by three officers. We introduced ourselves as I surveyed the area and kept a close vigilant of the cells. The officers took notice and saw I was ready to work and ready for the unexpected. The introductions began.

"I'm officer Mojo; this is officer, Joe and officer, John."

"How you doing, I'm officer Bermudez, and I'm ready fellas."

"Ready, for what?"

"Whatever you guys want…take no names, kick some ass and take down these mutts."

"Oh, so you're ready to fight these mutts."

"Ready when you are, that's right," I said courageously while cracking my knuckles.

The officers looked at one another, and for several seconds huddled like football players trying to come up with a strategic plan. They looked up to a cell while mumbling their words and mentioning my name on several occasions. They all appeared to agree on something and broke the huddle with smiles on their faces.

"What did you say your name was again?"

"The name is Bermudez, B-e-r-m-u-d-e-z."

"Ok, that's what I thought you said. Can you do us a favor officer?"

"Sure, no problem, what's up?"

"Go up to cell 1-F-5; tell him to come to the cell door. Show him your nametag and tell him these words. Yeah, that's right. I'm a family member ass-hole."

"Who the hell is in cell 1-F-5?"

"We'll tell you later, just go up there and tell the convict what we instructed you to say?"

I exited the bubble making sure my baton and equipment were in place. I cracked some knuckles again and made my way to cell 1-F-5. As I approached the cell I notice other convicts who were standing by their doors walked away. I sensed they were somewhat afraid of me, and why not? I was young, in shape, clean cut and could project a tough-guy image in a drop of a hat.

I quietly reached the cell and looked inside. Sitting on the bed was a black male convict with a notorious look on his face.

Ugly son of a bitch, I thought to myself.

He obviously knew of my impending arrival and was staring at the door as I stepped up.

"Hey, convict, come to the door?"

"Come to the door for what?"

"Come to the door because I said come to the door."

The convict got up from his bed, walked toward the cell door and looked at me with a hateful and disgusting look.

"Yeah, what do you want?"

"You know how to read?"

"Yeah, I know how to read."

"Good, now look at my nametag. Yeah, that's right Bermudez and I'm a family member too."

The convict's eyes opened up to the size of cup saucers, and while letting out a loud scream he reached through his cell door and tried to grab my uniform shirt ripping off a button. I immediately jumped back and fell to the floor landing on my rear end. The baton flew out of its baton-ring, my pen and writing pad fell out of it pockets. My gun-ho attitude went right out the fucking window, instantly converting me into the soft Pillsbury Boy. I reached for the stair railing and lost my balance slipping on several steps. I managed to pick up the baton, went back to the cell door and raised the baton at the convict who quickly retrieved his arm back inside his cell. I could hear laughter coming from the unit. I looked toward the bubble and saw three red faces laughing their heads off.

I knew then I've been tricked. This was a lesson I would learn from and one I would never forget. Just another life's lesson taught through hands-on life experience. I can feel the shame being displayed through the rush of blood to the face and warmth to the ears. I remember thinking to myself.

"Par carajo, nunca mas," (Hell with that, never again).

I entered the bubble as the convict kept screaming.

"Come back motherfucker, come back!"

I looked at the officers and thanked them for the encounter.

"Holy shit fellas, what's up with that? The convict tried to grab my shirt and rip my heart out."

After several minutes of trying to regain their composure the officers asked me to sit down and explained the circumstances surrounding the convict's violent and spontaneous outburst.

On April 15, 1984, in Brooklyn, NY, the convict entered a home on Palm Sunday, with a firearm. In the home were a family of two Latina women and eight children. His target was a man name Enrique Bermudez, but he was not home at the time. The convict then killed the two women and killed the eight children execution style by shooting them all in the head. One child managed to hide and survive the massacre. Most of those killed in the apartment had the same last name, Bermudez.

"Oh, shit, I remember that incident. That's the ass-hole that killed all those people?"

'Yep, that's him," said officer Mojo.

"I see. So seeing my name Bermudez, led him to believe I was a family member."

"Oh, yeah, now you're going to have to be careful everywhere you go in this jail. That convict is going to remember your face, so stay on your toes."

"Yeah, no shit. That son of a bitch ever comes close to me I'm going to let him have it."

"That's if he doesn't get to you first."

After recovering from the encounter with the convict, I understood the reason for his outburst. The last I heard this killer was scheduled for parole in 2010. That's very little consolation for those family members who are still with us and the one child who witness and survived the massacre. I seriously doubt he'll survive a year out on the streets if paroled. Another killer was the NYC Zodiac, a serial killer who I had the pleasure of conducting a routine cell search on. He was being treated like a Hollywood celebrity and being provided with personal necessities by nonprofit organizations and college students. The catch was simple: let us write about your life as a serial killer or interview you, and we'll send you free US postal stamps, notepads, envelopes and anything else allowable in prison for the rest of your life. Other convicts have funds put into their accounts with personal checks or money orders by private parties, while others receive food packages, clothing, cosmetics items, holiday goody bags (gifts) and many other items as a form of payment for their participation in telling their stories without any of the victims or their families ever knowing about it.

During the holiday season while conducting a security patrol in B-block, I was approached by an older convict who walked with a cane. He apparently was upset because a holiday goody bag was not placed in his cell. I explained not all the goody bags were given out on the gallery and informed him he may have to wait until the following day for a goody bag; that was when the next shipment was expected to arrive. The convict became upset and grabbed his walking cane.

"Yo, officer; if there's ever a riot I'm going to look for you and rape your ass."

Quite naturally this made me extremely angry. However, in a cool, calm and collected voice, and making him feel as though his threats were successful, I stated the following.

"I tell you what, let me double check on that goody bag for you, I'll be right back,"

"Yeah, that's what I'm talking about, do that, get my fucking goody bag."

After conducting a background check with a few reliable sources, I discovered the convict; between 1973 and 1974, at the Park Plaza Hotel in New York City, committed the acts of burglary, robbery, attempted robbery, rapes and multiple murders, thus being labeled by the news media, the Park Plaza Hotel serial killer. During the course of these crimes, he intentionally caused the death of nine elderly women by way of suffocation. Now he wanted a goody bag for the holidays, or he'll rape me in the next riot. One hour later I went back upstairs to have a talk with him and found him sleeping in his cell. I struck the cell bars with my baton, and he nearly fell off his bed.

He didn't like the idea of tapping on his cell bars with the baton and became boisterously vulgar; and so did I.

'What the fuck you do that for, your asshole or something?"

"What I do that for, because if there's ever a riot in this prison I'm going to forget I'm an officer, come directly to this cell, take that cane and shove it nine inches up your old ass. I figured you're never too old for being someone's bitch and nine inches in your ass for the nine elderly women you killed, you lowlife prick. You still want that goody bag?"

"You can't talk to me like that. I'm old enough to be your fucking father. What's your name, I want to know your name?"

"The name is, Bermudez, ass-wipe." I didn't think my approach was professional by any means. The interpersonal communication skills technique went out the window, but there were moments in prison where negotiations, communications, comprehension and understanding wasn't an option, and stooping down to another's level was the remedy of the day. The convict went back to sleep and never spoke to me again, at least not directly. Convicts in Sing-Sing and throughout NYS, receive holiday Christmas goody bags containing toothpaste, tooth brushes, soaps, shampoos, conditioners, deodorants, mouthwash, combs, tissues, notepads, pencils and other items, all compliments of an American nonprofit organization. Other well known nonprofit organizations donated holiday cards throughout the year and Christmas toys for their children. The countless of toys are given out to the children while visiting the convicts in the prison during the holidays. Other toys are brought to their homes or arrangements are made to have them picked up by their families. Again, no such program that I'm aware of are available for crime victims or their children.

When convicts are newly incarcerated and brought into a state correctional system, they are supplied with green uniform coats, jackets, hats, two different color sweatshirts, two different color shirts, pants, t–shirts, underwear, socks, sneakers, boots, belts, blankets, sheets, pillow cases, pillows, laundry bags, envelopes, writing pads, pencils, pens, toilet papers, soaps, tooth brushes w/case, toothpaste, matches, rule books, a Bible and ID card. Other free professional services include counseling, radiological exam, physical exam, medical exam, psychological exam, eye exam, and dental care. It's all part of the state correctional reception process. While sitting in an office at Downstate facility kitchen, a convict from the streets of Coney Island approached me at the office and told me he needed to show me something of importance. I allowed him to enter the office.

"Hey, officer Bermudez, take a look at this?"

He showed me a million-dollar smile, an entire prosthodontic oral reconstruction and then some. As a result from many years of neglect, he was suffering from gum decease, stained, broken, cracking and missing teeth.

Doctors at the facility were able to create a perfect smile for him that included form, function and beauty. Reverse engineer bite surfaces, tooth shape for inlays, onlays, veneers, crowns, bridges, the whole works. It was a streamline dental reconstruction process with very little discomfort, little recovery time and the cost was in the thousands. As I sat there looking at him, it reminded me of a single stay at home mom named Margarita Pereira Morales from Brooklyn, NY, who had no dental care her entire life. She struggled throughout her life trying to make ends meet. Her children were always her priorities and although her health was also important to her, many hospitals and dental offices didn't seem to think so and constant denial for medical care became part of her life. She never stopped seeking a remedy to her problems, never committed the smallest of sins and never blamed society as a whole for all the discrimination she endured throughout her life as a woman. When she did receive the dental care she longed for, it was only with the help of her sister Maria Martinez Pereira, who paid out of pocket.

Margarita was now faced with a new challenge, cancer. She became terminally ill and was hospitalized on numerous occasions only to recover and bounce back better than before. Margarita was from Monte Santo, in Vieques, Puerto Rico. She was a woman of great wisdom, tough and beautiful. She didn't like criminals by any means, but for some-odd reason, she didn't like correction officers either. Margarita was a firm believer; if you can't make it in United States of America without a legitimate physical or mental disability, you shouldn't be here. She sincerely believed this land of opportunity was becoming the land of the opportunist. Recent downfalls of powerful private corporations and CEO's confirmed her theory. When she finally began to feel better and her health improved, she moved to central Florida where she began a new life. She needed health care soon as possible, so she decided to apply for a job at a nearby department store, Ross. She was delighted to discover they actually gave her an employment application without questioning her age. So on July 16, 2002, she quickly went home and delightfully filled out her application. She began putting her plans in motion, searching for local dentists, health insurance providers and discussing all the potentials and possibilities of a new life in Florida.

The thought of finding new employment at her age sixty-four, was enough to somehow trigger a positive chemical reaction inside her brain that would result in a dramatic physical and spiritual improvement. She was a fighter; there was no doubt about that. Just like many others who have nothing, yet know the value and importance of appreciating the smallest of things in life, it didn't take much to make Margarita happy. On January 07, 2003, less than six months later, Margarita Morales Pereira died from cancer complications. She was my beloved mother; my heart, my inspiration and my connection to family roots. These are the descent people of America, who are ignored and forgotten. Should she have decided some time during the course of her life to commit a heinous crime; she would have never experienced the numerous medical care denials. On a contrary, she would've had her oral reconstruction done years ago. Her children would've been cared for in one form or another by social services, and most importantly, she would probably be alive today. As I sat there and observed the convict who entered my office at Downstate facility kitchen with his brand new ten-thousand smile, my first thought was to put fist through his mouth.

While the incarcerated are receiving upscale quality dental care, with no borders or barriers of bureaucracy in its process, I'm battling endlessly in an attempt to find a dental office that will accept our dental insurance here in Central Florida. When I finally did find a dental office that was willing to take my money, 'not my insurance' my diagnosis was beyond gingivitis and in the early stages of periodontal disease. The total out of pocket expense for rectifying my little problem went beyond a thousand dollars and the bouncing around throughout Central Florida in search of doctors who specialized in my particular area of dentistry was similar to that of a pinball machine. Before receiving the dental care I so desperately needed I was informed by a doctor, who evaluated my condition.

"Don't worry Mr. Bermudez, most doctors would agree that after a good scaling procedure, deep cleaning and some good root planing, you may not require any further active treatment, including surgical therapy. But always keep in mind; you will require ongoing maintenance therapy to maintain healthy gums, like flossing every day, even twice in one day."

If flossing four to five times daily as I do and brushing after every meal is not maintenance, I don't know what is. Naturally, everyone knows or should know smoking only exacerbates the problem and contributes to periodontal disease. When I did smoke, this was the main cause of my periodontal disease and professional opinions, and instructions were short of an insult. When I didn't smoke, it was attributed to a heredity gene and about half of the patients who entered a doctor's office were associated to this risk factor. If you had no history of periodontal disease in your family then quite simply put, your inability to correctly perform maintenance led to your poor hygiene. No one was willing to care for me until I paid cash or had insurance they participated in. After finally receiving the perio scaling care and surgery I needed, I discovered a new meaning for the word, butchered. For almost two years I was left in substantial pain and drinking out of a straw like a patient with a broken jaw. I asked myself, whatever happened to "*Primum no Nocere - First, do no harm*," the oath all Dentist swear by?

Frustrated, I gave up and contacted those at the Florida Department of Health and Florida Board of Dentistry expressing my concerns, grievances and unfortunate experiences. The moral of the story is, if prison convicts were subjected to the same healthcare bureaucracy that the average American experiences, you can rest-assure that prisons throughout this country will riot.

STORY CONT:

I came down from S-gallery after warning the convict of his family photographs in law enforcement uniforms and reported it to the block sergeant who later ordered the convict to remove the photos off the locker. I found the officers warming up their lunches in the coatroom where a microwave is kept. They had very little time left before the convict meal was called. There's no such thing as a lunch period or lunch hour in prison for correction officers, although they do find the time to eat. Hopefully, they won't be found eating state food, (meals served to convicts). If an officer is found by a supervisor eating state food and is written up, it could cost them a two hundred fifty dollar deduction on their payroll check. *

208

That's another one of those things about correctional food policies I never understood. I can remember working on numerous occasions in a wall post sixteen, located just outside of a messhall loading dock where all the trash is dumped into large steel dumpsters after every meal. I've seen hundreds of plastic cases of unopened bread loafs, fresh onions and peppers being dumped into the trash. Yet, we insisted and instructed convicts during the meals not to take more than four slices of bread, six if the extra two slices are end caps. I once asked a convict worker standing outside on the loading dock.

"Excuse me, what are you guys going to do with all those vegetables?"

"We're going to throw it away officer, why you want for your family and friends?"

Other convicts began laughing as though there was something wrong with the question.

"No, I don't want for the family; although I'm sure they wouldn't mind. I was just wondering why it's not taken to a local homeless shelter and used for their dinner instead."

"Damn, officer, you're right. I never thought of it that way."

"I guess not, neither did the state. And you know what, by the time we're done talking about this, one child around the world already starved to death—food for thought!"

The convicts looked at me, as though I was some sort of hired humanitarian activist from a nonprofit group or organization filing a verbal grievance or voicing my opinion for the sake of humanity. They all walked away without anything further to say.

STORY CONT:

The officers were now done with their lunches and the half-hour of conversing. All the morning documentation was completed, and the afternoon count was submitted and verified. Now the whole routine repeated itself over again, afternoon messhall workers report downstairs for work and convict population steps back into their cells in preparation for the afternoon programs. The block sergeant in the messhall got the clearance for movement and the officer on the bridge, who has the list of galleries in order, contacted me via telephone for the commencing of messhall operations. I in turn, notify the gallery officers via loud speakers and telephone.

This morning's messhall movement was bottom to top galleries Q/V, R/W, S/X, T/Y and U/Z. The afternoon will be the opposite, top to bottom galleries. Convicts like this idea and it makes them feel as though favoritism doesn't play a part in the messhall operation. The meal was in progress, and galleries were entering the messhall. The block convicts appeared to be very quiet and lawful in their movement and activity for some unknown reason. When this code of silence usually happens, it spells trouble. I even received phone calls from several officers who took notice of this unusual behavior.

"Good afternoon, officer Bermudez speaking."

"This is officer Rosenblum, from U/Z gallery. I notice the block has been very quiet?"

"It is quiet. I received calls from other officers, and they too are wondering what's going on. Let me call the block sergeant and see what he makes of it. I'll get right back to you."

I made the call to the messhall-bridge and spoke with the supervisor in command.

"B-block messhall-bridge, this is Sergeant Johnson."

"Sergeant, this is officer Bermudez. I don't know if you noticed, but the block convicts appear to be very quiet this afternoon?"

"Yes, officer Bermudez, I noticed that too."

"What do you make of it sergeant?"

"Well, I think with all the keeplock commotion we had in the last couple of hours, the fighting and stabbing, the convicts probably think we're all a little on the edge. I guess they realized we've had more than enough of our share of violence for one day. This is their way of saying, 'leave them alone."

"Okay, sergeant thanks. I'll pass it on to others."

That was sergeant, Carl Johnson a man of wisdom, knowledge and professionalism at its best. *

He was indeed, one of the best supervisors and human beings any person could ever work with and work for. He had since passed on, but left in our hearts and in our minds countless of positive memories. As a supervisor, he did not only show us all how to be good correction officers, but honorable and respectful people. Cool, calm and collective, Sergeant Carl Johnson never sidetracked from his character under any circumstances.

His level-headedness and control made the difference in quelling disturbances, isolated incidents and keeping his officers in their places. His sharp appearance and extremely polished shoes set the stage for many other officers who worked B-block. For those who didn't know Carl Johnson and entered B-block half dressed, he would make it clear they're uniform appearance didn't have to be as sharp as his, but you better damn well come close to it the next time you're assigned to his housing block. He certainly will be missed by all, but most importantly missed by his loved ones. I was fortunate to have worked with such a man, befriend him and experience through him the process of honorableness. His partner, Sergeant Donavon Sherrod was no exception. He too was a great supervisor to work with and work for. Notorious for his southern accent and those jerry curls, that somehow seem to surpass time, we all looked forward to seeing him daily. Years would pass on and those jerry curls somehow seemed to fit right into the latest hair styles. I'm afraid he may have also found the fountain of youth. I recently saw Donavon Sherrod, who's been retired now for several years and still look like the same person I saw back in 1985, when I first met him. As supervisors and men, Donavon and Carl had many similarities in their demeanor. His level-headedness and control also made the difference in quelling disturbances, isolated incidents and keeping his officers in their place. Donavon's sharp appearance and extremely polished shoes also set the stage for many other officers who worked B-block. It was obvious to all the officers and many supervisors, Sherrod and Johnson were a unique team and when they worked together, we all worked together.

L-R Judy, Donavon, Lydia and Al, photo by Bermudez

One without the other in a day's work was like entering a classroom in school and waiting for your favorite teacher to arrive, but getting a substitute instead. God most definitely broke the mold when he created those two men. Donavon recently and sadly lost his beloved wife Judy, of twenty-four plus years, she'll be missed by many, but let us also remember:

"Like many others before us; as our eyes close forever we won't know we're gone like those who stand looking down at us; we won't know this life ever existed, like those who stay behind us. What we should know and for what it's worth; is that I can't imagine honorable, decent and productive human beings not being blessed with the resurrection of another life and finding themselves in the company of their loved ones once again. We hate to see them go and unselfishly suffer their permanent absence. However, always remember when it's your time to leave this world; it's also your time to enter there's in unification, as others will enter yours at their demise. You will not resemble who you were, nor will you know you both existed in this life, but you will surely reunite and start your lives together again as two completely different people in appearance, yet with the same heart and soul."

Like Carl Johnson and Donavon Sherrod; there were many other honorable people who I crossed paths with during my lifetime and haven't forgotten.

In the late 1970s, into the early part of the 1980s, I was employed at a shoe factory in Coney Island. Unfortunately, for two consecutive years, just weeks before Christmas, I was laid off. The layoff period was only for a couple of months, until after the holidays, but the financial hardship that would follow was detrimental to the family and to our Christmas spirits. In early September 1981, it happened again. The layoff slips came down, only this time it was two months before Thanksgiving Day, and this layoff period would go far beyond February 1982. Times were hard again—the monthly rent was past due and I had to make good for the family or we wouldn't eat. Our combined weekly household income was just above ninety-eight dollars, and several months have already lapsed with no signs of employment in sight. We had no vehicle, no bicycles and no funds available for public transportation. I walked many miles daily and for many weeks in search of employment. I looked through neighborhood garbage cans for thrown out newspapers that contained the classifieds and employment sections. It was on a Tuesday morning in November, when I decided to walk from Avenue X, north on McDonald Avenue. I stopped at every business establishment that was open on McDonald Avenue and off the many side streets asking for work, but nothing panned out. I reached 18th Avenue and continued on toward Avenue F, until I reached a horse relish manufacture. I walked inside and applied for a job. I filled out an application and was told they would call me. That small sense of hope was better than no hope at all. As I exit the establishment, I remembered leaving out an important source of information on the application and immediately went back inside. As I made entry, I observed the factory foreman discarding my application in a trash pail and to his surprise, I witnessed it. After stuttering several of his words in an attempt to come up with an excuse for his action, the foreman informed me he was given orders by his supervisor to discard the application; then he apologized. Shattered and torn, I left the premises and walked over to a nearby neighborhood park bench on McDonald Avenue and Avenue F, where I sat and collected my thoughts.

L-R: George Lubin, Jimmy and Joey 1986

I remember feeling helpless, hopeless and sense of unworthiness in being a husband and father to my family. I rested in preparation for the three mile walk back home. As I sat there I looked across the street and notice an automotive business establishment called, "Colonial Carburetors." I didn't know much about automotive, let alone carburetors, but I also knew I was a fast learner and didn't have a choice. I took the chance, went across the street and walked inside. I was met by one of the business owners, a tall gentleman who instantly approached me as I entered.

"Can I help young man?"

"How you doing sir, my name is Al Bermudez, and I would like to know if I can get an application for a job?"

"What do you know about carburetors?"

"Honestly, nothing. But I'm a fast learner, and if you gave me the chance, I'll prove it to you."

214

"How long you've been out of work."

"It's been several months now."

"Do you have any kids?"

"Yes sir, I'm married and I have a son?"

"What did you do at your last job?"

"I manufactured shoes, creating outsoles and cutting out leather patterns."

"Why did they let you go?"

"The factory always layoff its workers two weeks before the holidays, but this time the layoffs came much sooner and no news on when it will open up again."

"I tell you what, today is Tuesday, and we're closed until Monday for the Thanksgiving holidays. Why don't you come back on Monday the thirtieth and we'll put you to work?"

"Yes, sir, thank you so much!"

"No problem young man, write your name, address and telephone on this paper, and we'll see you then."

A sense of relief was felt throughout my entire body and the efforts in endlessly searching for work have finally paid off. I knew I would be going home with great news. Someone in the heavens had finally heard my prayers. I quickly grabbed the pen wrote down the personal information and gave the owner a great big Kool-Aid smile. I thanked him and began making my way out the door when he called me back in.

"Hey, Al, is it ok I call you, Al?"

"Yes, sir, that's fine, Al is fine."

"How long did you say you've been out of work?"

"About three months."

"And you said you have a family?"

"Yes, I have a son and a wife."

"Hold on there for just a moment young man."

The owner walked away into an office riddled with automotive books and carburetors parts, reemerging with a small white sealed envelope in his hand and a smile.

"Here, take this. It's one week's worth of pay. Now don't disappoint me and make sure you're here bright and early Monday morning, Happy Thanksgiving."

L-R: Al / Ret. FDNY Barney Santangelo 1985

His name was Mr. Barney Santangelo, co-owner of Colonial Carburetors in Brooklyn and retired New York City firefighter. I knew someone up in the heavens had finally heard my prayers, but I didn't know an angel would be the savior of my financial and emotional hardship. I shook his hand with a vice grip hold and promised him I would be there rise and shine Monday morning. I remember walking home and momentarily stopping at Washington cemetery off McDonald Avenue to catch my breath as I kept thinking more and more of Mr. Santangelo's sympathetic and thoughtful gesture. I cried that early afternoon just underneath the Bay Parkway Avenue train station. It was a long and well deserved cry though. I guess I couldn't believe such kindness still existed in people, especially toward a young Latino who didn't matter much to other employers. There were many happy faces of joy and filled stomachs on Thanksgiving Day, November 1981.

216

We even went all out and purchased a couple of bottles of wine for the occasion. All this made possible by one man, Mr. Barney Santangelo, who looked into my eyes and saw a human being in need. He didn't ask what nationality I was or what neighborhood I came from. It didn't matter to him, because his honorableness and his heart was his direction. Barney had two sons: Buddy Santangelo, who was a New York City fire marshal, and now an executive officer with the NYC fire marshal's office and President of the NYC Fire Department Columbia Association; still active today after thirty-three plus years of service and dedication. His other son was Michael Santangelo, a New York City police officer. Mike was laid off during the 1970s fiscal crisis. He returned to the force with the improvement of the economy and move up through the rank and files to the level of sergeant and later retiring as lieutenant. Mike had lots of good NYPD stories, some hilarious and others detrimental. He once told me a story many years ago concerning a rookie officer. They were on patrol in their squad car when they observed suspicious activity. Upon reaching the location it was obvious to them this was a crime progress. As they both were preparing to exit the vehicle for a possible foot pursuit, the rookie officer decided to remove his service revolver from his holster before exiting and the gun went off inside the vehicle. Mike stated he heard police sirens in his head for months, just like on his patrol car. He once instructed the rookie officer, "Hey, do me a favor and turn off the sirens."

The rookie answered back.

"Sirens—what sirens?"

We laughed hard that day at Colonial. Buddy and Mike, two men who served their father well and who would make any parent proud. Barney was later struck and killed with a motor vehicle driven by a lowlife male with twenty-two suspensions on his license. The lost of Barney was tragic for many, and my family was no exception. His kindness and his story will forever be passed on to others. He lives in our hearts, in our minds and in many of our family holiday gatherings and conversations reminiscently. Barney Santangelo, Carl Johnson and Donavon Sherrod, were just some of many decent men in my life that I had the distinctive pleasure and honor of knowing.

Even now as I sit here writing this book, I sometimes wish I could spent just one more day with those three gentlemen. I would thank them all for their knowledge and for showing us all how to be men when circumstances were at its worst. In Sing-Sing there were many supervisors, but very few like Carl Johnson and Donavon Sherrod, who I can personally speak positively about. They were supervisors from of all ranks and walks of life. They're daily ritual was to break down officer's morale at any cost and break down the very existence of unity among them. Many of those supervisors were minorities who forgot where they came from, and several still work at Sing-Sing today. The added stripes on their uniform sleeves or bars on their shirt collars gave new meaning to the pejorative term, 'Uncle Tom.' In their eyes, we were uneducated minority officers incapable of entering other fields of law enforcement and extremely fortunate to be employed.

Sing-Sing officers were men and women capable of controlling and successfully managing a maximum-security prison with over 2,250 plus convicted felons. They were family men and women who outside the prison managed other forms of business establishments and life's important responsibilities. However, many supervisors didn't see it this way. Like one particular sergeant who walked around the prison on a daily basis with a brown stained empty plastic cup of coffee affixed to his uniform belt. He was unfortunately held hostage in a prison riot. He somehow thought in his mind that all the correction officers owed him something for his unfortunate encounter. Being held hostage is a traumatic experience for any human being, and no one should have to be subjected to such devastating circumstances, but unfortunately this is not the society we live in. As previously mentioned in this book, I've witnessed firsthand, people being held hostage and later escape their captors. Unlike that sergeant, I'm sure those hostages didn't take their anger or frustration out on their family members or coworkers. I wondered what would happen if correction officers held him hostage next time around. Maybe he'll redirect his anger at the convicts instead. I once read a love letter sent to a Sing-Sing female officer from Buffalo, NY, by this happily married supervisor, who I might add recently retired. In the letter was a photograph of his son in a little league baseball uniform while holding a bat.

The Buffalo officer was the live-in-wife of an officer who worked the same prison, the letter read.

"If I could take the world, put it in a box and wrap it with a bow for you, I would."

Aw, how nice. Talk about being a snake in the grass from Washingtonville, NY. The Buffalo officer, who was also a crisis intervention member, eventually left her man, (The officer) for a convict serving twenty-five years to life. She had no choice, her nude photos were found in his cell during a routine cell search at Shawangunk correctional facility, catching everyone by total surprise. She apparently wasn't the flying nun everyone portrayed her to be. Many supervisors who got wind of it, from Sing-Sing to Downstate, ran to their local medical centers for complete physicals and blood tests. She was playing the field more than we could have imagined, and was actually worse than the snake in the grass. She eventually married the convict she was having sex with at the prison and who's still serving his sentence. She later applied for a position with the City of Newburgh, police department, but was turned down when they discovered the reasons behind her discontinued service. She eventually went back to Buffalo, NY, with her drunken stupor personality, and I think she and her convict are both living happily ever after, although not under the same roof.

One female officer originally from Sing-Sing named Bend-These-Knobs, who is now at Fishkill facility, was aware of the sexual encounter between the officer and convict prior to its discovery as she mentioned to other female officers. She gave the Buffalo officer her blessings and told her not to concern herself of what others may think or say because is her words, "Convict or not, he's still a man." There were many cover-ups by supervisors on all levels concerning this Buffalo officer, simply because many of these low self esteem supervisors, who were sexually involved with her, were married men and didn't want their secrets revealed. She was allowed to resign and was not fired like many others before her. I've often wondered, not only about the competency of those supervisors, but of those state promotional examinations, its methods of scoring and hiring process. Some of those supervisors didn't know how to tie their own shoelaces, let alone supervise correction officers in a para–military organization. If you ask me, some should have never passed a psychological exam.

Then again, some of those elite few who rose to supervisory positions in Sing-Sing were members of a click who had personal contacts and connections to supervisors. However, not just any supervisor, these were supervisors who not only had access to the new upcoming promotional exams in Albany, NY, but participated in the preparation and development of these exams. So it's no wonder why all those involved in this click may have reached to the level of captain and are now walking the prison system with their heads so far up their asses that they forget where they came from.

STORY CONT:

After getting the information from Sergeant Johnson, I passed it on to all the gallery officers to ease their minds. The messhall was coming to end and the last gallery was finishing up their afternoon meals. Convicts were unusually cooperative and those who returned from chow were stepping into their cells without being instructed to do so. Galleries were already secured even before the messhall was completed. There was no screaming, no running, no questions and no stragglers left on the galleries. This was unusual, but definitely acceptable. We don't always get full voluntary cooperation and compliance by convict population without instructions. Officer Cradle returned with her reports and placed the convict, who had screamed at her earlier in the day, on keeplock status. She notified the gallery officer who in turn informed the convict while manually locking his cell door. She walked over to movement and control office and placed a red tag on the convict identification card so that other officers know of his keeplock status. She then went into the OIC office, opened up the keeplock board and added the convict's name and number to the list. If he's found guilty, the smallest disposition could be a work detail imposed by the block sergeant, worst case scenario is confinement for thirty days in his cell, in addition to thirty days loss of privileges, packages, commissary and phone calls. The convict began calling me from his cell.

"Officer Bermudez, come over to the front of my cell, I need to talk to you!"

I came out of the office, walked over to Q- gallery south and looked up to his cell, "Yeah, what's up?"

"Yo, she (Officer Cradle) locked me up, but I don't care. I'm probably better off in my cell anyway, considering all those damn diseases flying around in this place!"

"That's one way of looking at it. I'll chat with you later!"

I walked away and headed back to the OIC office fully understanding what the convict was trying to imply. *

Since I've been a correction officer, I developed many illnesses of my own in B-block, from skin fungus, ringworms and fevers, to unknown sores and depression. I even tested positive for the tuberculosis in 1996. While working as a transportation officer, I had to transport many sick convicts to different hospitals and medical clinics. Many of those trips were emergency transports with medical conditions unknown to us. The medical staff were not allowed to inform us of any convict's health condition, but it was quite obvious to us some of these convicts were seriously ill. Many of my medical transportations included trips to St. Clare's hospital in New York City's Westside, St. Agnes in Westchester County, Westchester County Medical Center, Albany Medical Center, Phelps Memorial hospital, St. Luke's in Newburgh New York, Helen Hayes hospital and countless of other places. Many of these convicts had their faces covered with breathing masks. Medical staff informed us it was to prevent the convicts from catching any diseases or infections from us during the trip. Many of the sick convicts coughed uncontrollably in our state vehicles, and some even coughed out large blood clots. There were times we opened our vehicle windows to air out any airborne bacteria's and other times we couldn't because of cold weather. Some convicts didn't have the strength to get in or out of the vehicles and had to be literally carried on and off. With all the blood donations I've given and physical examinations I've taken throughout my lifetime and my career with negative results, you could only imagine how upset I was to learn I tested positive for tuberculosis, but nothing to worry according to a nurse from Sing-Sing's facility hospital.

"Oh, don't worry about that officer. You just probably came into contact with someone who may have had the tuberculosis disease—that's all. It doesn't mean you have it and look at the bright-side, that means you don't have to donate anymore blood, isn't that great?

Just go to your local doctor who will prescribe 300 MG, of Isoniazid medication for six months, get yourself a lung x–ray once a year, and you'll be just fine."

For that instant as I looked at her, I mentally saw myself smiling at her, picking up a contaminated syringe filled with blood and stabbing her right in the eyeball while saying,

"Oh, don't worry about that nurse. You only came into contact with me—that's all. You'll be fine. Just go wash out your eyeballs, get yourself an x–ray once a year, and pop some pills for good measure."

Transportation of ill convicts was not the only form of contact while working in Sing-Sing, another area was the AIDS unit at the prisons hospital forth floor. While assign there I once saw a convict patient who was a gym worker and housed on one of the galleries in B-block. This guy was approximately six feet tall, two-hundred plus pounds of solid muscle and strong as an ox. He was a married man who always told me of his regrets and remorse for his conviction. Now he was approximately one-hundred pounds, a little less than six feet tall, weak, frail and skin-and-bones. When he called out my name, I couldn't recognize him until he told me his name and what gallery he was from.

"Hey, officer Bermudez, you remember me?"

"Yes I remember you," I said, making sure I didn't say anything that would hurt his spirit.

"I got the monster, (slang for AIDS) and look what it's done to me."

I couldn't believe what I was seeing and what this disease was capable of.

"I'm sorry to hear that buddy; I hope you get better soon."

"Nah, officer Bermudez, that's not going to happen anytime soon. I feel so weak man. I can't even get up in the mornings or eat solid foods."

"That's so unfortunate," I said, looking into his eyes that clearly showed his worries of death. I had to think of something fast to say and change the course of our conversation.

"Hey, so you're not as strong as you used to be I see?"

"Nah, officer B, I'm not."

"You know what that means?"

"What, I'm not going to live long enough to see your gallery again," he replied in a hopeful and regretful voice.

"No, not that, I figured; now that you're weak and not as strong as you used to be, when you come back on my gallery and cause a problem, I'll just beat your ass and throw you in your cell."

The convict stood there for a second, took a large gasp of air filling his lungs and let out a loud laugh.

"You're crazy, but I respect that. You're one of the best officers in that block and the brothers up there know that. But they're not going to tell you, you know what I mean?"

"Yes, I know exactly what you mean. I know convicts like when officers do their job. It gives them a sense of being safe and secure."

We ended the conversation when a Latino convict, who spoke no English, approached me. His skin was as yellow as a pencil. He was suffering from cirrhosis of the liver as a result of many years of alcohol abuse.

"Oye, oficial Bermudez, tu bebe," (Hey, officer Bermudez, you drink)?

"Yo bebo un poco, porque," (I drink a little, why)?

"Tu eres un hombre bueno Bermudez no bebas. Mire lo que sucedió comigo, ahora necesito un hígado," (you're a good man Bermudez, don't drink. Look what happened to me, now I need a liver).

"Me recordaré eso pana, gracias y que Dios bendiga los dos," (I'll remember that buddy, thanks and God bless you both).

I then left the AIDS unit. I've seen many convicts enter the prison system with the AIDS virus. Some noticeable and others you couldn't tell if your life depended on it. Most were heroin users on the streets and others were involved in unprotected sexual practices. Regardless of whom they were and how much money they had, or how high of a reputation they held on the streets; once other convicts suspected or learned they had AIDS, they were immediately outcast. Others disowned convicts were those who suffered from different illnesses, but displayed similar physical characteristics to the AIDS virus, like stomach viruses, which may cause weight lost and physically obvious. Some of those convicts, who turned their backs on the ill, were also caught having unprotected sex with other convicts. One of those convicts I personally knew from the streets name Pipo. I spoke with him on several occasions and in one conversation he mentioned to me the nature of his conviction.

223

"Hey, B, look at me man, my wife gave me the AIDS papa. You believe that shit? I got myself checked out and when I was told I had it, I went home that same day and stabbed her. I stabbed that bitch five times and the knife bent, so I grabbed another knife and stabbed her seven more times. I stabbed her twelve fucking times."

I couldn't believe what I was hearing; then again, I personally knew Pipo's violent past and knew of his family reputation on the streets of Bedford Stuyvesant.

"I stood there staring at her for an hour or more as she bled papa. Then I decided to go to the bodega, (grocery store) and buy some beer. I went back to the apartment, and she was still there on the floor unconscious and bleeding. I stood there looking at that bitch while she was dying. I drank all the beers and left her there, but you know what?"

"What," I said, as though I was waiting on a punch line.

"That bitch lived, bro. She lived and testified against me in court. You believe that shit?"

"Yeah, I believe it Pipo."

"I'm talking to her now, and she accepts my collect calls. I'm trying to convince her to tell the District Attorney she lied in court, so I can get out. I'm dying from AIDS anyway, so if they let me go, I'm going back to finish the job. Only next time I'm going to kill her, her mother and her sister."

"Let it go Pipo, and make your peace with God while you still have the time. Beg for his mercy and forgiveness so that you can be resurrected with a new and meaningful life next time around?"

"You really think that shit will happen, B, after all I've done?"

"That's officer Bermudez, Pipo, not B. But yes, I'm sure it will happen. As far as you're concern this life is over for you, why not look forward to a new and meaningful one next time around?"

"Did you know that bitch had sex with my nephew Georgie and he died of AIDS too? I can't forgive her for that."

"Listen, Pipo, read the whole Holy Bible and while doing that put aside all your negative thoughts and anger?"

"Yeah, you're right, B—I mean, officer Bermudez. I'll hit the Bible tonight."

"Good move," I said, and the conversation ended. I never saw Pipo again.

Sometimes I wondered where I got the courage to stand by and listen to some of these horrific stories without prejudice. Whatever higher power allowed me to do so, I was glad I did it without having to recognize the intense aversion of it all. Pipo was a career criminal from Bedford Stuyvesant, Brooklyn. He was no stranger to violence and as far as I could remember, Pipo stabbed many people on the streets and in the Marcy housing projects. On several occasions, Pipo confronted me in an attempt to corrupt me and have me mail letters for him or bring in boxes of donuts. He also wanted me to pass on information to his family members on the outside or 'his people,' as he called them. In one occasion, he asked if I could bring drugs into the prison system, simply because we once had a friendship and knew one another from the streets. I finally got fed up with it and put a stop to his bullshit on R-gallery in B-block. I made it clear I was not for sale. I wouldn't put my family's livelihood on the line for a convict and found it very disrespectful he would even consider such a request. I made it clear to him if he ever approached me again with a request like that he would regret it. I was not only going to write him up and sent him to a special housing unit where he would lose all of his privileges, but I would put my foot up his ass in the process. I didn't expect anything less from Pipo, who once lived upstairs from me in apartment 6-A. He was a hardcore criminal with little to no remorse for any of his actions, and his brother was no different.

We once heard a knock on the door at 121 Nostrand Avenue where we lived. My mother got up and went to answer it. When she opened the door, there was an upstairs neighbor from apartment 6-B, standing there with a machete protruding from her chest. My mother began screaming and became hysterical. I clearly remember her verbal request to my mother in Spanish.

"Margarita, por favor cuidame mis niños hasta que mi familia llegue," (Margarita, please take care of my children until my family arrives).

She slowly walked back upstairs and later died on a bed in her bedroom. I never knew the reason why she was killed. I did know the scumbag that killed her was Pipo's brother. He was also recently released from state prison and was a butcher at a local meat market. I distinctively remember her as a very attractive and decent woman, but that didn't matter to people like Pipo and his brothers who were natural-born killers.

225

However, knowing of Pipo's criminal history and heinous crimes; and seeing the physical deterioration caused by AIDS, that almost seems to fit the consequences of his actions; I couldn't help but feel a little sympathy for him and many others like him who suffered from AIDS.

I was once jogging during twilight time, heading east on Avenue Y, then I turned right heading south on Ocean Parkway. As I continued jogging, I was approaching Coney Island hospital to my left. I momentarily looked up trying to focus in on the 8th floor and wondered about someone who was being hospitalized there. I continued jogging toward my destination 28th Street and Neptune Avenue, but only reached Neptune Ave and Shell Road. Something told me to head back toward the hospital, and I did. I began jogging up Shell Road to Leif Ericson Drive toward Ocean Parkway crossing the six-lane parkway into the hospital. I picked up my visitors pass and took the elevator up to the eighth floor. I entered the room and to my complete horror, I saw what was a normal one-hundred seven-five pound man, just twenty-four hours ago, now a ninety-pound man of skin and bones. He appeared as though he hasn't eaten in months, but the cause of this deteriorative physical transformation was dehydration. Someone wasn't doing their job in the hospital and wasn't providing him with the saline solution and other medicines needed to combat his deteriorating condition. I became extremely angry and boisterously demanded to see a nurse. His wedding ring fell off his finger and onto the floor as he tried to get my attention while muttering sentences,

"Don't worry Al, I'll be ok. Just because I look like this doesn't mean I'm not a capable man."

I picked the ring up off the floor, slipped it onto his finger and said, "I know you're a man, and I also know you need to be cared for."

The medical staff finally walked into the room and provided him with the care he desperately needed. I decided to stay with him the rest of that night. Several hours later his lungs collapsed. He couldn't breathe and was turning blue on the face. The bed alarms in the room didn't work, and I again became extremely angry and boisterously demanded help. They came in moments later, administered oxygen, and he pulled through.

226

Deusdelid Bermudez, Jr. 73 photo by Elaine Bermudez

I finally fell asleep and woke up at nine a.m. the next day to the presents of a normal one-hundred seven-five pound man looking back at me. I can't remember if I jogged back home the following day, but I do remember falling apart as I made entry into my home. He died several years later in 1990, and for ten years I was devastated and suffered his lost. He was my oldest brother Deusdelid, (Duce) Bermudez, and he was thirty-three years old. He taught much in life, but taught me most of the catastrophic and devastating effects AIDS can have on a human being.

Chapter Five

~~~

STORY CONT:

The messhall was completed. The convicts were locked in their cells and officer Mama left the area after placing the convict on the keeplock board. The supervisors were in their office, escort officers were gathering up in the OIC area for their next assignments. The one-to-nine shift officers were entering the block. Convicts were allowed to see a movie, located in the chapel, so arrangements were being made to clear that area of any stragglers. This afternoon the front galleries were scheduled for the movies. The back galleries would attend the gym and yard recreation. The announcement was made via loud speaker.

"Gallery officers, let out front side for the movies, Q-R-S-T and U galleries report down to Q south for the movie run!"

All the convicts came running down like they were being called for parole release. *

Chapel, white cross (below-right) marks infant burial site

The first ones to make it in front of the line had choices of seats. Convicts love watching movies, especially when a police officer was being killed on screen, you'd think a baseball team won the World Series with all the cheering. Another thing I notice about moviegoers was the gay convicts. They always seemed to find a spot right in front of hundreds of other convicts, even if they were the last one to come down. I also notice they tend to look very girlish on movie days. They wash up thoroughly, wear homemade lipstick and threw on homemade perfume with colorful clothing, almost as though they were going on their first prom date. We knew what the deal was as soon as the lights were turned off in the chapel. We also knew we had to pay close attention to those particular convicts. When the lights were off, the chapel auditorium was very notorious for throat slashing and deep throating. It was also a place of prayer, peace and forgiveness, but that didn't matter to others who saw the Chapel for what it was, a prison building for mischief opportunities and pleasurable entertainment. Church volunteers who came every Sunday for services were not aware of how many convicts had their throats slashed or manhood taken the previous week. In their eyes, it was a house of worship and a place to save others, but we knew better. The projection room located above the chapel just past the chapel entrance gates to the right, was a room of many stories.

229

Female officers back in the 1980s were having a sexual escapade up in the projection room and some charging fifty dollars a head. One female officer was having sex with several convicts at one time, while others watched and waited their turn. She was discovered in a doggy style position with no clothes on, while one convict penetrated her vulva, a second penetrated her anus and a third her mouth. She worked the three-to-eleven shift, had an attitude toward male officers and always threatened them with sexual harassment. Her discovery led to the fall of many others. It was a domino effect that would eventually land many of them in prison and with long sentences. A couple of those female officers were pregnant and married to officers who worked in the same prison. These lowlife skanks had their men convinced it was their babies, when in fact, it wasn't. They were babies being fathered by convicts in a prison environment. One of those female officer's married to an officer at the same prison had her baby fathered by a convict who was convicted of killing a Federal Agent during the 1970s. Others were also bringing in alcohol, marijuana, cocaine, heroin, cigarettes, money and anything else you can think of as illegal in a correctional institution. Many were running a well organized prostitution ring. Several women officers were prostitutes on the streets of NYC, who had no previous arrest or convictions. They took the corrections written examination, successfully passed it. They attended the Academy, successfully passed that, and became correction officers. They then entered Sing-Sing, learned the prison ropes and ran their undercover prostitution scheme on the inside. This was done under the careful watch of their pimp, who coincidentally enough, was incarcerated at the same prison and being hospitalized at the facility. This hospital area was infested with these uniformed prostitutes, which also explained why their pimp was hospitalized on the same floor with numerous stabbed wounds. It was later discovered through an internal investigation the pimp's wounds were self-inflicted.

'Prior to all this scandal a senator name Ruiz, "who was a frequent critic of the state Department of Correctional Services," in an eighteen-page report urged state prison officials to investigate a series of allegations, including charges that a corrections officer, Thomas Connaire, was murdered in 1984, because he threatened to blow the whistle on his co-workers.

He charged, among other things, that there have been seven known cases of sexual relations between convicts and female corrections officers and that the black female officers in the cases were disciplined more harshly than their white counterparts. He also said in an interview that while Hispanic convicts constitute thirty-two percent of the prison population, less than three percent of supervisors are Hispanic. Ruiz, who fought with the commissioner in 1983, over who to hire to staff a proposed state prison in the Bronx, complained that few Hispanic candidates had been recruited,' (*Arenberg, 1988*).

While attending a training class at Sing-Sing during the late 80s, I was approached by a fellow female officer who had some bad news. She appeared very disturbed and needed desperately to talk about her problem. This was our brief conversation.

"Hey, Bermudez, I need to talk to you."

"Yeah, what's up Lin?"

"No, B, we have to talk in private."

"Okay, let's go in my car."

We went to my car parked in front of the training building and she appeared shaken up. I knew something was wrong, but I didn't know just how much trouble she was in.

"You know what's going on with those female officers at the chapel and the hospital area?" Yes, I answered.

"Well, Bermudez, I'm also a part of that."

"What?" I was totally surprised and caught off guard. She was the last person I thought would ever do anything closely resembling a violation, let alone a crime.

"Yes, I'm a part of it. I have three kids and I needed the money bad, Bermudez. I was bringing in alcohol and marijuana."

"How did you bring in the alcohol without being detected?"

She removed a hairpin, let down her hair and showed me how she managed to slip a half-pint of whiskey in her hair and roll it back up covering the bottle. Her hairpin held the bottle in place somehow. Since she had lots of hair, it was almost impossible to see.

"I'm going to turn myself in to Ossining police."

"No, don't do that. Go to the deputy of security's office first, explain what you told me and let them decide what to do."

"Okay, then, I'll do that. I don't know how I got myself into this mess."

231

"You were the last person I ever thought would do something like this Lin. But you can make it right again, just go to the Dep's office," (Deputy of Security).

"Hey, you know what? So did I, I also thought I would never do something like this, but I did."

We went back to training and sometime during the course of our lunch break she left the prison grounds and turned herself in to Ossining police. I guess she could no longer live with her constant guilt.

Another female officer, who was extremely attractive with light skin complexion and hazel eyes, worked the front gate administration area. She was also accused of bringing in a kilo of marijuana, in addition to other contraband. She was well liked and respected by her fellow officers. Her kindness was her way of projecting an image in an attempt to hide any suspicion. She was also named in the indictment, but before state police and inspector general investigators could apprehend her at the prison, she was arrested on the streets of Long Island purchasing drugs from an undercover officer. She was probably purchasing it for the convicts. Another officer was performing oral sex underneath a kitchen serving steam table in the messhall while convicts were preparing meals. One convict would serve meals while others watch and help to conceal him while she was underneath the steel cabinet. She would remove a circular plate from the inside, open the convict's zipper, pull out his penis and begin her symphonic playing. When she was done, another convict would take his place and so on. By the time the messhall meal was completed she played enough brass to fill up a symphony orchestra. She charged fifty dollars per head. A total of ten convicts in two hours would net her five hundred dollars cash. Not once did any of them considered the possibilities of sexually transmitted diseases. AIDS in the early 1980s wasn't given much thought—therefore sex ran amuck with no real concerns. Sometime in the latter part of the 1980s, AIDS began surfacing in the prison system and many were discovering it when it was too late. Back in those days adequate medical care, psychological treatment or education on AIDS was almost nonexistent. AIDS eventually became the topic of everyone's conversation and those involved in high risk unprotected sex inside the prison were literally praying they wouldn't catch the "Monster."

232

Pamphlets on AIDS began surfacing in the school, hospital, chapel, counselor offices and anywhere the administration could think of. Convicts were reporting in record numbers to the facility hospital emergency for the slightest cough or sniffle. Some convicts would sneeze or cough and others jokingly yelled out, "Oh shit, you got the Monster!" The facility chapel is where church volunteers to this day continue visiting every Sunday in hopes of saving, at the very least, one life. But it's also a place where lives were snuffed out, manhood taken and where homosexuals were made. If walls could talk, I wonder what the chapel walls and all its religious statues would say.

STORY CONT:

The chapel officers and convicts were ready for the movie. They were released out of the block and off they ran like a bunch of greyhound dogs after an intimidating electronically operated jackrabbit. Of course, all the girlies with their pink sneakers were upfront. I made sure to inform all the officers at the chapel of the large gay turn out. I can't recall what the movie was at the time, but I do remember it had something to do with a gay actor. The movie was in progress, officers were at their post, and it was all downhill from there. The day was winding down and many of us had our fingers crossed we wouldn't be stuck (mandatory overtime). I went into the office and placed a call to the lineup room sergeant. I was curious to know if any large number of officers from the three-to-eleven shift called in sick. Officers were allowed to call in sick up to one hour prior to their official duty, so I still had some time. Mandatory overtime showed no mercy to anyone. If your shift ended on Christmas Eve, and you were called back for another eight hours, you were mandatorily obligated to complete those eight hours at a moment's notice, holiday or not. There were no sick calls made on the three-to-eleven, so mandatory overtime was not a concern. At that precise moment officer Ortiz, (aka Big O) entered the block.

"Hey, B, how are you?"
"Good, Big O, what's up buddy?"
"Who do you have in cell number Q-31?"
"A keeplock, his name is Suarez."
"That's him; I need him for a urine test." *

233

Officer, Raymond Ortiz, (Big O) was a Disciplinary and Adjustment Committee Officer with many years of experience. He was an extremely loud individual and an expert in his field. His job included; taking drug test of convicts through urine analysis and other methods. Putting together all case files related to disciplinary hearings, documentation, witnesses, evidence preparations and interpreting. In existence, New York prison convicts have two different types of State prison disciplinary proceedings and delineate rights at disciplinary proceedings guaranteed by the Supreme Court. All New York prisons must publish and provide prisoners with copies of rules of behavior before a convict may be disciplined for infractions. In addition, prisons may not punish convicts for breaking illegal rules nor levy illegal punishments, such as suspending rights guaranteed by law or New York prison regulations. New York holds two types of disciplinary proceedings: superintendent proceedings for more serious infractions and adjustment committee proceedings for less serious problems conducted by lieutenants and above.

Very minor infractions may be conducted by sergeants. In Wolff vs. McDonell, the US Supreme Court established rights of prisoners at disciplinary hearings, which are applied in New York to superintendent proceedings. These rights include the right to twenty-four hours notice before a hearing, to counsel, to a copy of the hearing decision, to an impartial observer at the hearing, to immunity and a limited right to call and cross-examine witnesses. In New York, adjustment committee hearings only give convicts the right to written notice and the opportunity to appear at the proceeding. Superintendent hearings also differ from adjustment committee hearings in that they may levy greater punishments and use different procedures. Further discussion of the adjustment committee hearing covers procedures for bringing issues before it, possible punishments, and appeals,' (*National Criminal-justice Reference Service, 2008*).

Basically, the adjustment committee, to an extent, serves as the judicial system within the confines of a prison system. As a transportation officer and seeing firsthand the many adjustment committee officers throughout the State of New York, I have never come across another correction officer who possessed or exhibited such knowledge and professionalism in his field of work as did officer, Raymond Ortiz.

Many supervisors throughout the state of New York would agree, when Big O, is on official duty at the adjustment committee, not only is seventy-five percent of their work done before the commencement of any hearing, but their state of being safe is of no concern. When I was a rookie officer I was once instructed by a hospital supervisor to closely monitor a convict in a bathroom as he urinated. I did, but obviously not close enough. Big O, who was in the area, formally introduced himself.

"How are you, officer? I'm Officer, Ortiz."

"I'm fine, thank you. I'm Officer Bermudez."

"Officer Bermudez, are you watching the convict piss?"

"Yeah, I'm watching him officer, Ortiz."

"Well, I'll tell you the truth, you should be inside watching him and looking directly at his penis."

"At his dick—are you kidding me?"

"Nah, officer, as you get to know me better you'll discover I'm not a kidder when it comes to these things. You have to make sure the convict is releasing urine from his penis."

"Of course it's coming from his penis," I stupidly stated. And I began to laugh while adding, "Where else would it come from; unless he has a vagina."

Ortiz looked at me as though to say, *you poor little fool.*

"Follow me into the bathroom rookie officer Bermudez."

"Sure," I replied and we went inside.

Big O gave the convict an intense stare, like an African lion stalks his prey. I noticed the convict began shaking and Big O quickly moved in and a verbal command, "Put your hands up on the wall and don't zipper up."

I couldn't believe what I was witnessing. After a quick search of the convict officer Ortiz had him pull out a soap dispenser bag containing someone else's urine. The bag resembled a hospital intravenous bag with a long plastic tube and a removable cap at its end. The convict apparently had it strapped to his waistband with duct-tape. His body heat kept the urine warm and the tubing was protruding through his zipper for easy accessibility. I not only ate my words, but looked up to Big O ever since. I learned fast and discovered you can't question experience and hands-on knowledge. The next time I was faced with similar circumstances, I remembered that incident and what it taught me.

I made sure never to let my guard down, regardless of the type of watch being conducted, which brings me to another form of watch, the dry cell. The dry cell watch is a physical and visual surveillance of a convict in a cell with no running water or plumbing. This type of watch is conducted when a convict is suspected of swallowing drugs, jewelry or other foreign objects. Once the convict defecates—and if he doesn't pick up and swallows it—the officer then puts on a mask, gloves, removes it and searches through the feces with a wooden tongue depressor for contraband. During my career, I personally had the honor of conducting many of these searches. Thanks to politics, palace guards and those who brown-nose their way they're entire career. In those searches, I discovered gold necklaces, wedding bands, loose cigarettes, matches, razor blades, drugs, love letters and other items. Most contained in balloons or wrapped in different sorts of plastics. New technology recently introduced to federal authorities allows a convict to defecate into a dry steel toilet. The toilet automatically washes away the feces exposing only the hidden contraband with no bacterial residue. It then dries the contraband with heated blowers, and the officer is never exposed to anything.

STORY CONT:

Officer Ortiz got his man; convict Suarez and left the block to the disciplinary office for his drug testing. This convict was young, probably twenty-one, but looked seventeen. I was beginning to notice convicts entering the prison system were coming in younger and with heavier sentences. Young convicts were meeting up with uncles, brothers and fathers who were already incarcerated. It was almost as though entering the prison system was part of growing up or a family tradition being followed. *

Every Thursday in Sing-Sing, a group of young people are brought into the prison system as part of an alternative to violence program called, 'Scare Straight.' Most of these youngsters are heading down the wrong path, and this program provides them that alternative. Ironically, many of those who were brought into B-block were greeted by incarcerated family members. To some, it was a family visit or reunion without all the red tape.

236

I remember one fourteen-year-old kid brought in by Scare Straight counselors. A convict up on a gallery looking down asked him a question.

"Hey, Shorty, are you sure you want to come to this place?"

The fourteen-year-old looked up and replied with a few words of his own.

"Mind your fucking business, yo. If I wanna come here, I'll come here motherfucker! So mind yours before I tell my peeps (his people) to shove a fig, (knife) in your ass!"

We actually had to rush the fourteen-year old out of the area before other convicts, who heard what was said, came running up in retaliation. Many older convicts with long sentences like younger convicts like this, with no facial hair and large lips; this kid was no exception. In prison, convicts already know, upon admittance of a young convict, who will be his slave or bitch. Others jump right to it and make their move in a bathhouse by forcibly sodomizing the convict. A bitch convict usually stays with one man, while a slave convict is used to clean up, sew, do laundry, cook and ordered to have sex with others. Slaves also bathe their man, while bitches are more like jailhouse wives. Some of these young convicts were already spoken for without their knowledge. It's easy to fall into the trap.

A good example is when a young convict enters a messhall and another convict offers his food. The process repeats itself day after day. Then come the cigarettes, envelopes, stamps, soda and so forth. Before you know it, the younger convict is in a debt he never knew existed. It's called payback time—when he will have to start paying back in one form or another for all the kindness and gifts he received. That could be, either with similar items, or something physical in return. Chances are if you don't have money or materialistic things to surrender in return for the debts you owe, your buttocks or your lips will do just fine. If that doesn't work for you; you can either sign yourself up for voluntary protective custody or fight your way out, while at the same time building a reputation for yourself. Which reminds me; while conducting a pat frisk on a convict, I noticed an unusually large and deformed scar across his face. It didn't appear as though medical personnel may have applied them. A closer look revealed the convict stitched up the unreported wound himself.

Apparently, the convict took it upon himself to apply the homemade sutures with common thread in an attempt to avoid a trip to the facility hospital and disciplinary action. It was later discovered, through an internal investigation, that he was extorting a younger convict. When he tried to take the younger convict's manhood, the younger convict surprised him with a razor. As a result of his attempt to try and toss the other convict's salad, (slang for rape) he received a slash across his face, which required approximately twenty five stitches to close the wound. The extorter then courageously went back to his cell, pulled out some thread, a needle and stitched up the wound himself. The convict then had others sign up for sick call and steal the needed medication to prevent any infection. Because of incidents like this, many young convicts in prison have to walk in wolf packs, (groups) or associate themselves with gang members through conversations so that others stay away. If you're a young convict loner, minding your own business and just want to serve your time, ninety-nine percent of the time you'll be noticed. Others will and test you, either through threats, extortion, robbery, harassment, stares, attempted sodomy and any other form of intimidation you can think of.

Many young convicts try to ignore gang recruitment, while others are left with no alternative but to join for protection, it's all part of the prison survival process. A young convict loner in state prison, who just wants to serve his time, doesn't stand a chance in hell. Like on our streets, gangs in the prison system are many and there seems to be no end in sight in its recruitment process or the creation of new gangs. Unlike the gangs of the 1960s and 1970s, in today's society, children as young as eight years old are being recruited, shown in photographs and being displayed in public gatherings with identifying gang characteristics. By the time some reach their tenth birthday, they have already learned to use a firearm or have already shot someone in the absence of public and law enforcement knowledge. The innocence of their angel faces are eventually replaced with fearlessly hardcore and deadly delicacy of expression. The photo depicted of a gang member walking down a flight of steps is that of a former gang member name Papo, also known as Duce.

Motorcycle Member Papo, 1980

Since childhood Papo always had an interest in gangs, once receiving a beating as a kid by the Spanish Kings of Brooklyn, NY, for wearing a red handkerchief around his head. He later moved to Williamsburg, Brooklyn and with a guy name Johnny, (aka Tank) started a gang called the Phantom Lords in a tenement basement on South 4th Street in 1972. Johnny was crowned Pres, (President) and Papo physically fought his way to War Counselor. Walking through Union Avenue several months later and while flying his colors, Papo was once again confronted by the Spanish Kings, received a serious beating and his colors were taken. Discovering his colors were being display in their social club, Papo infiltrated recruitment into the Kings.

239

When the time was right, he retrieved his flying colors and returned to Williamsburg. The Phantom Lords eventually faded, and Papo later became a Brooklyn Ching-a-ling. He was actually a family man who could not seem to break away from his passion of gang activity. This was one of many gangs during this era. During my career, the New York prison gangs I was aware of and just to name a few, were the Latin Kings, Netas, Crips, Bloods and Five Percenters, now considered a religious organization which split from the Nation of Islam in 1964. Growing up in the neighborhoods of Brooklyn during 1960s and 1970s, the gangs I remembered most were The Young Lords, Black Panthers, Myrtle Avenue Brothers, Filthy Mad Dogs, Spanish Kings, Bachelors, Savage Skulls, Dirty Ones, Dirty Dozen, Dirty Riders, Phantom Lords, Apache Hewes, Satan Souls and Crazy Homicides in Coney Island.

Bicycle choppers with forks as long as six feet and in some cases longer, were the vehicle of choice. The identifying gang fashion were the leather or denim jackets with fur wrapped around its collar. Torn and worn out jeans with an old lumberjack shirt were a favorite, along with a leather or denim vest and handkerchief around the head. For footwear, a pair of combat boots with white laces was good, but a good pair of leather engineer boots; also known as Abners or Stompers, were the top of the line footwear, it didn't get bigger than that. The weapons of choice were large wooden ax handles, baseball bats; some with nails hammered through them, 2x4 lumber, pipes, chains, large belt buckles, knives, brass knuckles and a large meat hook. Names like Savage, Little-Man, Deadeye, Pichon, Outlaw, Batman, Apache and Tank, just to name a few, were the most popular during that era.

Unlike the gangs of yesteryear, some of today's gang initiations involve slashing someone's face, preferably law enforcement, civilians or other gang members. Today's modern day gang, members prey on just about anyone. Although don't wear flying colors on their backs, they usually wear other identifiable items like red or blue handkerchiefs, beads and similar color clothing. Unlike the 1970s, today's gang members boast about themselves on the internet sites like MySpace, Facebook and You-Tube. Gang members can be seen revealing pertinent information, posing in photos with families, firearms, drugs and money.

They brag about their rivals, past criminal acts and reveal first and last names of their members. This is a great information cyber line for law enforcement. In the 60s and 70s, gang members formed an Apache Line as a form of initiation recruitment. New gang members walked through a double line of men, some with weapons, and take as many punches, kicks, slaps and hits as you can. In today's senseless gang rules, many target helpless innocent people. Children are recruited for acts of homicide, drug transactions and transporting; since they're not of legal age and the consequences of their actions are much less strenuous with the criminal-justice system. In the Marcy projects of Bedford Stuyvesant, the most obvious gang members were the Bachelors with their flying colors of Red, Black and Green target circle affixed to the back of their jackets.

The Myrtle Avenue Brothers were a much smaller group as I can remember. The Black Panthers I seldom seen, but when they did step out it was quite obvious to everyone who they were with their black gloves, pants, turtlenecks, shoes, jackets, shades and trademark black berets. In Williamsburg, on the Southside of Brooklyn were the Satan Souls, Savage Skulls, Dirty Ones, Apache Hewes, Phantom Lords and a gang that use to chase me down Union Avenue past Lorimer St, Middleton St, Harrison Avenue and as far as Lynch St, just before Broadway; those maldito (Damn) Spanish Kings. Separated from my mother, my father resided on the Southside of Williamsburg, Brooklyn. Every Friday I was sent there for a financial support visit, and they would chase me up Broadway. I later discovered the member who initiated the chase was named Pichon, (Bird). He knew my schedule and knew I'd be passing through just like clockwork every Friday. But after being chased many times before by other gangs throughout my childhood, Pichon didn't know just how good of a runner I was.

Come to think it, I too should have been named Pichon, because just like un Pichon, (a bird) I flew my little Spanish ass down Union Avenue like a NYC pigeon flying away from its prey. Incidents involving gang initiations, territorial conflicts and disputes are always followed into the prison system from the streets. In prison, you can't hide like you can out on the streets. Prison convicts have a very reliable informational pipeline that runs across New York State, from Attica to Sing-Sing and Rikers Island City Jail.

241

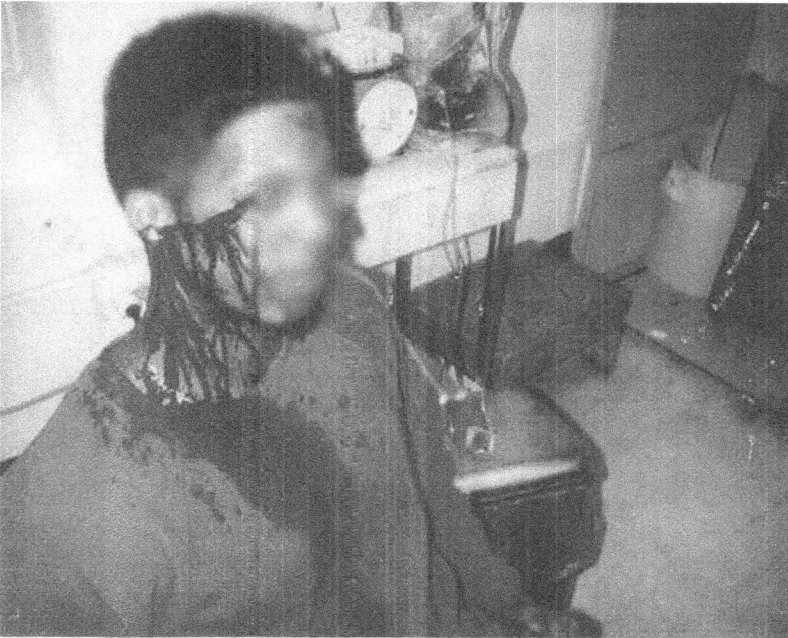

Slashed Gang Member, photo by Bermudez 2000

Their assaults are not just limited among themselves. Many correction officers, supervisors and civilians have been slashed or stabbed, and these assaults continue to this very day. Most assaults like these are the results of young blood gang members' initiation. Others are to prove their loyalty to the gang or to build up a reputation. The convict shown in the blood-stained shirt was a blood member who was slashed by another gang member. The other gang member apparently didn't like the way he stared him down, (looked too long). The result was hundreds of stitches to close a couple of gashes that ran from his right eyelid to the right ear and from behind the right ear down to his neck. The slashes you see in this photo are basically the same slashes seen on many other convicts and officers, which of course run in many different directions and other parts of their bodies. Slashes are more common than stabbings, it leaves the victim alive with something to look at and think about for the rest their life. A stabbing, on the other hand, is usually mean to kill or permanently disable the person. Other Latino convicts, who originally formed gangs in the 1970s, were called the Asociacion Neta.

These were convicts whose main concern was to stop an increase of violence between convicts at a prison in Rio Pedras, Puerto Rico. Some would also say the Netas was formed by convicts who were actually innocent of their convictions. One of their most identifiable marking is a heart shaped tattoo on their hands with the letter N inside of it. The Netas are still within the prison system, but choose to keep a low profile, unlike other Latino gang members who don't mind bringing attention to themselves, either through self–advertising or some other form of public display. Like the gangs of the 1960s and 70s, violence against security staff and other law enforcements, involving rules of engagement and initiations by Netas, Latin Kings and other gangs, are few if any. Their initiation rules do not have a place in law enforcement and innocent civilians.

During the 1990s a small riot broke out involving Latino gang members in Sing-Sing's B-block yard. Everything appeared normal on this day. Convicts were hanging around in the baseball field, basketball courts, some playing handball, others watching television and nothing appeared out of place or unusual. The ground officers kept a close watch of their surroundings. Wall post officers kept a close watch of all activities and in wall post seventeen, Officer Santo Martinez was officially recording the entire yard recreation activity. From his video, we could see convicts walking around in groups of five, some in groups of four, others in groups of three. Some convicts began slipping on plastic garbage bags over themselves. Officers thought there might be a passing cloud of rain, but after careful observation, nothing was seen in the sky. The convicts who were walking in groups all met at the same location and began running in one direction. They ran toward the baseball area and broke up in a circular pattern surrounding a group of other convicts. Shanks was pulled out from every direction and without any warning, quickly the stabbings began. The Latino convicts who were walking in a group began stabbing other Latinos and Black gang members. Some managed to escape the attack. When the stabbing was done the convicts who initiated the assault ran as close to the prison wall as possible and began throwing their shanks over the wall. Then they removed the garbage bags and threw themselves on the ground in surrender.

The plastic garbage bags were used to prevent splatter and shanks were tossed over the prison wall to prevent confiscation of evidence. All the convicts involved were in their 20s, and the attacks were a message being sent to the other Latinos, not to negotiate with blood gang members. One of those convicts stabbed received multiple stab wounds to the heart. I was the officer who transported him to the hospital. While I was standing over him at St. Agnes hospital in Westchester County, I witness the doctor open the convict's chest, then plug the hole in his heart with a finger and massage the heart with his other hand. Blood sprayed in every direction, and the convict miraculously survived. Through all this ordeal and chaos, no officers were injured intentionally or otherwise. During my career, I've learned a lot of things from young gang members and other young convicts who were incarcerated with more than twenty-five years. These are their circumstances and reasons for their incarceration, told to me through conversations and questioning. Some blame the problems on their parent's absence and lack of supervision or parents who worked to support their family and were never home.

Others lived in households with no fathers or father figures and even when the father was present, the love was absent. I've learned many of these young convicts were in need of love and attention, or needed to be spoken to as you would do with a friend. Many of these young people don't mind discipline, they actually approve of it because it reinstates and instills in their minds the understanding that you are the parent and caretaker. According to many I've spoken to, the most common behavior that builds hatred was the constant physical abuse, verbal torment, degrading statements and toe-to-toe challenges and confrontations. The kind of behavior which crumbles their self-esteem, builds hatred and anger in which they learn to live by. This is the same hatred and anger they later use against others as a form of relief, literally a recycled behavioral process. I've learned their complaints involve their parent's abusive relationships, that they're parents had some prior knowledge of it, had doubts or suspicion that their relationship may not work, yet decisions to enter these relationships were made regardless of all the red flags. Many grew up in homes where they witnessed or became victims of sexual abuse at the hands of their own parents, relatives and family friends. Ghetto life is tough, not only on the streets, but in their own bedrooms.

244

Most if not all young convicts I've spoken with grew up in households with some form of substance abuse. These were households where drugs, alcohol and sex were the norm and where monthly welfare check concerns took precedence over children's needs. Where refrigerator shelves meant to hold beverages, vegetables and wholesome food, were instead filled with wine and forty oz beer bottles. A convict from W.27th Street in Coney Island once told me he had hundreds of large cans and pickle bottles filled with roaches. The roaches were later used for human consumption because the family had nothing else to eat. Many are left with no other alternative but to live a life of crime if they are to survive. Going to prison guarantees three meals a day, there's no guarantee they'll ever eat on the streets. These are the unfortunate circumstances and conditions in which many of our American people live in, and where education ceases to exist. How do you educate a man who can't read or write when his family is in need? What do you think he sees when he's presented with a job application and the English language looks foreign to him? Should society educate him before, during or after an incarceration? A young convict once approached me in Downstate facility and asked me the following.

"Officer Bermudez, can you do me a favor and write my home address on this envelope? I live at 111 Nostrand Avenue, Brooklyn, NY. 11206."

I replied, "But you just gave me all the information you need to put on the envelope. What's wrong, you have a broken hand or something?"

"No, officer, my hands are fine. I just don't know how to write. I could make mistakes in the letter, and my family won't mind because they'll figure it out, but not on the envelope because it will never get there."

Dumbfounded, I answered back, "No problem young man. Make sure you keep the address I write down for future use and when you arrive at a permanent facility sign up for school."

And the conversation ended. Personally speaking, I don't agree with college education for confined criminals unless their capable of paying for it. However, I sincerely believe a common education, would not only help those who want to help themselves, but allow people like the young man mentioned above, to simply understand what a job application is.

245

This instills in their minds the potential for corrective possibilities. However, education is not the only thing which ceases to exist in their households, so does respect. Respect is an extremely important issue for many of these young convicts. Most, who do not receive respect at home, demand it on the streets. Many parents don't realize it's so much harder for a child to disrespect their parents when their like a friend, then it is to disrespect a parent who's constantly bickering, degrading and torturing them. I'm not the perfect parent by any means and far from it, but involving myself in their conversations and understanding most of their problems, helped me to improve my imperfections as a parent. Unfortunately, parenting or the lack thereof for those who are raised in an impoverish environment wasn't the only issue. Liquor stores and billboards advertising cigarettes and alcohol, which litter every street corner don't help matters either.

For many, joining law enforcement or becoming a soldier was not an option, nor is it instilled in their minds by others, especially those with a criminal mentality. A factory worker, construction worker, janitor or even a prison convict was more of an ineluctable fate for many. Personally, as I matured and learned the facts of life, I discovered that by passing on my life experiences, my problem solving solution and the enjoyment that sometimes came with working, my son's and neighborhood kids would have an advantage over many others who found themselves in an impoverish environment. My theory was simple, to engrave in their minds the consequences of misbehaving, the potential rewards for good behavior and playing a small part in their everyday lives. These were key elements for me in building an indestructible bond of trust. Not every parent can be there for their children during these important times, and not every child possesses the leadership needed to deter the most common disreputable temptation. It's also up to family members and neighborhood people to give a moment of their time, but not to misconstrue a moment of their time with babysitting. If all adults in our neighborhoods and communities throughout our country gave kids the privilege to discuss what's on their mind, threw a baseball occasionally in their direction, and share their most important life experiences with them, the bond between the two would be extremely difficult to break.

246

As such, you would no longer be looked upon as a neighbor, but as a trusted friend. Unfortunately, many lowlife pedophiles have adapted to this theory, and it has become very difficult to know who the honest neighbors are and who the lowlife pedophiles are. I once decided to get a haircut and went to a local barbershop off Ocean Parkway and Neptune Avenue in Brooklyn, called Alberto's. As I sat there, my chair was turned slightly to right, and I was now facing the front window of the establishment where I had the view of passing pedestrians and kids heading to a nearby school. A group of rowdy teenage kids approached the barbershop window, placed their hands over their eyes to block the glass reflection and started looking into the barbershop.

Some could be heard talking on the other side of the glass.

"Yo, let's go inside and get a cut."

Two other teenage kids soon joined the group with cigarettes in their mouths. They too placed their hands on the glass to look inside, but only one opened his eyes to the size of golf balls and the cigarette in his mouth dropped like a towering pine tree in a forest. The facial expression was a classic. I gave him a great big smile, acknowledging my presence, and he moved away from the window.

"Yo, that's my uncle on the chair."

The facial expression was enough to confirm he was up to no good, and I immediately suspected he was not where he should have been, in school. He quickly gained his composure, boost up his courage and opened the barbershop door sticking his head inside.

"Hey, Tio, (Spanish for uncle) how are you? I'm on my lunch period and doing some walking around in the neighborhood with my friends."

Of course, I knew it was total bullshit, but I played along and told him to be careful. The barber looked at me with a smile while saying.

"He mentioned he was on his lunch period, but his facial expression was more like that of a girl experiencing her first period."

We laughed like heck in the barbershop that day, and I never told his mother Joanna, my sister. It was my nephew Al Pagan, who fifteen years later as an adult admitted to skipping class.

247

The bond between us did not allow me to tell on him and should I have broken that trust, we probably would not have the relationship we enjoy today, we'll never know. I had no knowledge of any excessive school absences on his part. If I thought his behavior was one of a criminal nature or a repeated offense after an advice on my part, then quite naturally I would have approached it differently and would have told his parents. I've witnessed many family members, and neighborhood kids cut classes or play hooky from school from time to time. Although this behavior is not acceptable by any means, sometimes utilizing your trust by simply giving them a little advice can have better results than subjecting them to the fear of what their parents would do if you disclosed their secret. We don't expect every child will be a civil servant worker, join the armed forces; become an executive, an athlete or movie star. And in today's society, we're extremely lucky if our child avoids a local stop to prison. Sometimes a simple application of adult responsibility through conversation and work can have great results. That's if the kid doesn't take your trust for granted and many do. We've been extremely fortunate to have two good-hearted sons, Al Bermudez, Jr., and Carmine Bermudez, who never fell through the cracks of our criminal-justice system or found themselves in the dependencies of substance abuse. Son's who never forgotten the meaning of their parents wedding anniversaries or birthdays.

As a Father to my sons, I truly believe I demanded a lot from them. My discipline as a parent was somewhat extreme with intolerable rules. Timeouts didn't exist during my adolescences and long counseling conversation and negotiations was out of the question. You broke a rule you lost a privilege, broke the same rule twice, and you'd wish you hadn't. Although I did not pass on the full brunt of my disciplinary experiences and abuse as a child, and if I had to do it all again; my parenting skills would have been different to some extent. Naturally, there are some regrets with how I fathered, but nothing in life with such importance as my sons could ever camouflage the love I have for them or sacrifices I'm willing to make. My sons are our pride and joy, they are a reflection of what goodness means in people. I would give my life for them in an instant. Watching them as they enter manhood makes me proud to know, 'they are an exception.'

L-R: Carmine, Al and Al Jr. 2008

The common values and morals implemented during their childhood are the tools needed to live a productive and sensible life. They're not perfect by any means or distinguished by perfectionism. They're two extraordinary caring young men with fundamental principles, respect and honorableness that will someday make any woman proud to marry them. Someone once asked me, if you had to do it over again, would you change anything? My answer was no. Now looking back in hindsight; I would overturn that answer with a definite, yes. I would have been a better son to my parents, a better man to my wife and a better father to my sons.

'Maturity comes too late in life for many men, but better too late in life is immaturity, then the absence of fatherhood, love, care and support,' (*Al Bermudez Pereira, November 21, 2008*).

In today's society cutting classes or playing hooky doesn't seem so bad, when you consider all the children who are sexting and posing nude on the internet for millions to see around the world. In many cases, even their own parents are posing nude and setting the stage for this corrupt behavior. Children's desire for fame and attention has replaced family morals and values. Can you blame them?

Most children who are acknowledged and phrased by families and teachers are those who graduate high school or college, while those who are displayed on television as celebrities and athletes are honored and worshiped by all. While many young people are seen on the local news media committing crimes and being arrested during their glorified fifteen minutes of fame, thousands of other law-abiding and decent young people, who are volunteering their time in society for the sake of humanity, are not.

Simply put, the more we publicly focus on criminal behavior as entertainment, the more public attention they desperately seek through imitation. Public television networks and production companies throughout our nation need to stop targeting our children and do away with programs that glorify gangs, violence, vehicle pursuits, sex and love of money. I don't expect this will happen; the buying power of American children is much too high to ignore. There are only two forms in which your voice can be heard in this country, the abundance of unity among people and the power of money. As it stands, American children's buying power is estimated to be at approximately fifty billion.

During my life, I've had the privilege and honor of crossing paths with many youngsters and have been blessed with an abundance of nieces and nephews who never chose the path of self destruction. Many of these young people and family members are now in law enforcement in every level of government, in the armed forces and others in civilian capacity. None that I'm aware of ever entered the criminal-justice system through incarceration or presently experiencing any form of substance abuse. Many young people today unfortunately look down on law enforcement and the feeling of strong dislike seems to be on the rise. Their respect toward law enforcement is almost nonexistence. I strongly believe that by indoctrinating our youth on daily basis to law enforcement activities and making them aware of, not only of our judicial system, but of the laws of our states, they're understanding and respect for the law will not only result in being law-abiding citizens, but will continue on to other generations.

STORY CONT:

B-block was once again quiet. Convicts were in the movies, and others were out in the yard and gym. The phone rang in the OIC office. It was Officer Leo Coletti, Jr, (Aka, Leo 'The Pinky' Coletti).

"Hey, Al, it's Leo. How are you?"

"I'm fine, Leo. What's up buddy?"

"Hey, I heard you put in for a wall post?"

"Yes, I did. I put in for wall post fourteen."

"No, shit. That post is closed, but they'll shift you around to other towers."

"What's it like working up there?"

"Ah, shit. It's easy. You don't do shit. Just keep your eyes open that's all, especially for those stuck-up sergeants."

"No problem, hey I have to go, but before we hang up, I wanted to tell you I'm going to buy a house up in Newburgh. Maybe you can fill me in on what I need to do or what to expect?"

"No problem, buddy. When they put you up on a tower give me a call in wall post eight, and I'll fill you in."

"Sounds like a plan. I have lots of questions."

"Yeah, I hear ya. I'll talk to you later."

"You got it Leo." *

While out on a convict work-related injury, my compensation case was controverted by a Downstate prison administrator in 2001. As a result, our life saving was depleted nine months later, a vehicle confiscated and our immediate future looked vague. As the bills began piling up and mortgage went into default, we knew we were heading toward disaster. Supreme Court foreclosure notices began appearing in our mailboxes and creditors were hounding our telephone on a daily basis. But just when we thought there was little to no hope in our financial recovery and dilemma, someone stepped up to the plate. In one surprising and promising phone call and without hesitation or prejudice, this individual put me and my family back on track. Thanks to the generosity and honorableness of one man, Leo Coletti, Jr. There were many who turned the blind eye to our unfortunate circumstance.

Although I hold no animosity or hostility toward those who found a rock in which to hide under during my hard times, their betrayal and deceptive hypocritical friendship will never be forgotten. I still personally keep in contact with Leo after all these years. I even consider him a brother, maybe because Leo has given me more support than my own biological father has ever given me in one lifetime. Sing-Sing have many good people from all walks of life, people with different morals, values, characters, nationalities, cultures, traditions and languages. It is a small melting pot of diverse human beings who for eight hours a day manage to put aside all their differences and opinions for the sake of peace, unity and cooperation. I often think of all the fellow officers, civilians and friends I left behind from Sing-Sing to Attica. I wish them and their families well and can only hope that others in state government and in the general public would recognize and honor all that they do. Their loyalty, commitment and dedication to their work are the important components that keep the surrounding communities safe from the evil that lurks just behind those prison walls.

STORY CONT:

The shift was finally coming to an end. Recreation was terminated and convicts would have to lock in for the next tour, the three-to-eleven shift. The movie would go beyond three p.m. so officers from the next shift would have to be sent to the chapel to make their relief. Convicts were running around the other galleries for their last minute borrowing. The block sergeants were gone and left to the watch commander's office where they would turn in all of their paper work for the day. The officers could easily be heard yelling at the convicts to lock in their cells. It's almost as though two-thirty p.m. gave them all a second wind. They know it's time to go home and there's nothing that will stand in their way. Other officers secured their galleries and were reporting to the OIC office where they turned in their radio and keys. Some officers liked to sneak out early before anyone else. It's up to the front gate officer to stop them from doing so. However, who would want to stop an officer from leaving the confines of a prison environment after such a strenuous eight-hour shift?

The three-to-eleven shift officers were now entering the block and all equipment, along with any vital information was being passed on. This information included unusual incidents, drafts, keeplocks, population count and any other information encountered throughout the day. As I stood in front of the OIC office exchanging my information, I heard the same voice that called me first thing in the morning, call me again at the end of the day.

"Hey, B, let's go, Papa. Coño bro, (damn brother) don't you want to go home?"

It was Gonzo again, but no moving of the chest this time, at least not until we got to the locker room.

"I'll be right there Gonzo," I replied as many officers hurried out of the block and into the corridors. As I exited the block, I looked down the corridors and saw many officer's feet moving a mile a minute as they were heading toward the front of the prison. Those were the same feet I saw every morning dragging up the hill to the prison blocks. We finally made it to the locker room, and everyone there was making plans for the night. Some were even contemplating calling in sick the next day.

"Yo, Bermudez, let's go out tonight," came a voice from three aisles back.

"Nah, that's okay buddy. I'm going straight home and staying there," I replied.

Another voice echoed from the background in response to my reply.

"Ese tonto tiene una bola con cadena en el locker, chequealo," (That chump has a ball and chain in his locker, check him out).

Half the locker room started laughing. This was the kind of peer pressure you could either give in to and go out with fellas, or stand your ground and answer as I did.

"You got me fellas, I do have a ball and chain in my locker, but that's not all, I have a pink skirt too."

Everyone laughed again and the locker room became a standup comedy show. Another officer spoke up in Spanish.

"Oye, Gonzo, tu vecino por fin salió del closet," (hey, Gonzo, your neighbor finally came out of the closet).

Gonzo spoke up in my defense.

"Yo, that's my boy B, don't mess with him!"

I smiled as I finished dressing up. I looked over to Gonzo and replicated his words used earlier in the day.

"You tell them Gonzo, and thanks for looking out brother, but next time, I don't need you to speak up for me."

Gonzo shockingly gazed over at me.

"Oh, shit; it's like that B, after I just spoke up for you?"

I gazed over at Gonzo one last time before walking off and courageously stated,

"Behind this chest that doesn't move up and down like yours, is a heart surrounded by muscles— that shit will do that to you G. That shit will do that."

Remembering the morning encounter with Gonzo, I thought I give him a little taste of his own medicine. Gonzo smiled and ended the conversation with a last few words of his own.

"You got me B; you got me."

We all met at the parking lot for one finally despedida, (Farewell). Ninety percent of the Latino officers lived in the Bronx, many of the African American officers lived in Harlem, and most of the New York City Caucasian officers lived in Long Island. Unfortunately, for the upstate officers, ninety-nine percent of them lived on prison grounds and couldn't go home. It was hard for those individuals who had wives and children back home, especially during the holiday season. I always wondered how they did it, I guess when you're a responsible human being, there's nothing that will stand in the way of providing for your family. Many of them swapped their days and worked endlessly in hopes of combining and accumulating enough time to spend with their families. It worked for many and most we're happy to know they would spend those days with their families.

After leaving the parking lot and traveling over an hour, it was now four-fifteen p.m. and I was now entering the FDR drive from the 3rd Avenue Bridge. Traffic as always, was at a crawl, smog filled my lungs with its polluted particles and unseen potholes littered the roadway. Horns blew endlessly and road rage came from every direction. I slowly entered the FDR drive with lots of room to spare when in that instant I was cut off by another driver. I immediately hit the brakes and swerved my car in an attempt to avoid a collision. I took a deep breath and angrily thought to myself.

"Wait a minute, I'm going to catch up to this prick and give him a few words he won't forget. My day had been too rough to put up with more bullshit out on the streets."

I put the pedal to the metal and caught up to the driver who had cut me off two miles back. My driver-side window was slowly approaching their rear passenger-side window. I could see it was a female driver, but I'll be damned if I'm going to let that stop me from at least flipping the bird, (Middle finger). As I approached the passenger-side front window, I looked over to the rear of her car and couldn't believe what I saw. There was a little child sitting in the back seat with the saddest look on his face. His eyebrows were slightly tilted, as though he was in so much pain. Next to the child was a green oxygen tank connected to a clear plastic mask that was attached to his face. Just when you think you have it bad, there's always another much worse off. That encounter was the start of many inspirations in my life yet to come. I felt bad for the kid, and I'm sure I would have felt a lot worse if I had gotten the chance to say what I shouldn't have. I slowed my vehicle down, took a couple of breaths and thought to myself.

"Heck with the traffic and all the negative bull-shit associated with it. Surely, it's not worth the heartache."

I moved over to the center lane and began driving the speed limit, which of course is not recommended in places like NYC without pissing someone off. While driving, I noticed a police car creep up alongside of me, and I momentarily looked over. The officer returned my look with an angry stare as if to say, "Hey, you want a piece of me?"

I looked over at the patrol car again. I was curious to see if any of its windows were opened and if the air-conditioning was turned on. Sure enough, windows are closed and the air-conditioning appeared to be on. *So what's his beef?* He was sitting in an air conditioned RMP cruiser and that alone would make me want to apply for a position with NYPD. It beats working inside a maximum-security prison with no air-conditioning, no weapons and constantly running up and down the galleries eight hours a day while serving one hundred twenty plus convicted felons as though you were their personal housekeeper. Not knowing what kind personal problems this cop may have been experiencing, and remembering the child I just saw on the rear seat, I continued driving and paid no mind to other drivers.

I finally reached Battery Park in Manhattan, WUI Plaza on Washington Street, where I stopped every late afternoon to pick up the wife just before five p.m. My usual parking spot, between the Frankfurter man and the Battery Tunnel utility building was available, so I parked. I sat in my car and gazed up at the World Trade Center as I've done for nine years. A Wall Street executive leaned on a three-foot fence in a dark suit while smoking his marijuana joint as twilight slowly moved in and the twin towers began to illuminate in a spectacular glow. As I sat there, I wondered to myself.

"How in the world are they ever going to take down those two buildings? I guess I'll never see it in my lifetime."

I was wrong; I saw it along with millions of other people on September 11, 2001. After picking up the wife, I began the final trip home from Manhattan into Brooklyn via the Battery Tunnel. *

We lived in an Italian neighborhood which bordered Bensonhurst and Gravesend off McDonald Avenue and Avenue X. It's been our home for over ten years. Before moving to this neighborhood, my wife told me how sweet and quiet it was and how friendly all the neighbors were. On moving day 1983, I loaded a rental truck with our furniture. We moved from 65th Street and Bay Parkway in Bensonhurst, to Avenue X in Gravesend. As I pulled up, I noticed numerous police cars and ambulances. A body bag was being carried out by two police officers from our new next-door neighbor's home. Since my wife picked out the neighborhood, I looked over at her and said,

"Yeah, nice neighborhood, I can't wait to see what Christmas is going to bring."

Word on the street was—the kid next door was a troublemaker. He apparently often went to a popular club called The Plaza Suite around the corner off 86th Street and caused problems there. His name was Anthony 'Tony' Bermudez, same last name as ours. He met up with a couple of wise guys who were no fly by nights, and ruffled their feathers. Under orders, they apparently went to the house, up to his apartment and into his bedroom. They then ordered the wife to keep quiet and shot him to death in front of her, as their baby who slept in another room. The Plaza Suite was a discotheque owned by the Gambino crime family and managed by underboss Sammy 'the Bull' Gravano.

256

The Plaza Suite was located on 86th Street. The building was originally owned by four legitimate businessmen who formed a corporation called "Enjoy Yourself Incorporated" in 1979 and obtained a liquor license. Two of the businessmen became involved with silent partners, one was a made soldier named "Salty" from the Genovese crime family and "Vinnie Sicilian" a capo from the Colombo crime family. The two other shareholders brought in Sammy Gravano for "protection" and "support." For this, Gravano was given fifty percent interest in the discotheque. When Gravano took over he became unhappy with what he considered sloppy management. He muscled his way into the business and took over the entire operation but kept the original arrangement with Salty and Vinnie Sicilian. After Gravano took ownership of the disco, he divided the ground floor of the building in half. Part was devoted to his construction headquarters, with a private office for himself and his brother-in-law Edward Garafola and clerical staff. The other section contained a display space for carpeting and hardwood flooring company Gravano had started to complement his various construction contracts. On the second floor of the building was his discotheque The Plaza Suite.

The disco was large and offered five-thousand square feet of space. The walls were burgundy and gray. By the front entrance was a long bar counter and banquettes surrounded the dance floor. In the back was a separate VIP designated lounge. Unlike his earlier night club ventures, Gravano now immersed in his construction business, was not able to be present at the disco every night. He fired the bouncers and installed his own men, Michael DeBatt and Thomas Carbonaro. His manager of The Plaza Suite was Joseph Skaggs. Gravano hired local girls as waitresses. After he took over The Plaza Suite it became one of the most popular discotheques in Brooklyn and had people lining up around the block to get in. Just before Sammy Gravano muscled his way in and took possession of the discotheque, one of the legitimate businessmen who formed the corporation was found beheaded in his apartment tenement off Ocean Parkway in Brooklyn. Until today, no one was ever arrested or brought to justice. This was obviously a tough neighborhood, and I had my work cut out for me. Although many told me I looked Italian, I still knew my last name was Bermudez, and hoped it would not be confused with the deceased Tony Bermudez.

Some of Gravesend neighborhoods during the 1980s, had a way of welcoming those who they thought didn't belong. In June 1982, an ex-marine who worked with the city Transit Authority and two of his buddies, went to a bagel shop on Avenue X near East First Street. The three black men, off-duty from their jobs as subway-car maintainers at the nearby Coney Island yards, bought some beer and left. When the three men got to their car, a white man from the neighborhood approached them, shouting, "Niggers, get out of here." Words were exchanged. Seconds later, twenty young men and women ran over from the schoolyard of PS 216 across the street, throwing bottles and other objects. Two of the victims managed to get out of the car and run for help, but not before suffering minor cuts and another with a bad gash on the head from beer bottles. The third Willie Turks was caught by the white mob. Turks, unarmed, tussled with one of them, and then he was hit on the head with a stick by another. A teenage girl yelled, "The nigger's got a gun," and the gang moved in, beating Turks with sticks, feet and fists.

By the time police arrived, he was dying, sprawled across a sewer drain with massive skull and brain injuries. NYC prosecutors would later say they had never encountered a killing so motivated by racial hatred. Residents resent the adverse publicity brought by the Turks killing. The people thought they were getting a bad rap for one incident that was isolated and can occur anyplace in the city. But Turks and his friends were not the first blacks to be attacked after leaving the Avenue X bagel shop. In May 1981, a gentleman named Roscoe Fountain got off work and was in the mood for something to take home, he was a NYC housing authority police officer and he too went over to the bagel shop, he's been there before, but never alone. He ordered the bagels and when he got outside he was hit upside the head with a bat. They were saying, 'kill the nigger.' They started pounding, beating and kicking him. Kill the nigger, they said, as he was lying in the middle of the street and as ten or more people came and began beating him. He was trying to get his gun from an ankle holster, but also had to cover his face from the beating. Finally he reached for the gun and was going to shoot the guy standing at his feet as he yelled, "I'm a police officer," and shot. But at the same time somebody kicked his hand and the bullet got his ankle.

With that they all scattered. Officer Fountain spent a month at Coney Island hospital recovering from the attack and retired on disability because of the injuries. He maintains bitterly that police failed to investigate the incident adequately, despite the fact that he was a police officer. In yet another incident, in April 1982, a black man named Frank Tyrrell was set upon as he left the bagel shop shortly after midnight. Tyrrell spent several days in a coma at Kings County hospital. There were no arrests in the Fountain and Tyrrell cases. In Gravesend, the name of Willie Turks the transit worker killed, brought frowns to the faces of some residents, who say their whole neighborhood was unfairly maligned by the media. In the bagel shop, employees refuse to talk about the killing. Some residents still repeat rumors that the men were carrying weapons and that they provoked the fight. These sentiments persist despite courtroom testimony to the contrary. Convicted in the killing of Turks were Gino Bova, Anthony Miccio, Joseph Powell and Paul Mormando. Whether Gravesend has changed really didn't matter much to Donald Cooper and Officer Roscoe Fountain. Both men said they stay away from Avenue X, they also said they learned the hard way that New York is a city of distinct neighborhoods and that perhaps it is wise for a person to know a little about a neighborhood before they venture into it, especially at night. A sixth person arrested in the Willies Turks murder case was Anthony 'Tony' Bermudez, the Plaza Suite troublemaker. He never made it to trial though, (*Ron Howell, 1986*).

However, Gravesend also had its share of good, working-class and decent law-abiding people as well. In the neighbor was an old-timer; a retiree who served over twenty-one years as a police officer in Italy. He once told me they never used mechanical restraints or handcuffs, but rather plastic flexible cuffs to subdue their prisoners. He didn't speak much English and would speak to me only in Italian. Although I couldn't speak the language, the similarity in dialogue was enough for me to understand what he was trying to say. As time went on, we became good neighbors, and we were all like family in a neighborhood that was once plaque with racism and hatred. Like all good neighbors, we shared many stories, conversations, gifts and good times. Across the street was another Old-timer; an Italian man named Joe, who grew grapes in his yard and always had a batch of homemade wine that would drop a man to the ground with two glasses.

His fried hot Italian peppers were another story. Down the street on McDonald Avenue was a neighborhood kid named Tony Gramegña, (aka Tony 'The Italian Stallion' Gramegña). He was the grandson to the retired Italian policeman. Tony was an amateur great kick boxer who was exceptionally good as a fighter. Tony invited me once to watch him in one of his fights just off Ocean Parkway. He was in the ring bouncing around and warming up for his fight. I was at ringside watching Tony warm up when I called him over and instructed him to tell the referee to announce his name as a professional boxer.

"Hey, Tony, tell the referee to announce your name as, Tony 'The Italian Stallion,' Gramegña."

Tony looked at me with the eye of the tiger and called the referee over.

"Hey, ref, (referee) how you doin? Do me a favor, when you announce the fighters, make sure you announce me as, Tony 'The Italian Stallion' Gramegña?"

The referee looked at Tony with a disgusted look on his face.

"What do you think—this is professional boxing, go back to your corner and sit down!"

Tony walked back to his corner and sat down with a confused expression on his face. He looked over the ropes at me as if to say, 'what the hell just happened?'

We all laughed like hell after that. Tony went on to win the fight. Tony had a younger sister who was also a fighter in her own way, her name was Marzia Gramegña. She learned to fight with her brothers, cousins and the neighborhood boys she ran around with. There were no girls on the block she could hang around with back then. Of course, with the exception of Eileen, but Eileen was much older. Another couple of Italian Stallions were Frankie and Fonzie Racanati, cousins of Tony and Marzia. Frankie was also into martial arts. There were not too many kids in Gravesend, who knew how to speak Italian, but these kids knew how and always spoke their native language around their family—it was a must in their household. They were tough kids, yet they were good kids with good hearts, good morals and family values. I remember one Halloween day I went to a local auto body shop, where I was having my car painted. I wanted to take the car home, but the owner insisted I wait another day or so. I couldn't, and like a fool, I took the car home.

That night eggs were flying all over the neighborhood, and although I did not see Frankie Racanati hit my car with eggs, the word was out on the street, 'Frankie did it.' The next day I couldn't believe what I was seeing. My car looked like a dog with rabies. Somehow, the eggs caused a foaming reaction. I approached Frankie's father Mario and graciously paid me one-hundred dollars for the estimate repair. However, just one week later my son threw a baseball through Mario's window and the cost for the repair, one-hundred bucks. Mario recently passed on and I'll never forget the honorable man he was and how he welcomed me into the neighborhood, *Rest in Peace Mr. Mario Racanati.*

In another Gravesend encounter, I can recall sitting on my building stoop with all the neighborhood kids and nephews. We were all reading the NYS penal and criminal procedure law books. I was actually trying to teach them a little about law, just in case they wanted a future in law enforcement. As we sat there discussing the differences in robbery and burglary, a neighborhood drug addict approached us while carrying a large color television. He offered to sell it at an extremely low price, but then noticed the law books in our hands.

"Hey, what's doin— you guys wanna buy a nice color television? I'll give it to you at a low price."

Then he noticed the law books in my hands began stuttering his words.

"Are you a cop or something?"

"Why are you asking?" I asked suspiciously.

"Cause this is my cousin's television, it's not stolen or nothin; he wants me to sell it for him, and if I can't sell it I'll just bring it back home."

"Oh, yeah, no kidding, nice television, but we don't need one."

"No problem," said the junkie and who quickly disappeared into the early night like the character Louie Dumps, in the movie Bronx Tale with actor Robert De Niro."

We all looked at one another and laughed. The neighborhood was an old-fashioned place where store credit was the shake of someone's hand and their word was as good as gold.

As far as I can remember, no other neighborhood kids ever came looking for trouble between X and W, on McDonald Avenue. The local troublemakers went to other neighborhoods with their mischief. However, the neighborhood silence soon gave way to an endless mob war. Bodies of dead mobsters were seen lying on the streets by neighborhood residents and kids on their way to work, to school or simply riding their bicycles. My son Al, Jr., who one day was on his way to school, came across a body with a plastic bag wrapped around its head. He came back home complaining about it and I didn't believe him. I thought he was trying to make up an excuse not attend school, but he was right, and the body was that of a mobster who was executed the night before. The news media was having a field day all over Brooklyn and news vans could be seen on many neighborhood corners.

According to news media executions brought to ten the number of Colombo and Bonanno crime family associates who have been killed over the past ten months in what federal investigators believe was a drug trade dispute. It would appear that some of these hits may have grown out of some narcotics dispute, and also there would appear to have been a further indication of a breakdown of discipline within the mob," said Andrew Maloney, U.S. Attorney for the Eastern District. Joseph R. Tekulve, thirty-three, of Bensonhurst, was found dead shot in the face and temple, on Village Road South between residential Lake Street and mostly commercial McDonald Avenue in Gravesend. A 25-caliber shell casing was found beside the body. Federal prosecutors identified Tekulve, a pizza shop owner, as a loan shark for Anthony Spero, who they described as a high-ranking member of the Bonanno family. Tekulve was out on bail, investigators said, pending an appeal of a 1984 conviction for conspiring to extort three-hundred thousand from a Manhattan businessman. Spero was named as an un-indicted coconspirator. Manhattan Assistant District Attorney John Fried had said the six-foot-two, two-hundred pound Tekulve was the strong-arm man in the extortion scheme. "Next time it might be you," Tekulve is said by officials to have told his victim after breaking up the businessman's video arcade. Maloney named Spero in a civil racketeering suit indictment that charged the Bonanno crime family with using legitimate businesses as fronts for illegal activities.

The suit alleges that Spero, as the crime family's counselor, was "running the family's day to day operations." City law enforcement officials said Spero's crew had been tied to four recent homicide investigations. Two reputable organized crime figures were gunned down on a Brooklyn street in killings authorities linked to the mob war. Carmine Varriale, described by police as a Luchese family soldier, and Frank Santora, said to be an associate of the Gambino and Bonanno families, were killed after walking away from Spero's club, Brooklyn detectives said. The car used in the hit was found parked in front of the club, police said. Varriale's brother, Pasquale, who investigators believe absconded with a ten-thousand dollar bribe intended for a Pizza Connection trial juror had been found murdered. Pasquale Varriale frequented Spero's social club, the Big Apple Two Way Radio Company, police said. Investigators believe Pasquale Varriale was murdered by Enrico and Vincent Carini, brothers who were found slain on June 12th. At least half the recent murders have been linked to the murder of Salvatore Scarpa, a reputed Colombo soldier. Although detectives investigating the individual homicides still carried on by the Scarpa murder as a botched robbery, investigators say it was a drug war execution. Authorities say Scarpa's younger brother, Gregory Scarpa Senior, runs a crime crew that lost a member, Joseph De Domenico, in a hit, (*McAlary, 1987*).

In Gravesend and Bensonhurst Brooklyn, the mob family wars continued throughout the 1980s, as other mob figures fought their way through the ranks. Many mobsters holding top positions were either jailed, died in prison, or were killed by other mobsters. Neighborhood people never blinked an eye and life in the neighborhood went on as it has always done. Through all the mob wars and bad reputation, the neighborhood continued to hold its own and businesses like your local mamas and papa's groceries, pizzerias and bakeries were as popular as ever. The people's determination to succeed when public scrutiny was at its worse was the common practice and mob wars wasn't going to put a damper on things according to an old Italian countryman named Joe, who also once said, "La Mafia è come il pane italiano, lei non si sbarazzerà mai di eso," (*The Mafia is like Italian bread, you'll never get rid of it*).

STORY CONT:

I finally reached home and just like I thought, no parking. I doubled parked my car between the steel columns under the elevated train. There was never any parking available for local residents, at least not until seven p.m. when all the automotive businesses closed up their shops. I went upstairs and sat in front of our television like many others do after a hard day's work. I stretched my legs, grabbed the remote and right on time the six o'clock news with its unwinding news of the day. A woman pushed onto subway tracks, vehicle accident on FDR causes major backups, three suspects fled a local bank robbery, and tomorrow's humidity is expected to reach one-hundred percent. I looked over my shoulder at a coffee table where all the mail was placed by the wife. On top was an envelope with big bold red letters that read,

'This is your last and final notice.'

I called out to the wife,

"Hey, Hon, what's the difference between last and final?"

"Sounds the same to me," she answered back.

"Yep, that's what I'm thinking."

"Oh, boy, Hon, they got you again!"

I knew what she meant; someone tagged me with a parking ticket. It was like clockwork and it never failed. They knew when I got home and knew my car. Once a week for the last six months or so, they'd come around, find my car and leave a pretty little yellow double parking ticket on my windshield wiper. What I couldn't understand was; McDonald Avenue had elevated train tracks and steel columns on both sides of the street which ran the entire length of McDonald Avenue and drivers rarely travel between those columns. I was not only getting tickets daily from local cops of the 61st precinct, I was also getting them from traffic enforcement agents and the cost of paying those tickets on a monthly basis was reaching in the hundreds. I couldn't understand for the life of me how I kept getting those tickets when we periodically looked out of our window every five minutes. It was almost as though those cops were either hiding behind those steel columns, or they were repelling like Ninjas from the train tracks above, then repelled back up again. They were as good, if not better, then those yellow pages deliverers who are never seen dropping off those books—even with a surveillance camera affixed to your front door.

I reached for the bat phone and call my brother Cruz 'The Moe' Morales, who at the time was a NYC police officer. He was able to pull some strings, and I never got another parking ticket placed on my windshield. What can I say; the kid had juice, (slang for connections). The day was done, the car was finally parked, and the parking ticket was placed on the refrigerator door. Tomorrow was another day with another exhausting story to tell. *

Prison has a way of wearing a man down—then again—it has a way of wearing anyone down. Its seems as though no matter how long the trip back home might be, there's never enough time to unwind. During the many years of traveling to and from work I realized the most unwinding time of the day was the drive between Ossining where the prison is located and Mt Vernon. The rolling hills, forestation, wildlife and mountain views are spectacular, but once you begin to reach the outer boundaries of New York City, everything gradually changes. The rolling hills, forestation, wildlife and mountain views gave way to small homes, which gave way to building tenements, then housing projects and factories. Graffiti starts to appear on building walls, traffic slowly builds up and the quality of the air you breathe goes from being almost pure oxygen, to a heavy smug and clouds of pollution. Almost instantly, and on a daily basis, I begin to feel the headaches, sore throat, itchy eyes and breathing becomes shallow when I enter the city boundaries. Many who live in these large cities don't realize the changes, because many who live in these cities don't work outside the city limits or never leave its outskirts. However, all that worry about pollution, double parking, alternate side parking, tickets, crime, railroad spikes and tar falling on the vehicles would soon come to an end when we moved out of New York City and went two hours north to a place called Newburgh. Unfamiliar with suburban living, all its natural wildlife and environmental tranquility that came with living in a country setting, getting use to it took many years. No longer hearing the emergency vehicle sirens, the elevated trains roaring pass, the horn blowing, the vehicle misfires, the verbal road rage disputes and the sound of neighbors sitting on their building stoops while engaging in conversation, actually became an imperative necessity to me at times. But we soon realized we were in a most pleasurable and family orientated environment.

A knock on the door on one September day confirmed this fact when a neighbor name Mrs. Jo-Ann Pugh, greeted our family with a home-baked cake. Just one of many gestures of generosity and enjoyable experiences we encountered on Foxwood Drive in the Town of Newburgh. As time went on and as we began to adjust to our new neighborhood, I began to experience and witness things I've never seen before in Brooklyn. As I sat in front of my new home one Sunday afternoon, I saw three little children; a Caucasian boy, a Spanish boy and Black girl riding their bicycles together. Almost instantly I felt a spiritualistic feeling and was overwhelmed. A sense of belonging and an urge to smile interminably came over me. It was as though I was witnessing an illustration from the Holy Bible come to life before my eyes and the only thing I can think of was the scripture of, Isaiah 32:17-20.

"The fruit of righteousness will be peace; the effect of righteousness will be quietness and confidence forever. My people will live in peaceful dwelling places, in secure home and in undisturbed places of rest."

However, it didn't end there, three months later Christmas Eve 1994—another wonderful occurrence took place when a knock on the door surprised us all. A neighbor, Mr. Richard Verrette, along with his daughter Amanda Verrette, and other young ladies, sang a beautiful Christmas Carol. In that instant, I knew we were in the right place. This was a neighborhood of divine power and folks with spiritual quality, blessings and abundance of family values. The act of friendship on Foxwood Drive was as natural and pure as a summer breeze. The importance of family values, its unity and its blissful harmony can easily be witnessed, simply by looking outside your window during the holiday seasons. The sense of belonging and knowing you were in the right place was in itself, a righteous and spiritual confirmation of existence. The thought of waking up in this neighborhood every morning brought to surface a smile upon my face every night. How do you put into word's the kindness, thoughtfulness and serenity that came with living in such a neighborhood? Springtime in March, did not only bring out the people from their homes, it brought out the smiles. The conversations were endless and the landscaping capability challenges were conducted by everyone who had a landscaping idea.

266

Newborn babies were also formally introduced by parents who had their babies during the winter months. Neighborhood kids were always in delight knowing they only had three months left for the school season to end. Summertime brought out the neighborhood kids with their bicycles, baseball gloves and skateboards. I introduced several of the Brooklyn street games to Foxwood Drive that immediately caught on and became a favorite like; Skully and Hot Peas and Butter. What I found to be most tranquil and relaxing at the end of a summer day, was sitting on my deck and hearing in the background the screams of children having fun in the neighborhood or the pouncing of a baseball against a garage door across the street by a neighborhood kid name David Gizzarelli. There were many good kids like David in this neighborhood with extraordinary parents like little Tommy Quinn Jr. When September came around and those yellow school buses were on the road again, I use to sit in my garage and look out of my window every morning with a hot cup of coffee, while enjoying my observation of neighborhood children heading back to school. As the change of colors on tree leafs began to occur, it was a good sign summer was over and all the sweaters and jackets would come out of their closets once again.

Halloween was near and it was time for many to decorate the exterior of their homes with ghosts, pumpkins and goblins. A couple of large spiders affixed to a nylon string just above our front door were always a good idea too. Another popular concept for Halloween was an electric chainsaw, without its blades of course. I would hide behind a pine tree and patiently wait for my neighboring victims. When the time was right I switch on the motor while sporting a Jason Vorhees mask and let out a loud yell while swinging the chainsaw back and forth. I got them every time, although I must admit many neighborhood children were frightened to the extent where they wanted no part of ever visiting our home again. Even after the holiday seasons it was quite obvious they were a little skeptical in approaching. I even placed a human size Grim Reaper once in front of our home three weeks before Halloween, then got inside on Halloween night for the sole purpose of scaring the socks off neighbors. I won't admit the names of my two popular victims, a courageous NYS correction officer from Downstate.

The other was a brave NYC firefighter, who on separate occasions, did not only jump twelve inches off the ground, but also let out a yell similar to that of Blankman, where actor Damon Wayans yells while being assaulted by villains. I'm sure Jeff Jackson and Tommy Quinn will never forget those times, and neither will the kids and significant others. Halloween is a joyous occasion celebrated by all in the neighborhood and a remarkable time for witnessing little villains roam the neighbor streets in their memorable costumes. From little princess's and barbaric pirates, to small frogs and walking McDonald french-fries by Mark Pugh. But as we all know, the older we become the faster time seems to pass us by and with the end of Halloween came the ultimate holidays of all, Thanksgiving, Christmas and New Years. During the holidays the Gizzarelli family, as far as I can remember, was the first family to decorate their colonial style home with an abundance of Christmas lights. They're decorating ideas quickly caught on, started a domino effect and many followed behind the decorator responsible for this course of prevailing tendency, Joe Gizzarelli. Before you knew it, Foxwood Drive was becoming a Christmas light spectacular and everyone was enjoying the various decorations.

In 2008, CNN Money published the ten best small cities to live in America, of course Town of Newburgh was nowhere to be found and its city is riddled with crime. However, should there ever be a publication on the ten best communities to live in Foxwood Drive would have to win hands down for the greatest neighbors. We eventually moved from Newburgh to the state of Florida in 2004, after retiring from New York State corrections. Nothing could be further from the truth when I say we deeply regret leaving behind such an honorable and genuine group of people. To say our love for them was that of a family member would be the most precise definition in describing the immense appreciation we have for them all. As I sit here writing this book, I often get the feeling of wanting to move back to Foxwood Drive. Then-again, when I think of the bone-chilling cold, the snow falls, and shoveling that comes with it, the word, 'nah' seem to restraint that feeling and overpowers any thought to the contrary. We eventually moved and found a cozy little location in unincorporated Seminole. On any given day, you can see the most unusual creators anywhere in Florida.

Starbucks, Lake Mary Blvd, 2008

The abundance of wildlife that takes its daily walk along the perimeter of our property is spectacular. I recently sat in my backyard enjoying the natural beauty God has blessed us all with when a telephone call interrupted my never ending derived of sensory processes stimulating my mental contentment. I answered it and on the other side was a person who asked what I was doing. I explained that I was sitting in my backyard looking up at a towering pine tree with five extremely large woodpeckers that somehow resembled a 1950s Doo Wop Group. The red feathers on the woodpecker's heads were pushed back like some old pompadour hairstyle. She said, 'you need a life' and she was right. After getting accustom to my property and identifying with its wildlife, I began exploring the surrounding neighborhoods. I discovered a Starbucks Cafe off Lake Mary Boulevard, and made a decision to stop there. I quickly became addicted to its environment and quite naturally their coffee. The pleasant atmosphere and the quality of warmth, kindness and professionalism projected by its employees kept me coming back for the next five years.

There was something at this Starbucks that fascinated me, the close resemblance of many employees to today's Hollywood celebrities. The store Manager Brat Matlack, closely resembled Ty Pennington; employees Natalie, closely resembled the actress Angelina Jolie, Christine closely resembled singer songwriter Lisa Loeb and John Brocks, and Amalie didn't resemble anyone, but their unique and genuine peculiarities as a person won my respect, appreciation and admiration. These are people who without a doubt give new meaning to the words social comportment. Starbucks in Lake Mary became a favorite hangout spot for me, a place where I made many new friends, met people in high places and some in not so high places. On any given day at Starbucks, you may see pro-football players to pro-golfers. News anchor people to famous authors, musicians and other celebrities. In a world where high social status has no place for little pee-ons like me, it's good to know high-end professional individuals are willing to converse at any level. From New York State to Puerto Rico and Florida, I've encountered some of the best human beings this society has to offer. They come from all walks of life, all levels of education, employment, cultures and religions, people who without knowledge and conscience touched our lives in the most positive and benevolent manner.

All who are mentioned in this book in honorability are prime examples of goodness, people of principles and righteousness. People who without selfishness implement on a daily basis the ethic of reciprocity to, "Do unto others as you would have them do unto you."

Looking back in hindsight, there was something good after all that came from working in a maximum-security prison environment, the appreciation and gratitude in knowing decent productive members of society and of this great nation, still do exist and dwell all around us.

THE END

www.ingramcontent.com/pod-product-compliance
Lightning Source LLC
Chambersburg PA
CBHW022102280326
41933CB00007B/229